CHANGE IN PUBLIC BUREAUCRACIES

MARSHALL W. MEYER

Professor of Sociology, University of California, Riverside

# CHANGE IN
# PUBLIC BUREAUCRACIES

CAMBRIDGE UNIVERSITY PRESS

CAMBRIDGE

LONDON · NEW YORK · MELBOURNE

Published by the Syndics of the Cambridge University Press
The Pitt Building, Trumpington Street, Cambridge CB2 1RP
Bentley House, 200 Euston Road, London NW1 2DB
32 East 57th Street, New York, NY 10022, USA
296 Beaconsfield Parade, Middle Park, Melbourne 3206, Australia

© Cambridge University Press 1979

First published 1979

Printed in the United States of America

*Library of Congress Cataloging in Publication Data*
Meyer, Marshall W
Change in public bureaucracies.

Bibliography: p.

1. Public administration.  2.  Local finance.
3.  Organizational change.  4.  Bureaucracy.  I.  Title.
JF1411.M49   301.18′32   76−47193
ISBN 0 521 22670 8

# CONTENTS

108303

# PREFACE

Like any successful organization, this book is a product of cooperation among many people in many places. The research reported here began in 1965 as part of the Comparative Organization Research Program, directed by Peter M. Blau, at the University of Chicago. Data for the first wave of the study of local finance agencies were collected in 1966 and early 1967 under the auspices of CORP. A panel or longitudinal design was not envisioned at the time. The longitudinal study was planned and the 1972 data collected while I was at Cornell University. The analysis of the data and preparation of articles and this work were undertaken at the University of California, Riverside.

I owe intellectual debts to a large number of people who have contributed to the development of organizational theory and research in the last decade. Most are cited in the bibliography. Some people making direct contributions to the design and execution of this research as well as to the analysis require specific mention, however. One such person is Peter Blau, now Quetlet Professor of Sociology at Columbia, who stimulated by example and suggestion the transformation of a cross-sectional study comparing organizations at one point into longitudinal research comparing organizations over time. Charles N. Halaby, now at the University of Wisconsin-Madison, and M. Craig Brown, now at SUNY

Albany, provided substantial intellectual input into this work as graduate students (at Cornell) and as departmental colleagues (at U.C. Riverside). Brown, it should be noted, is co-author of the original version of Chapter 6. John C. Anderson of UCLA and Richard H. Hall of SUNY Albany read the manuscript with great care and provided detailed comments and suggestions for improvement. I am especially indebted to Anderson who took several hours to discuss his suggestions with me after I had had a chance to review them. I thank these people for their help and absolve them of responsibility for the flaws remaining in the book.

A number of organizations have also contributed to the research reported here. The National Science Foundation has supported the enterprise throughout. The 1966 study of finance agencies was funded as part of the Comparative Organization Research Program under NSF Grant GS-553. The 1972 wave was supported by NSF Grants GS-33509 and SOC73-05688. These grants are gratefully acknowledged. Put simply, the work could not have been undertaken without them. The field staff of the National Opinion Research Center conducted the interviews of finance officials for both the 1966 and 1972 waves. NORC also did the initial data processing for the 1972 wave. I am indebted to Eve Weinberg, then NORC's field director, for her diligence and graciousness in undertaking the task. The Municipal Finance Officers Association of the United States and Canada also contributed to the research by its endorsement of our studies and by allowing me access to their records and meetings of their Executive Board. My special thanks go to Donald W. Beatty, Executive Director of MFOA.

This preface would not be complete without the acknowledgment of the cooperation of a large number of city, county, and state finance officials throughout the United States in the interviews used to gather data for this research. Over 97 percent of the assigned cases were completed, and interviewers noted consistently the care and thoroughness with which responses were given. One could not but have the impression that the finances of most U.S. localities are managed by highly competent and considerate people.

Ande Deaver and Terry Herrity typed the several versions of this manuscript, always with good cheer. I am grateful to both of them.

Three others collaborated in this project, often unknowingly. My wife, Judith Meyer, aided in the legal research that was done in connection with Chapter 6. More importantly, Judy usually kept her sense of humor long after I had lost mine. Sons Joshua and Gabriel Meyer behaved like most academic children. Sometimes they prodded. And sometimes they interfered. This book is dedicated to Josh and Gabie with love and with the hope that their books, in turn, will be dedicated to their children.

Marshall W. Meyer

# INTRODUCTION

This book is about the process of change in some government bureaucracies of cities, counties, and states in the United States. The bureaucracies are finance departments, comptrollers' offices, controllers' offices, departments of administration, and the like. These agencies are ubiquitous because the accounting and auditing functions are needed in all local governments, but they are hardly known to the average citizen because their activities are routine and rarely excite controversy. We can only begin to describe finance departments and similar agencies in this Introduction, but because the entire book concerns these organizations, the reader should have a sense of familiarity with them by the end.

This book is also about organizational theory and research. Theory, of course, is a body of abstract principles meant to apply to a variety of organizational forms and settings, and research is a procedure for testing propositions. The research study that generated this book was grounded in theory, or better, a theory that might be labeled the Weberian,[1] administrative, or closed-system model of organizations. As the study progressed, the theory became somewhat less plausible, but so did all organizational theories. The discussion of theory like the description of finance departments is necessarily sketchy in this first chapter, but it becomes more developed as we progress. If the reader finds the results of the research as consistent and convincing as I perceive them, then his skepticism of theory—or at least of theories purporting to describe all organizations without reference to their histories and social or institutional contexts—will grow with his understanding of finance agencies.

The place to begin is in the basement of a Reconstruction-era city hall in the spring of 1972 where I am interviewing a finance director. He is a man in his mid-sixties of southern extraction. His daughter is present and taking notes. During the interview, a two-way radio remains on and occasionally interrupts when a dispatcher sends fire equipment to answer a call. The finance director has made a hobby of monitoring fire calls. He was instrumental in campaigning for a professional fire department in his city and is proud of his accomplishments. He is also proud of his own finance department and finds it well organized and efficiently run. Part of the interview went as follows:[2]

> *Interviewer:* Mr. B., I came here to see you partly because your department is a bit unusual. You have sixty-one employees, but twenty-eight of them, nearly half, are in the data-processing division. Can you explain to me why so many of your people are in data processing compared to your other divisions?[3]
> *Finance director:* There is no secret about that. The computer does all of our accounting and payroll work, of course. But it is also used for other things. You see, we have a large military installation nearby, and there are many temporary residents of the city. Because there's so much turnover, we have to send utility bills monthly—the city supplies electricity and water. In addition, we have to collect traffic tickets very, very quickly or lose much of the revenue from them. We use the computer to send out notices after fourteen days. We are also about to computerize all of our hospital records.

> *Interviewer:* Will you need more people or a larger machine?
> *Finance director:* The present computer—I think it's a 360/40 will be replaced by a larger one, a 360/50, which is faster and has greater capacity. And since we want to move to three-shift operations, some more computer operators will have to be hired.
> *Interviewer:* You mean that more than half of your people will be in data processing?
> *Finance director:* That's right.
> *Interviewer:* Do you anticipate any changes—other than the new computer and three-shift operations—in your department?
> *Finance director:* No, none at all.

I later talked with the head of the data-processing division and covered some of the same points. His answers were initially like his boss's, but he sensed my disbelief. The following is from memory.

> *Data-processing manager:* Would you turn off the tape recorder please?
> *Interviewer:* I'll be glad to.
> *Data-processing manager:* Look, the truth is that I'm going to the city manager the day after tomorrow to ask that data processing be made a separate department.
> *Interviewer:* Good luck. But why?
> *Data-processing manager:* Partly because we're growing—with three shifts we'll have at least thirty-one people—but mainly because much of our work no longer has anything to do with finance.
> *Interviewer:* Can you tell me more about this?
> *Data-processing manager:* Sure.

The head of data processing went on to explain that much of what used to be purely financial work has become increasingly managerial, extending beyond the traditional limits of finance administration. He cited several examples of how this shift has occurred, but most vivid was his account of how the chief of police began using information from parking tickets.

> *Data-processing manager:* As you know, we've computerized our traffic tickets—we write about 100,000 a year—in order to dun violators within fourteen days.
>
> *Interviewer:* What information is on the ticket?
>
> *Data-processing manager:* There's the date, time, location, and type of violation, tag number of offending vehicle, and there's the officer's star number. We put all of these into the machine. Now our police chief who looks a bit like Broderick Crawford came to me one day and asked, "Bill, I'd like to know who my productive officers are. Can you give me a listing of citations by officer?" I said, "Sure enough, Chief" and had it for him by evening. The next morning the chief was back at 8:00 A.M. and requested a listing of citations by officer and location. "Sure enough, Chief." He was back at 7:00 A.M. the following morning wanting a listing by officer, date, location, and time. That took a lot of paper. The next morning at 6:00 A.M. he held a meeting with his patrolmen. He had discovered that virtually no parking tickets were being written between 2:00 and 4:00 P.M., and that most between 1:30 and 2:00 in the afternoon were in the vicinity of movie theaters. The chief told his men what movies they had been watching and that it would have to stop. It did. And to keep things honest, I now send the chief a productivity report on his officers every month.

Several themes in these conversations will recur throughout this book. One is that finance officials tend not to anticipate much change in their organizations. Their orientation is toward accounting, and they view innovations such as electronic data-processing and sophisticated budgeting techniques as new means of attaining old ends. This attitude is well founded. Bureaucracies, as will be argued, are generally not in the business of promoting change. Their work, which consists mainly of enforcing rules, and their members' career orientations tend entirely in the opposite direction. A second theme is that when change occurs, it is determined not so much by internal processes in bureaus as by external events. In the example above, the data-processing director concluded that his boss had failed to take advantage of the managerial potential of the computer once he saw how the police chief used it. Whether or not he was right is unclear. On the one hand, the data were not being fully utilized; but at the same time it is questionable whether, from the finance director's perspective, it was desirable to mix fiscal with managerial functions. A characteristic of bureaucracies, I shall argue, is that most decisions result from administrative or political judgments rather than technological imperatives. For this reason, and contrary to stereotypes, bureaus tend to be very open or vulnerable to their immediate environments. A third theme, one not directly evident from interviews with the finance and data-processing directors, is that increasing bureaucratization of public agencies through additional rules and layers of hierarchy results in part from their openness to the environment. This has some implications for the scope and structure of bureaus at all levels of government and also for their capacity to respond to genuine needs for change arising externally. These implications will be pursued in the last chapter.

### A description of finance agencies

Before turning to organizational theory and procedures for testing theory, the subject of the next two chapters, a descriptive account of the setting and work of finance agencies is in order. Finance agencies of local and state governments are almost always located in city halls, county administration buildings, or state capitols. They are almost always alongside the office of the head of government—the mayor, manager, or governor. Sometimes these quarters are old and drafty—I spotted a spittoon in one—and sometimes, especially in growing suburban areas, they are in modern low-rise structures spread across government "campuses." The proximity of the finance director or comptroller to the head of government is not accidental. In theory, the chief financial officer is the chief executive officer's advisor in all fiscal matters, which excludes little of the business of city, county, and state governments. In fact, some finance officers have immediate and frequent access to their superiors, but some have little access or are forced to compete with others for their boss's ear in fiscal matters. We shall explore reasons for differences in influence of different financial officers in the chapters to follow. Interestingly, at least in cities and counties, finance offices often serve the public directly as well as the head of government. Many, for example, are responsible for collection of taxes and fees as well as, in some instances, parking and traffic fines. The functions performed by finance agencies, then, range from fiscal planning and advice that cannot be accomplished following fixed procedures to operating cashiers' windows where virtually no discretion can be permitted.

When one enters a finance department, he is struck by its similarity to other administrative organizations. Virtually all work, save for reception, is done at desks, most of which are in undivided offices, some behind partitions, and a few in the private offices of the department head, his deputy, and the division chiefs. Almost half of the nonsupervisory employees in public finance agencies are women, but almost all division and department heads are men, and few are minorities. For many of the women employees, their jobs are means of earning needed second incomes to support their families. For the men, there are incentives of civil service tenure and benefits, advancement within the organization and, in recent years, numerous opportunities for employment in other localities. Work hours, including lunch breaks, are fixed. And, whereas the frenetic process of a stock brokerage or exchange floor is never observed, there are periods of intense activity, especially when budgeting and fiscal year deadlines are approaching. My impression is that the staffs of local-government finance agencies are highly competent, but also somewhat conservative in appearance and demeanor, with the exception of data-processing personnel. Their political views, when expressed, are similarly conventional. The one finance director whom I remember expressing strong opinions on public issues had been appointed partly for his political views and was not actively involved in the management of his department. In short, finance agencies typify in most respects the medium- to large-sized administrative bureaucracies found at all levels of government; and their appearance and organization may not differ substantially from administrative bodies in the private sector.

Work routines in finance agencies are not easily described, because there are very many of them and they vary somewhat across jurisdictions. The core function, accounting, for example, can require checking of a request for payment (usually originated by another department head) for appropriateness, for availability of funds, and for evidence that the goods or services to be paid for were in fact delivered or rendered. Depending upon the size of the request and its nature (e.g., whether or not a contract is involved), more than one approval may be needed. Treasury and debt administration, also core finance functions nowadays, are not so easily routinized because they entail money-management decisions that are largely in response to changing marketing decisions. Data processing and budgeting activities are partly routine, but they also demand technical skills of a highly specialized nature for those in supervisory positions.

Finance agencies may also have responsibility for property assessment, itself another specialized activity, management of government-owned property, and the purchasing function. The reader, no doubt, has some sense of the nature of these activities. The diversity of activities taking place within finance agencies, importantly, is a challenge for both the observer who wants to describe them economically as well as for the administrator who wishes to manage them simultaneously. Indeed, the diverse and occasionally disparate nature of finance functions provide some impetus for change in these agencies.

*Organizational forms for the finance function*

There are three basic organizational forms for the finance function in cities, counties, and states—the comptroller's office, the department of finance, and the department of administration. Sometimes the term controller or auditor is used in place of comptroller, but the organizational forms associated with these names are essentially similar. The comptroller's office is the oldest form for the finance function, the finance department is of more recent origins, and departments of administration have begun to emerge only recently. The three types of local government finance agencies should be described briefly using materials drawn from interviews, observation, and informal discussions with a large number of finance directors in both their offices and at professional meetings of the Municipal Finance Officers Association.

*The comptroller's office.* One city comptroller suggested that the organization of his office reflected a "Depression mentality," and most of his colleagues agreed. By this he meant that the comptroller's job is regulation of expenditures−limiting budget requests, limiting disbursements to amounts and for purposes budgeted, debiting accounts when obligations are incurred (as opposed to when paid), and minimizing long-term indebtedness. Some of the more aggressive comptrollers conduct detailed audits of local agencies, which generate some savings and, occasionally, publicity. The comptroller's main activity, then, is bookkeeping. He is involved in policy only when fiscal safeguards and regulations are needed. Not surprisingly, a comptroller's outlook is like that of a traditional accountant. Financial data are examined for internal consistency and are not linked directly, if at all, to the level of government services. Thus the scope of activities of comptrollers is not large, but what they do is essential and cannot be reduced much. All of this would suggest little change in comptrollers' offices over time save for a growth trend due to accounting requirements of new programs, particularly federal categorical grants and, now, revenue sharing.

*The finance department.* If the comptroller's office is a creature of the Depression, then the finance department reflects the perspective of the 1940s and 1950s. The finance director, like the comptroller, is responsible for accounting and auditing of government funds, but these functions are subsumed under an organizational structure that includes a number of other activities such as revenue collection, purchasing, treasury management, investments, and the like. Although the finance director examines all expenditures to make sure that they conform to budget requirements, he is often more concerned with finding the resources needed for local-government services. The finance director issues all bonds and other obligations. Part of his job is to develop close ties with the banking and investment communities to ensure that funds will always be available when needed.[4] Needless to say, the finance director is more involved in policy than the typical comptroller, for he must determine whether funds can be raised for proposed projects and then find the money. This is especially the case where he has charge of budgeting.

The finance department was the logical outgrowth of the comptroller's office, and its functions were initially well defined. Almost all fiscal activities were consolidated in a single office, and questions concerning fiscal policy were meant to be referred to the finance director. By the 1960s, however, the distinction between financial administration and the nonfinancial aspects of local government began to be questioned, and it has all but evaporated now. This is due in part to the replacement of line-item budgets that take no account of policy outputs with program or performance budgets that link outputs to expenditures. The introduction of large-scale computing has also blurred the line separating fiscal management from operations. Data once used only for financial purposes now have other applications. For example, assessment records showing dwelling type and construction (as well as value) are helpful to fire departments in dispatching equipment. As local governments move toward integrated data bases and as financial data are merged with other kinds of information, the separation of finance from other administrative activities becomes even more tenuous.

*The department of administration.* Departments of administration are relatively new. Almost all have been formed since 1960, and many comptrollers' offices now reorganizing switch to the administration rather than the finance model. The department of administration completes the subordination of accounting and auditing activities to other housekeeping functions, especially data processing. Unlike finance, the concept of administration leaves no ambiguity about the location of the computer and budgeting. Both fit squarely within its mandate, as administration connotes linkage of financial with nonfinancial data—of cash inputs with policy outputs. The personnel function is usually placed in administration along with property management and other activities that do not fit clearly in one of the operating departments of government. Indeed, his scope of responsibilities can make the director of administration a second city or county manager.[5] The functions of administration departments are broad and expanding at the present time because of their newness, incorporation of computer technology, and modern budgeting concepts. Whether administration departments will develop the same internal strains as departments of finance remains to be seen. Most likely they will, but not for some time.

### Forces tending toward change

Even though finance agencies are essential to local-government administration, they are not invulnerable to change. Within finance agencies, work is becoming more diverse. This trend is due largely to computerization and modern budgeting techniques requiring both technical expertise and guesswork, and which are very different from traditional accounting. The external environment has also induced change in finance agencies. Federal actions have had profound effects upon local communities through a variety of programs. Because the subject of this study is organization rather than the implementation or impact of specific federal programs, we shall focus upon federal actions and other developments occurring nationally with immediate implications for organization.

*Strains arising from centralized administration.* Prior to World War II, fiscal responsibilities were usually divided among units such as the comptroller's office, the treasurer, and departments of revenue and purchasing. In the 1940s and 1950s, the concept of centralized finance administration under a single director of finance emerged. Administration was to be streamlined by having a chief financial officer responsible directly to the head of government. The Municipal Finance Officers Association of the United States and Canada has long advocated centralized administration, and most finance directors share this preference. But in the last few years, centralized financial administration has become increasingly difficult to manage. What were in the 1950s fairly similar and routine tasks have become disparate—some still routine and predictable, others fraught with uncertainty and requiring technical skills beyond a knowledge of accounting. Two developments brought about this change. The first is computerization, which raised the issue of who was to control data-processing facilities and thereby the key pressure points in the information flow of local governments. Initially, finance agencies retained control of the computer, but they are slowly losing their monopoly as other government agencies recognize the potential of electronic data processing. The second development is new budgeting techniques variously labeled systems analysis, PPBS, cost-benefit analysis, and the like. All of these depart from conventional line-item budgeting because they attempt to link costs to outputs and to identify the least expensive means of providing satisfactory levels of services. They also entail a level of uncertainty that is distasteful to the traditional accountant; hence, some budget units have been moved out of finance departments.

A general trend exists, then, toward contraction of the responsibilities and administrative structures of finance agencies. As the following chapters show, a number of conditions affect this process. Certain conditions minimize the effects of the environment on the size and structure of finance departments so that they remain essentially stable over time. Under other conditions, environmental demand attenuates growth and leads to loss of functionally specialized subunits. Contraction and dedifferentiation of finance departments are accompanied by growth of other agencies serving local governments. Some evidence of this latter process will be shown toward the end of Chapter 4.

*National developments.* So many events in the larger society affect local governments and local fiscal conditions that it would be impossible to list, much less trace, the implications of all of them. Two developments important for local government finance, it should be noted, did *not* occur until after the studies reported here were completed—namely the flow of unrestricted Revenue Sharing funds to local government entities, which began in 1973, and the New York City fiscal crisis, whose proportions became evident in late 1975. During the period when the research reported here was underway, 1966 through 1972, the Vietnam war grew in intensity, but so did national concern with urban problems, which was triggered by the riots of the late 1960s and incorporated into federal policy as part of President Johnson's Great Society program. The flow of federal funds to localities and subsequent expansion of government services increased the demand for finance administration; but the effects of increased demand upon individual finance agencies were only indirect and mediated by some organizational mechanisms to be discussed in Chapters 4, 5, and 6.

Two developments directly affecting finance agencies were the shift in local government personnel practices, hence in the personnel practices of finance agencies, mandated by the federal government, and federal subsidization of local-government payrolls. The Intergovernmental Personnel Act of 1970 called for the extension of "merit" principles to all levels of government, whereas federal merit requirements had previously not applied to locally funded programs. Other suggested changes in personnel practices were formulated at roughly the same time by the highly influential National Civil Service League. The 1970 edition of their Model Public Personnel Law sought to exclude policymaking officials from civil service coverage, a reversal of an earlier position. The history of civil service laws in the United States, the provisions of the 1970 Intergovernmental Personnel Act, and the 1970 Model Public Personnel Law are discussed in some detail in Chapter 6. The 1971 Emergency Employment Act authorized federal funding of local-government positions in an effort to ease high rates of unemployment. Most finance agencies had small numbers of Emergency Employment Act workers by the time the 1972 survey was undertaken, whereas such jobs did not exist in 1966. Despite contraction of responsibilities and administrative structures, employment in finance agencies increased between 1966 and 1972, partly due to EEA funding. Chapter 3 discusses patterns of growth in local finance administration.

### A note on the organization of this volume

If there is a single guiding idea in this book, it is that the structure and behavior of public bureaus are largely shaped by environmental forces, especially forces in larger social and political environments. Internal processes are at best loosely connected, whereas interchanges between environments and organizations exhibit some regularities and appear to be of more substantive significance than relations among variables describing organizations themselves. It should be noted that this pattern is not viewed as either aberrant or dysfunctional for public bureaucracies. Quite the opposite, it may be that government agencies are properly more open to external pressures than popular beliefs about them would suggest. The only thing for which this description is aberrant is the view of bureaucracies as rigid, closed, insular systems.

A number of specific hypotheses flow from the guiding idea that bureaus are more open than closed, and that they are more loosely coupled than is commonly believed. First of all, the concept of organizational structure becomes subject to close scrutiny if it is more labile than is usually supposed and is more of an outcome than cause of other things. This issue is taken up in Chapter 3, following the discussions of theory and methods. A second broad hypothesis is that environmental effects may be mediated by a variety of mechanisms in organizations, including the nature of leadership positions and of unprovable claims to domain asserted by public agencies. The exploration of environmental effects begins in Chapter 4 and continues in Chapter 5. A third hypothesis posits that apparent effects of history on organizations are but the residues of much larger differences due to origins, less substantial environmental effects since. Chapter 6 addresses this problem. A fourth hypothesis is that despite pervasive environmental effects, many ongoing organizations do not change fast enough, hence are rendered inconsistent with the environment, and are eventually replaced. Reorganization is hypothesized to be in the direction of consistency with external demands. Parts of Chapters 5 and 6 concern these ideas. The last chapter summarizes results of the research and suggests implications for organizational theory, for the management of public agencies, and for sociological research. In sum, the thrust of the book is that organizations should be studied dynamically rather than statically, that dynamic approaches yield a complex pattern of interchanges between environments and organizations, and that key environmental elements are as often located in larger social and political context as in immediate task demands.

# 1

## Issues in organizational theory

A large body of literature on organizations exists, much of it falling under the rubric of theory. Organizational theory has a mixed character. It contains elements of prescription, prediction, and historical analysis. All of organizational theory need not be explored here, but some of the issues germane to public bureaucracies must be given consideration. One question, first raised by Max Weber, concerns the efficacy of bureaus as authority systems. Another issue, more current, is whether organizations ought to be treated primarily as open or closed systems, and, if the former, what the relevant dimensions of the environment are. A third issue, one that has not been given a great deal of systematic attention before, is whether theoretical statements can be made about organizations generally. This is not a question of technique (e.g., qualitative versus quantitative) but one of methodology in the broadest sense of the term: Does one aim for predictive statements, or does one settle for description aided and informed by the tools of the social sciences? All of these issues meld together nicely toward the latter part of this book, but they should be treated separately to begin with.

### The efficacy of bureaus as authority systems

Max Weber's (1946) classic essay on bureaucracy signals its development as a distinctly modern form of administration, but the essay also contains important hypotheses about the behavior of bureaus. Let us put aside the debate as to whether or not the ideal–typical model of bureaucracy elaborated by Weber can be tested at all. Weber said not in his *Methodology in the Social Sciences* (1949), but most investigators have ignored his stricture and I shall also. A syllogism of sorts operates in the essay on bureaucracy. It is roughly this: Bureaucracies have many distinctive features (e.g., hierarchy of authority, written rules) compared to earlier forms of administration, and bureaucracies are more efficient than earlier forms. Hence the distinctive structure of bureaucracies accounts for their superior efficiency. It is ironic that although the premises of this syllogism are accepted uncritically by most scholars, the conclusion has never been tested carefully. If anything, bureaus are regarded as inefficient rather than efficient; and the culprit is usually identified as multi-tiered hierarchies and elaborate regulations, which are, according to Weber, modern rather than primitive features of organizations.

Let us first present the theory as Weber did. Weber began by delineating what he considered to be the distinctive features of bureaucracies: division of labor ("fixed and official jurisdictional areas") and hierarchy of authority such that each official has one and only one superior; a specialized administrative staff; written rules and regulations; selection and promotion of employees according to objective criteria be they seniority, educational qualifications, or a combination of the two; lifetime careers for most officials; and pecuniary compensation. All of these are commonplace in modern organizations. Indeed, it is difficult to imagine organizational arrangements from which such patterns are absent.[1] Weber did not limit his concern to internal administrative characteristics of bureaucracies. He also dealt with linkages between bureaus and their environments, although he did not use this language exactly. Weber noted, for example, that bureaucracies require separation of home from office, of personal from official interests. Like the internal features of bureaucracy, this is taken for granted nowadays in all but family-run businesses. Weber also noted that the technical requirements of bureaucratic work demand expertise that can be obtained only through formal education, hence the close connection between peoples' educational attainments and their position in the bureaucracy, and between higher education and public bureaucracies as institutional structures. Finally, Weber underscored the power position of bureaucracies vis-à-vis elected officials and the public. The politician stands as a "dilettante" opposite the bureaucratic expert.[2] So far as the public is concerned, democracy consists not in popular control of the bureaucracy, which would be rule by the *Demos* or mob, but rather in its "leveling" in the face of the omnipotent bureaucratic apparatus of the state. This is not the place to discuss whether Weber was an antidemocrat or whether bureaucracy is inherently antidemocratic. Suffice it to note that Weber saw bureaucracy as an equalizer that reduced both the latitude of elected officials and demands for privileged treatment of clients.

Whatever Weber's feelings about democracy, his work is centrally concerned with the problem of authority and indeed smacks of a fondness for authority from time to time. I find two distinct questions raised by Weber's discussion. One concerns the bases for legitimacy of authority—what distinguishes authority from power?—and the other raises the issue of effectiveness—what administrative structures are best suited to maintain a system of authority considered legitimate? As to the former question, contemporary quantitative research can say little. Weber distinguishes three kinds of legitimate authority: charismatic based on belief in a single leader, traditional based on what has been customary, and rational—legal based on a belief in supremacy of abstract principles of law and administrative regulation. Development of rational—legal authority is the quintessence of the process of rationalization of all institutional forms that Weber saw as the common thread of much of Western history. Because rational—legal authority has displaced other types in modern societies, studies of different bases of legitimation of authority are necessarily historical and comparative, similar to Weber's work and beyond the scope of quantitative analysis undertaken in this book.[3] As to the latter question, that of the most appropriate organizational structures for administering rational-authority systems, some tentative conclusions can be drawn from analysis of existing organizations. A convenient way to begin is with the questions or hypotheses posed by Weber.

Basically, Weber elaborated two hypotheses in his theory of bureaucracy. The first lies in his delineation of the "ideal—typical" characteristics of modern bureaus—division of labor, hierarchy, and regulations, written files, and the like. Weber was saying, simply, that modern organizations based in rational—legal authority are more likely to have these attributes than earlier forms. Weber does not say, though others have read this into his work, that there exist functional interrelations among these attributes such that change in any one implies change in some or all of the others—for example, the more division of labor, the more elaborate the hierarchy of authority. (See, for example, Blau, 1963.) This part of Weber's theory of bureaucracy is primarily historical and does not describe short-run organizational processes. The test of this first hypothesis, like the study of the bases of legitimate authority, lies primarily in historical and comparative analysis, but a partial test is possible with contemporary data about organizations provided that information about origins are available.

What I read as Weber's second hypothesis is somewhat different from the first and may be testable, if only indirectly. The second hypothesis links bureaucratic attributes to organizational efficiency. The hypothesis is subtle: Weber does not make simple causal assertions such as the more hierarchy and the more rules, the more efficiency. Weber does hypothesize, however, that the more an organization conforms to the bureaucratic model, whatever the constellation of elements in it, the more it will conform to the ideal of efficiency. But efficiency is always with respect to specific goals or ends. It does not stand apart as an element of organization independent of others. Hence, a test of Weber's second hypothesis requires one to ask what bureaucracies are intended to do, or in the broadest sense, what their goals are. A difficulty with this second hypothesis, as will be seen, is that the goals of bureaucracies are elusive, hence so are efficiency measures. This does not mean that bureaus have no goals or only contradictory ones, but it does mean that models portraying bureaucracies as maximizers are unlikely to be accurate.

As far as I can tell, Weber saw the work of bureaucracies as mainly administrative: that is to say, concerned with implementing laws and policies rather than making new rules, coping with recurring crises, manufacturing goods, or performing any of the myriad instrumental activities that may be demanded of organizations. By assuming the administrative character of bureaucratic work, some of Weber's statements that on the surface seem inconsistent become understandable. But the nature of bureaucratic work distinguishes it rather sharply from other kinds of work, thus a theory or model of bureaucracy may not fit all organizations. Several examples illustrate the limitations of bureaucratic theory. Weber claimed, for instance, that bureaus function most effectively when officials' authority is strictly delimited. A whole literature on alienation and job satisfaction argues otherwise.[4] Indeed, the dominant tendency nowadays is to enrich or enlarge jobs so as to minimize the effects of low morale upon productivity. The literature on job enlargement, it should be noted, pertains mainly to industrial settings. Weber's essay on bureaucracy, I believe, does not.

Let us turn to another example. Weber has a preference for hierarchical reporting relationships, strict super- and subordination, monocracy, and the like, such that officials are constrained to vertical links with subordinates and a single superior and not allowed lateral relations with others to whom they are neither superior nor subordinate. Again, the contemporary management literature does not recommend this arrangement in all instances because it can stultify initiative and block rapid responses to changes in the environment. So-called matrix or team organizations are suggested as alternatives in which people are grouped both by specialty or function and by project or "team" depending upon the task. A worker's team, hence team leader, may vary whereas his specialty and functional superior do not change. One should ask whether matrix or team organization, needed in settings where the technological climate is volatile, is equally appropriate for administering organizations whose work requires a high degree of continuity. A final example will perhaps suffice to underscore the importance of understanding the special character of bureaucratic work in interpreting Weber. Weber denies emphatically that fundamental differences exist between private and public administration, between business firms and government agencies. This flies directly in the face of a rich tradition in political science and economics that makes much of the distinction between firms and bureaus and argues that because bureaus do not operate in a market with voluntary quid pro quo transactions, they cannot evaluate their performance and hence are prone to inefficiency. At the risk of redundancy, I will raise the question of whether the gap between Weber's work and others' does not reflect different assumptions about the work of bureaus. The neoclassicists fear that bureaucracy will replace the profit motive in private enterprise. They do not recognize that many activities of firms—for example, the administration of insurance and pension plans—are necessarily run much like Weberian bureaus, and the kinds of things bureaus do not typically do (e.g., manufacture steel, at least in the United States) may be organized very differently.

Weber's work on bureaucracy, then, should be treated as

limited to administrative units. Like most scientific theories, theories of organizations that are nontrivial are also partial; they hold only under specified conditions. Weber's work becomes an example of an organizational theory applying to administrative units but not necessarily elsewhere. This occurs because the characteristics of bureaucracy Weber thought conducive to efficiency are in fact efficient for a limited class of organizations—those that must hold their members strictly accountable for nearly everything they do. The requirement of strict accountability means, in effect, that rules become ends in themselves for bureaucratic agencies. This is not the same as Merton's (1940) claim that adherence to rules for their own sake is a dysfunction or a pathology of individual bureaucrats. Quite the contrary, rule enforcement becomes paramount in administrative bureaus because of a strong normative presumption that the rules should be administered fairly and impartially by bureaucratic structures designated as appropriate instrumentalities for accomplishing this. Weber's phrase was *sine ira ac studio*, without hatred or passion. The normative principle of fairness is so embedded in bureaucracies that everyone who makes a decision—that is, implements a rule—must have authority and, at least in principle, be accountable for his action. Organizational structure is thus constructed by assigning only limited responsibilities to officials and requiring that the work of each be reviewed by a superior who is then also accountable. In other words, the requirement that rules be administered fairly, which is characteristic of modern societies, gives rise to bureaucratic structures to implement these rules because specialization and super- and subordination ensure that officials are acting within their authority and can be held to responsibility for their actions. Bureaucracy is in this sense closely linked to egalitarian beliefs, whether or not they are democratic.

On the surface, it would appear that the bureaucratic model is well suited for its purpose of administering fairly various codes and regulations. Weber, perhaps, was correct: Bureaucracy may be the most efficient means of carrying out administrative activities. Like the well-oiled machine, bureaucracy does predictably what was intended once it was set into motion. Weber waxed poetic about this quality of bureaus: "Precision, speed, unambiguity, knowledge of the files, continuity, discretion, strict super- and subordination, these are raised to the optimum point in the bureaucratic type of organization, and especially in its monocratic form" (1946:214). What Weber did not discuss and perhaps did not realize was the tendency of bureaucracies to grow due to increasing interdependencies in modern society, the need for rules to govern these interdependencies, and the increasing strain toward egalitarianism, which demands fairness in the application of rules. Just as there appears to be no alternative to bureaucratization, there may be no limit to it either.

Weber's statements about the superior efficiency of bureaucracy, then, create a paradox requiring exploration. For bureaus to do their jobs well, firm delineation of authority and lines of responsibility are required. But the principles of hierarchy and limited jurisdiction mean that levels of organization and the numbers of specialized subunits will increase with size.[5] This means that structure proliferates as the tasks of bureaus do. The result is that bureaus with relatively simple tasks eventually find themselves nested in larger agencies with more complex goals. For individual bureaus, then, the environment shifts from one dominated by constituencies to one where both constituencies and numerous other bureaus have to be dealt with. For government organization as a whole, the result is proliferation of hierarchy.

Both proliferation of hierarchy and fragmentation of the environment may have adverse consequences for efficiency—if not for the ability of bureaus to carry out their assigned tasks altogether. Extension of hierarchy slows and distorts communication, hence allows suboptional behavior to go undetected at higher levels. Fragmentation of the environment can obscure goals totally. Restructuring or reorganization may be the only way to bring about a closer match between external demands and internal administrative patterns if normal growth processes extend hierarchy and complicate the environment. A somewhat indirect test of Weber's assertion that bureaucracy tends toward efficiency rather than inefficiency, then, is possible by comparing ongoing agencies to instances where reorganization has occurred. If the former drift gradually toward inconsistency with the environment while the latter move rapidly toward consistency, then the implications of Weber's theory—if not the theory itself—would seem to have validity. If, by contrast, reorganization occurs with apparent randomness, without improving the fit between organizations and environments, then rethinking of the implications of Weber's theory may be required.

Whether or not Weber's theory of bureaucracy is correct becomes moot in light of this brief discussion. The ideal—typical model of bureaucracy is probably an accurate portrait of agencies whose mission is to administer rules fairly whether in the public or private sector. In all likelihood, it is less adequate as a description of other organizations where strict fairness, hence accountability, are not so important because other outputs are more visible. Weber's statements about the importance of authority and of super- and subordination likewise have partial validity. Insofar as they describe relationships between bosses and subordinates, Weber's statements are correct. But whether Weber meant to extend the idea of authority relationships to the interplay between bureaus in large governmental structures is, at best, uncertain. Finally, the issue of effectiveness of bureaus is especially difficult. If one wants to construct, *de novo,* organizations in which the level of accountability is sufficient to ensure impersonal application of abstract rules, then the bureaucratic model seems appropriate. But with new rules and greater demands for impartiality in their application, new bureaus and layers of authority are created; and they inevitably demand the attention of ongoing bureaus and thereby fragment the environment. The result may be that the effectiveness of bureaucratic structures may be self-limiting in the absence of continual reorganization aimed at restoring correspondences between organizational structure and the environment. To develop this notion further, some discussion of what is meant by *organizational environments* is required; and the distinction between immediate organizational and larger social environments in which bureaus operate must also be introduced.

### "Open" systems versus "closed" systems

A second central issue in the literature on organizations concerns whether organizations are to be treated as relatively closed, insular entities, or whether they are and should be viewed as open to their environments and influenced primarily by them. Weber's theory is usually viewed as a prototypical closed-system model in that it says relatively little about how external forces intrude upon organizations. A number of theoretical statements about open systems have been made, but they are not synthesized in a single theory as is Weber's. This occurs for a number of reasons: partly because the open-system approach is just that, an approach or perspective which is not grounded in a larger theory of social change; partly because of a paucity of concepts identifying the relevant environments of organizations; and partly because of some logical difficulties in dealing with the causal principles underlying open- versus closed-systems thinking. Open-systems theory is not usually connected with studies of bureaucracies. It is more often applied to firms operating in environments that are threatening or uncertain. I am devoting attention to open-systems theory because a careful analysis of its concepts yields conclusions that run counter to most stereotypes—namely that bureaucracies may be more open and vulnerable to their environments than firms, and that their rigidity and proliferation of layers may be more of a response to openness rather than evidence of closedness.

We should first ask what is meant by an "open" as opposed to a "closed" system. Organizational theory is rife with similar polarities. Aside from the open−closed dichotomy, theorists speak of natural- and rational-systems models (Gouldner, 1959), organic versus mechanistic organizations (Burns and Stalker, 1961), and the like. The open, natural, or organic system is viewed as complex, subject to inputs from environment, and possibly unpredictable. The closed, rational, or mechanistic setting is one where behavior is programmed in advance, the environment intrudes minimally and is neutralized when it does, and a modicum of technical rationality prevails. Causally, then, the open system is one that cannot control all of the forces affecting it, whereas the closed system either does not change or maintains feedback mechanisms permitting correction for environmental disturbances. Because perfect stability is rare in organizations or anywhere else, closed systems will be for the most part self-correcting rather than static ones. This view of a closed system does not fit intuitive notions of what a "closed" organization is like; but it is much more accurate than the notion that closed systems block environmental inputs, hence can be analyzed without regard to external factors. Because environments are ubiquitous, the question is not whether, rather how, their effects operate. Of some importance is the nature of causal processes between environments and organizations.

Let me present two models illustrating different types of organization−environment interchanges. One is a simple causal model: The environment shapes organizational goals, which in turn give rise to patterns of formal structure. The other is more complex because of a feedback loop: The environment shapes goals, and goals give rise to structure as before; but organizational structure in this model can be adjusted to maintain performance or attainment of goals such that the greater the deviation from desired performance, the greater the modification of organizational structure aimed at restoring performance. The two models are illustrated in Figure 1. Common to both models is a simple causal path from the environment to organizational goals. It is possible to add a path from the environment to structure directly without affecting the logic of either model, and it is also possible to posit paths from goals and structure to the environment, but we do not expect organizational goals or structure to affect the environment very much. Indeed, the relative (although by no means total) absence of feedback defines the environment for organizations. What distinguishes the two models is the causal path between structure and goals. In the simple causal model, no such path is present, and shifts in the environment lead, through goals, to corresponding shifts in structure. In the model incorporating feedback, there is a path between structures and goals, and its sign is the opposite of that connecting goals with structure. (This is denoted by $\pm$ and $\mp$.) Here, organizational structure maintains the capacity to attain goals. Disturbances in performance arising in the environment or changes in goals arising internally cause structural alterations whose ef-

Figure 1. Organizational environment, goals, and structure.

a. A simple causal model

b. Model incorporating feedback

fect is to restore outputs to the desired state. Environmental changes, then, may affect organizations with negative-feedback mechanisms, but there is no simple correspondence between what occurs in the environment and its long-run impact on organizations. Indeed, the best prediction is that stability will obtain where feedback mechanisms operate effectively.

The two models in Figure 1 demonstrate that intuitive classifications of organizations can be misleading unless their underlying logic is understood. The lower model, the one with the feedback loop, might seem to be more "organic" or "natural" than the simple causal model above it; but it is also one in which organizations are least disturbed by environmental changes, hence are most closed and most able to buffer their cores from the vicissitudes of the environment. In this sense, the model in the lower section of Figure 1 is more like a "rational" system than the model without feedback in which uncontrollable changes in the environment cause uncontrollable organizational changes. The latter, shown in the upper section of Figure 1, appears to be most "mechanistic" because of the presence of only simple causal links. It is also the model most like bureaucracy. Goals arising in the environment give rise to organizational structure, but elusive performance criteria render the link between organizational structure and goal attainment either slight or nonexistent. For this reason, the simple causal model in the upper section of Figure 1 yields organizations highly vulnerable to their environments. In the absence of self-correction, new demands from the environment trigger elaboration of existing organizations or formation of new organizational units without immediate attention to cost or to implications for existing programs. For this reason, organizational systems pervaded by simple causal logic are most open. A weak link between structure and goals, then, opens rather than closes public agencies to external pressures; and elaborate administrative structures and rules become understandable as responses to openness rather than evidence of closedness.

A third causal model of relationships among environments, organizational goals, and structures does not appear in Figure 1; but it nonetheless deserves mention. This is a positive-feedback system in which effects of environmental disturbances increase rather than attentuate over time. Crozier's (1964) discussion of the vicious circle of bureaucratic dysfunctions is one example of a positive-feedback model. Crozier observes that four elements in bureaucracies—centralization, rules, strata isolation, and parallel (i.e., nonhieriarchical) power relationships—feed upon one another so that public agencies alternate between periods of inefficiency and crisis. Whether Crozier's idea of the vicious cycle is meant only as a metaphor or as a causal statement is unclear. Positive feedback—that is to say, a self-exaggerating rather than a self-correcting causal pattern—is rare in organizations surviving over long periods of time. Sooner or later, correction must take place or the system will "explode" with ever-increasing values of variables.

What, then, remains for the distinction between open and closed systems? First of all, the open-systems approach stands as a directive, for it focuses attention on relations between environments and organizations that are most likely to operate according to simple causal logic, hence are most easily detected. The closed-system perspective, which focuses on relations among internal organizational attributes, may yield straightforward results, but only where equilibrium processes are not expected. Second, the open-systems approach also raises the question of what kinds of organizations are most vulnerable to their environments. The discussion above suggests that such organizations are those where simple causal logic describes best relations among internal attributes. But the open- versus closed-systems polarity also yields some paradoxical results. Types of organizations usually considered most open turn out to have the least susceptibility to environmental influences because of feedback mechanisms. Organizations normally considered to be the most rigid and closed, such as bureaucracies, turn out to be especially vulnerable to the environment because of the weak or nonexistent causal link running from organizational structure to goals. The fact that the open- versus closed-systems distinction yields counterintuitive results suggests that it encompasses too much and that it may potentially obscure rather than illuminate relationships among variables describing environments and organizations. If in considering categories describing the environment one is engaging in open-systems analysis, then there is no quarrel with its precepts. But to think of open-systems analysis as something fundamentally different from the closed-system approach may divert one from more fundamental and important differences among organizations—namely whether or not they have feedback mechanisms that allow dampening or buffering of environmental disturbances. Bureaucracies generally lack these mechanisms; and in the absence of well-defined and accepted effectiveness criteria, their rule boundedness and tendency to elaborate structure can be understood at least partly as adaptive responses to intrusions from the environment.

### A partial resolution: organizations as open yet intendedly closed

A partial resolution of the open- versus closed-system debate has been proposed by the late James D. Thompson in his seminal *Organizations in Action* (1967). Thompson's formulation is this: Whereas instrumental organizations strive for technical rationality, hence closedness, they are in fact open to the environment and subject to uncertainty. Various mechanisms—such as buffering, stockpiling, and forecasting and deployment of personnel into specialized boundary-spanning units—help absorb uncertainty arising in the environment, and they protect an organization's technical core.

Organizational structure, then, is the joint product of internal arrangements designed to minimize costs associated with technological interdependencies and the placement of boundary-spanning units whose task is to cope with the environment.

Thompson's overall approach will be adopted here, although with some modifications. Following Thompson, and anticipating considerably more openness to the environment in public bureaucracies than stereotypes suggest, it is intended to focus upon mechanisms mediating environmental influences upon organizations. The organizational elements mediating the environment, however, are somewhat different from those anticipated by Thompson's theory. The hierarchical organization of finance offices precludes specialized boundary-spanning units; and buffering of the environment, when it is possible, occurs mainly through delay rather than organizational design. We will therefore turn to some other mechanisms potentially mediating the environment—including, most importantly, the nature of leadership positions, claims to "turf" or domain made by public bureaucracies, and organizational continuity as opposed to reorganization. Organizations are viewed as seeking stability but operating in environments compelling change. The means through which change is promoted or retarded are to be explored in some detail.

*Immediate versus larger environments*

The literature advocating open-systems approach to organizations hardly recognizes the multiplicity of environments to which organizations respond. (An exception is Hall's [1972] classification of environments as either general or specific.) Instead, variable properties of environments are described—stable versus shifting, homogeneous versus heterogeneous, placid versus turbulent, munificent versus threatening, and so forth (see Emery and Trist, 1965; Levine and White, 1961; Terreberry, 1968; Thompson, 1967). Complexity within organizations is assumed to arise from the level of complexity or uncertainty in the environment. Mismatches between texture of the environment and organizational structures impede effectiveness; optimal performance obtains when organizational and environmental properties correspond. Indeed, in some theories, the boundary between environments and organizations is all but discarded. Weick, (1969), for example, speaks of organizational enactment of environments to which organizations, in turn, respond. J. Meyer and Rowan (1977) claim that the structure of many organizations, especially those in "highly institutionalized contexts," are but relfections of societal myths about how organizations should be.

Aside from the near circularity of these statements—effective organizations are those most consistent with their environments, but consistency is judged by effectiveness; organizations react to environments they enact; organizational structure is little more than the concretization of myths defining organizations—their main weakness is in the failure to differentiate the various external elements to which organizations might respond. There is, of course, a link between an organization's purposes and the kinds of events triggering organizational action: Fire departments respond to alarms, stockbrokers to stock market fluctuations, and so forth. How closely linked purposes and relevant environments are for administrative bureaus is an open question, however. This issue arises in part because bureaus often have multiple goals. A candid projection of revenues and expenditures may contribute to the professional standing of a finance director but cost him his job if he proposes a tax hike in an election year. The structure of public agencies also blurs relevant environments somewhat. The imperative of hierarchy means that most bureaus are nested in larger governmental structures. Public officials, then, serve dual masters: a constituency and a boss whose constituency is somewhat different and who, in turn, may also have a boss. A city finance director, for example, must be responsive to the finance committee or council, to the local financial community, as well as to his mayor or manager. A data-processing manager faces different but equally complex demands from his boss (often a finance director), other department heads, and, again, the governing body of his community. An important question in studying public agencies, then, concerns not only which of these multiple environments affect bureaus most readily but also the nature of the response to different elements in the environment.

This formulation adds credence to the earlier argument that public agencies are, in fact, more open or vulnerable to external conditions than firms for whom the dominant element in the environment, although not the sole one, is the market. Multiple environments imposing multiple demands make organizational adjustments to any single demand problematic insofar as other pressures may be thereby exacerbated. It also suggests a rough classification of environments affecting government bureaus. One can speak of the immediate environment consisting of other bureaus of the same level of government and of superordinate agencies. This is much in contrast to the larger social, political, and economic environments that give meaning to the mission of a bureau and to which government structures most ultimately respond. The distinction between immediate and larger environments is by no means absolute. One can conceive, for example, of intermediate levels of the environment where social and political pressures operating on local agencies are backed by incentives or the threatened withdrawal of incentives from state and federal agencies. But the distinction does help identify a number of external factors influencing public bureaus; and it orders them in terms of their organizational if not physical proximity to the agencies that are the subject of research.

The distinction between immediate and larger environments also leads to a central hypothesis in the study: Much *short-run* variation in public organizations is due to forces in the immediate environment. This hypothesis is phrased so as to allow for the possibility of a number of other sources of organizational change, especially those located in the larger social and political context; but the intention is also to exclude others. Specifically excluded is the notion that the organizational structures of public agencies arise principally out of internal needs other than size or scope of activities. It will be shown later that, over time, most of the organizational attributes of the agencies studied arise directly or indirectly from identifiable, forces in the environment. A critical question to be explored here, and one which cannot be answered fully, is whether changes in larger social, political, and economic environments affect public agencies directly, or whether such changes occur only after forces arising in the larger environment have been filtered through interstitial structures. Our evidence indicates that larger social and political forces are usually mediated by immediate environments and buffering mechanisms in organizations, but that their effects are rarely avoided. *Long-run* variation in public bureaucracies, then, is hypothesized to arise in the larger environment.

Whatever the relative effects of immediate and larger environments on public agencies, the distinction between different levels of environment calls attention to the multiplicity of external considerations to which managers of bureaucracies are sensitized. Rather than a market, there is a mission, multiple constituencies, and superordinate layers of authority with which to deal. (Finance directors must also contend with bond attorneys, brokers, and rating agencies, all of whom were taken for granted until recently.) A central question for social science as well as for public policy is to which of the different layers of the environment bureaus are most prone to respond. Neither Weber nor open-systems theorists anticipated the problem, much less its implications. If bureaus respond almost entirely to the immediate environment of other agencies and superordinate authority, and feebly or not at all to forces in the larger environment, then sooner or later they will become wholly unresponsive to the public, and the epithet "bureaucracy" will apply with a vengeance. But if public agencies ignore their immediate environments and become captives of outside constituencies, then orderly administration is threatened and the question of whose interest is being served becomes salient. The tensions between demands of immediate and larger environments are ubiquitous, and I hope to be able to illuminate some of them.

*Internal change versus external selection*

A somewhat novel approach to environment−organization relations is offered by evolutionary models, labeled natural-selection (Aldrich and Pfeffer, 1976) or population-ecology (Hannan and Freeman, 1977) theories. Rather than focusing upon rational adaptation of existing organizations to changes in the environment, the model of change implicit in most open-system theories, the evolutionary framework claims that change occurs through selection of organizations best adapted to the environment and elimination of others. The evolutionary approach posits stages of variation, selection, and retention of organizations; the population-ecology perspective adds to this considerations of the carrying capacity of environments, niche width, and whether or not environmental variations are fine- or coarse-grained. In both of these theories, however, the environment operates mainly through replacement of organizations rather than change in existing ones.

Whatever the merits of evolutionary theories−and they may not apply meaningfully to public bureaucracies, as Aldrich and Pfeffer (1976:88) point out−it is not clear how the evolutionary approach can be compared to conventional open-systems views of organizations. Evolutionary theory focuses on populations of organizations, whereas individual organizations are normally the unit of analysis in the open-systems perspective. Evolutionary theory treats organizations as if they operated in common environments, whereas the more conventional approach is to compare organizations assuming that their environments differ in some significant dimensions. Evolutionary theory, additionally, requires that organizations be observed long enough for population changes to occur. The choice of units—populations or individual organizations—whether one assumes common or distinct environments, and the interval over which observations are made determine crucially which theory can be tested. Rational open-systems theory and evolutionary models need not be disparate, but they are difficult to consider simultaneously. But it should be noted that a great deal of open-systems theory, especially Thompson's, is based on the premise that organizations must behave rationally so that their survival is not threatened by evolutionary processes.

### Generality in organizational theory

Another bedrock issue in organizational analysis concerns the possibility of highly accurate, hence predictive, statements about organizations. My concern for this issue stems from the oscillations organizational theory has undergone in the past decade. We have witnessed on, the one hand, attempt to develop general laws of organizational behavior and, on the other hand, a reversion to case or "process" studies triggered by the failure of quantitative analysis to yield meaningful results. The earlier discussion of some dominant schools of organizational theory—Weberian analysis of bureaucracy and the open-systems approach—underscores the difficulty. Weber's theory, it was noted, describes only a limited class of organizations and may be considered by some to be of more historical and antiquarian than contemporary relevance. Open-systems theory, on the other hand, may be a truism masking the complexities of the environments with which organizations must cope. The limitations of theory parallel the sparseness of research results to date. There have been three main findings in the literature: Organizational structure proliferates with size; administrative ratios decline with size; but the administrative or overhead component grows with structural complexity. These empirical results hardly speak to the issues with which either Weber or the open-systems school are concerned. Quite the contrary. They reflect design or engineering considerations involved in constructing administrative structures, but not causal linkages between environments and organizations or within networks of organizations which are notable for their weakness or inconsistency in empirical research studies (Pennings, 1975).

What accounts for this chasm between theory and empirical work, or, better, the lack of reliable and *interesting* research results? One possibility is that both theory and research have been too macroscopic. Advocates of the microscopic approach treat structure as but reification or formalism, and the environment as a source of stimuli triggering action by individual people. The essence of organization consists of decision premises held in peoples' heads; administrative activity consists of applying these premises to actual cases. Microscopic theory can, in fact, account for the few relible research findings that have surfaced. If organizational structure is but formalism, then connections between size, structure, and administrative burden can be interpreted as necessary outcomes of rules whereby structural formalisms are established—unity of command, span of control, and so forth. Additionally, the paucity of documented environment—organization links becomes understandable. If definition of the environment depends mainly upon cognitive mechanisms of individual persons, the macroscopic properties of both environments and organizations are several steps removed from the actual causal nexus and only weakly linked. *Perceived* environmental properties rather than actual ones have causal primacy from the microscopic perspective.

Another possibility, and one that I favor, is that research on organizations to date has been too microscopic. From this perspective, the disjunction of theory and research and the lack of demonstrated effects of organizational environments arises from too great an emphasis on convenient but small issues at the expense of questions suggested by theory. Some of the larger issues not fully explored in organizational research have been suggested above: Whether variations in organizational structures are greater over time than across organizations at one point; whether environmental effects are due to elements in the immediate task environment or larger social, political, and economic environments; what interstitial mechanisms mediate environmental effects; and whether organizational change occurs mainly incrementally in ongoing units or more sporadically through reorganization or replacement of existing structures.

These questions have several common elements. First, they require comparisons of organizations over time. Second, they require a greater range of data about both immediate and larger environments than has usually been available to researchers. Some of these data may be qualitative rather than quantitative. Third, some attention to populations of organizations is also required in order to observe demise, reorganization, and replacement of existing structures.

There is a third possibility that students of organizations have preferred not to entertain but must be considered here—namely that a highly general theory of organizations is unlikely, even among organizations in a single society. The nomothetic/ideographic distinction—i.e., the argument that the cultural and social sciences differ from the natural sciences in that the former deal with noncomparable (ideographic) units—might be invoked in support of this claim. But it is possible to use the natural-science model in studying organizations and still conclude that general laws are improbable. If behavior in organizations is shaped by combinations of individual, interpersonal, structural, environmental, and historical forces, then there is little likelihood of uncovering causal patterns of high generality in a single empirical research study. If causal laws governing organizations change over time in response to broad economic, political, and cultural changes, then, again, the likelihood of finding general patterns is slight. It is ironic that although positivistic methods permit disconfirmation of any single proposition, they cannot confirm the hypothesis that very few empirical regularities will hold across diverse units and over lengthy intervals. For these reasons, researchers have always operated as if general laws existed even in the absence of evidence supporting them.

A highly general and predictive theory of organizations seemed possible at the time when this research on finance agencies began a decade ago. Relatively few quantitative studies of large numbers of organizations had been undertaken, and they were addressed primarily to two issues: the adequacy of Weber's theory of bureaucracy and the effects of size on administrative overhead. (Regarding the former, see Stinchcombe, 1959, and Udy, 1959; regarding the latter, see Terrien and Mills, 1955, Anderson and Warkov, 1961, Rushing, 1967, and Pondy, 1969.) The adequacy of Weber's theory is primarily an academic issue of interest to sociologists and political scientists. The effects of size on administration may be as much a matter for industrial engineering or operations research as for social science. But both questions seemed to be of sufficient generality to be worthy of detailed studies; and the first survey of finance agencies in 1966 was addressed to them, especially to the issue of the consistency of Weber's model of bureaucracy. By the time the second survey of finance agencies was underway in 1972, the central issues in organizational theory had shifted somewhat. Woodward's (1965) work on industrial organization had shown the importance of technology to organizational structures; Lawrence and Lorsch (1967a) had demonstrated some effects of environmental contingencies; and Blau (1970) had elaborated a formal theory of structural differentiation, largely the result of size, in administrative bureaus. Categories describing environments, size, structure, and technology replaced the Weberian model as the focus of interest; and the longitudinal research reported here was initially aimed at developing propositions concerning interrelations of these categories. Findings of some generality have emerged, but they are not those anticipated. This occurred partly because what we thought we were measuring and what was actually measured were different in many instances. For example, whether or not a finance agency operates its own computer has little to do with its level of technological advancement. It does reflect, however, the centrality of an agency in the information flow of local government and possibly its power relative to other departments. Agency names connote more than functions; they are implicit claims to domain that can help or hinder the augmentation of organizational resources over time. Organizational structure, it turns out, reflects very little. Save for one small effect—multi-level structures promote decentralized decision-making—formal administrative arrangements are dependent on other things and the cause of nothing; hence they must be viewed as mechanisms preserving the semblance if not the substance of orderly and rational management. Other unexpected findings hinge on meanings, based on qualitative considerations about finance agencies, which are attributed to quantitative data. These interpretations may be limited to a single set of organizations. Theoretical generalizations, then, though based on quantitative evidence, may also be limited to the organizations studied, although they are not necessarily so limited. The relatively large number of organizations discussed here and the use of tests of statistical significance should not mislead one into believing that the same empirical findings would hold necessarily for all organizations at all times.

## Summary

An analysis of Weber's theory of bureaucracy leads to paradoxical conclusions. Whereas bureaucracy arises due to demands for fairness and impartiality in administration, which are attained through rules and strict accountability, growth of bureaucratic structures results in proliferation of hierarchy and fragmentation of the environment such that effectiveness may be self-limiting and periodic reorganization needed to restore environment—organization correspondences. Open-system theory is, likewise, fraught with paradox. Organizations most open to the environment are also those lacking feedback mechanisms, whereas closedness is attained through simultaneous shifts in structure and outputs such that environmental disturbances in either are largely corrected. Since bureaucracies usually lack feedback mechanisms, openness to the environment is expected as is considerable change, much more than anticipated by traditional stereotypes. To the extent that change is governed by larger social and political environments that gave rise to bureaucratic structures in the first place, empirical laws describing relationships between properties of immediate environments and organizations may be highly contingent and time-bound. Indeed, in the chapters that follow, descriptive and historical materials are needed for interpretation and generalization from specific empirical findings.

# 2

# Organizational research

We now turn to the design of research studies whose results are reported in this book. The design of research, of course, depends very much on the ideas or hypotheses to be explored, but it also has consequences. In particular, the possibilities for unanticipated findings are very much influenced by design considerations; and it is in this sense that method governs the substance of research. Our account of the studies of finance agencies begins with a formal introduction to comparative organizational research and the differences between panel or longitudinal as opposed to more conventional cross-sectional designs. This discussion is methodological for it concerns techniques rather than ideas. We then turn to the design of the research on finance agencies and some consequences of the longitudinal design that had not been expected but that changed fundamentally the substance of the research. Why this shift occurred will be explored in some detail.

### The longitudinal approach to organizations
The longitudinal approach to the study of organizations is a natural outgrowth of developments in the field over the past two decades. The early sociological studies of large-

scale organizations, done mainly by students of Robert K. Merton just after World War II, were case analyses. (See especially Selznick, 1949; Lipset, 1950; Blau, 1955; and Gouldner, 1954.) These works had the virtues of depth and fidelity—no one could deny that they were accurate portraits of the organizations studied—but the scientific value of observations based on single cases is subject to question. In particular, drawing causal inferences about all organizations from evidence describing one or a handful is fraught with risk because of the high likelihood that an anomalous instance was observed or that the true causal variable or variables were obscured from the observer. Gouldner's observation that leadership succession is followed by proliferation of rules, for example, has not always been reproduced in studies comparing many organizations; Blau's claim that rules serve as functional substitutes for direct supervision and shift the supervisor's role from managerial to consultative has likewise not been substantiated in multi-case studies. A series of interesting *aperçus* were developed in these observational studies. In other words, the studies remained cases and did not become the foundation for a systematic theory of organizations. For this reason more than any other, research on organizations shifted from case to comparative analysis and from observational to quantitative methods in the mid-1960s.

### Major comparative studies

A variety of approaches to quantitative comparative organizational research were pursued at first; and any attempt to classify them inevitably introduces some distortions. Nonetheless, it is instructive to ask two major questions of some major research projects comparing organizations that were undertaken in the early and mid-1960s: What were the theories or theoretical propositions addressed in the research, and what data were adduced in order to test the theories? A brief review of the work of five groups of researchers suggests some of the virtues as well as some limitations of the comparative method.

*The Aston group.* Several researchers at the University of Aston, England (Pugh, Hickson, Hinings, Turner, Pheysey, and others), who were *not* primarily sociologists, studied a number of large organizations in the Birmingham area. The organizations surveyed were heterogeneous, ranging from government bureaus to insurance companies, manufacturers of chocolate bars, and manufacturers of motor cars. Altogether some fifty-four organizations with more than 250 employees were surveyed. Lengthy interview schedules requiring an average of one full week per organization to complete were administered by the researchers. The theoretical aims of the Aston group were not as ambitious as their data were massive. Schooled primarily in psychology, Pugh and his colleagues focused their initial empirical work more on classification and taxonomy than on testing causal propositions about organizations. In their later work, which went beyond the initial stage of classification, organizational size emerged as the dominant causal variable. The Aston researchers argue, for example, that size accounts for the structuring of activities in organizations, concentration of authority, and even, to some extent, the technology an organization employs. Some of the results of the Aston group have been questioned, especially the finding that apparent effects of technology vanish once size is controlled (see, for example, Aldrich, 1972). The work of the Aston group appears mainly in scholarly articles in *Administrative Science Quarterly* (see Hickson et al. 1969, 1971; Pugh et al. 1963, 1968, 1969a, 1969b).

*Peter Blau and his associates.* Blau's Comparative Organization Research Program (CORP) began at the University of Chicago in 1965 and conducted several surveys of relatively homogeneous sets of organizations–employment security bureaus, finance agencies, hospitals, retail stores, and manufacturing firms. The research was initially aimed at testing causal propositions derived from Weber's theory of bureaucracy and later to developing and refining a formal theory of differentiation in organizations. Briefly, the theory of differentiation states that structural differentiation in organizations increases at a decreasing rate with size, and, net of size, administrative overhead increases with differentiation. The major publications from CORP draw data primarily from the study of fifty-four state and territorial employment security bureaus and their subunits (Blau, 1970; Blau and Schoenherr, 1971). The theoretical generalizations developed from these data are tested and for the most part confirmed in the other data sets (Blau, 1972). The data sets were never pooled, however, and theoretical explanations for effects of organizational type and environments were not developed.

*Hage and Aiken.* Two researchers at the University of Wisconsin conducted intensive studies of health and welfare agencies in a midwestern metropolitan area in the late 1960s. Sixteen organizations were included in the initial research, the case base increasing to twenty-nine later on. Organizational measures were constructed by aggregating responses of individual members within each of the agencies studied. Some of the results of Hage and Aiken's research are as follows: The effects of organizational complexity are ubiquitous. Complexity (i.e., occupational specialization, professionalization) is related to decentralization of authority and program change. Decentralization and program change, in turn, militate against formalization as do nonroutine work roles. Complexity is associated with organizational interdependence as measured by joint programs. The reader is referred to several articles (Hage, 1967; Hage and Aiken, 1967; Aiken and Hage, 1968) and a book (Hage and Aiken, 1970) for the details of the research. Of importance here is that the key causal variable in Hage and Aiken's research is organizational complexity rather than either size or technology.

*Lawrence and Lorsch.* The theoretical sophistication of Lawrence and Lorsch's *Organization and Environment* (1967a) is perhaps as great as any research study of the 1960s. Lawrence and Lorsch attempted to trace links between differentiation in the environment, patterns of organizational structure, and organizational effectiveness. They evolved a contingency theory of effectiveness asserting that organizations with structures consistent with the environment—that is, organizational differentiation appropriate to the level of differentiation in the environment and organizational integration appropriate to the level of differentiation—were the most likely to be high performers. The data upon which these generalizations are based are, however, somewhat limited. The initial study in *Organization and Environment* concerned six firms in the business of developing, marketing, and producing plastics; it was then extended to an additional two firms in the container industry and two in the consumer-foods industry. The study was later replicated (Lawrence and Lorsch, 1967b) in six subunits of chemical companies. In *Organization and Environment,* direct measurement of environments was not attempted. Instead, environments were characterized by executives' perceptions of them, the plastics industry being most dynamic and differentiated and the container industry least so. Measures of differentiation and integration were also based on questionnaire responses. For this reason, Lawrence and Lorsch's results may reflect more about *perceived* connections than actual causal processes between environments and organizations (see Tosi et al. 1973 ).

*Woodward.* Joan Woodward and her associates (1965) studied some 100 industrial firms in southeastern England in order to understand the relationship of technology to organizational structure. Firms were classified as having small-batch, large-batch, or continuous-process technologies. Small-batch firms, on average, had squatter hierarchies, wider spans of control, and fewer administrative personnel than others; continuous-process firms had taller and thinner hierarchies and used many more expert personnel. Woodward also noted that firms with spans of control at or near the median for all organizations with similar technologies tended to be most effective. This result is consistent with Lawrence and Lorsch's conclusion that effectiveness depends upon the appropriateness of structure for a given technology or environment.

### Comparing comparative studies

An interesting result emerges when one compares these major empirical studies of organizations along two dimensions: the scope of data collected and the level of theoretical development. The scope of data collected encompasses the number and diversity of organizations studied and the number of variables measured. The level of theoretical development is judged by the range and generality of concepts used in interpreting empirical results. Quantitative assessment of research studies along these dimensions is not easy, but some qualitative rankings are possible. For example, the scope of data collected by the Aston group exceeded that of any other research study; Blau's empirical studies were more extensive than Woodward's; Hage and Aiken and Lawrence and Lorsch amassed the least data about organizations, although a great deal of information from individual people, in their analyses. The theoretical complexity of these major studies does not follow the same order, however. Lawrence and Lorsch is perhaps most theoretically advanced because it attempts to link organizational properties with environments. Blau ranks second because of the attempt to construct a highly general and deductive theory of organizational structures, albeit one that does not consider the environment. Hage and Aiken do not develop a theory of environment—organization relations like Lawrence and Lorsch or a deductive theory like Blau, but they do focus upon theoretically relevant categories such as complexity, formalization, and interdependence. Woodward's concern for effects of technology leaves her work less developed theoretically than Hage and Aiken's, but more so than the Aston group whose main contribution has been to the measurement of organizational properties. Figure 2 displays graphically the relationship between scope of data collected and the level of theoretical development of these four major comparative organizational studies. Clearly, there is no positive association between the scope of data and the level of theoretical

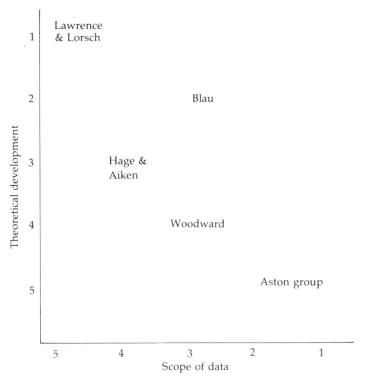

Figure 2. Relationship of scope of data to level of theoretical development of studies comparing organizations.

development, and there may be a negative association. Possible explanations for this outcome deserve careful exploration.

One cannot dismiss, at least initially, the possibility that studies that gathered the most data were not intended to test complex theories, especially theories dealing with environmental effects. Woodward's study, for example, was concerned explicitly with effects of technology, not of environments or of a myriad of other possible causes of formal organizational arrangements. For this reason, Woodward's theoretical contribution was deliberately limited. It is not certain that the same was true for the other studies under consideration, however. Both Blau and the Aston researchers wished to introduce environmental concepts into their work but did not succeed fully – Blau because he could not separate "scope of activities" from organizational size, and the Aston group because the components of the "technology—charter – location nexus" were also inseparable.

Another possibility, and the more likely one, is that comparative organizational studies proceeded by treating all organizations as comparable, ignoring two strictures fundamental to the social sciences. The first stricture is that invariant properties cannot explain variance in other things. In Blau's research, especially that reported in *The Structure of Organizations*, characteristics of the environment most salient for the agencies studied did not vary across them because state and local employment security offices are tied together in a Federal Employment Security System. The *national* unemployment rate and federal legislation affecting administration of the system (e.g., extension of eligibility for unemployment compensation due to adverse economic conditions) have in all likelihood profound effects on state and local employment-service and unemployment-compensation offices; but these effects do not change from place to place at any one time but only over time.

A second fundamental stricture is that comparative research requires comparable indicators. This problem is acute when studying organizations of different types, but it is rarely acknowledged by those doing comparative organizational research. For example, formalization in organizations may be measured by the extensiveness of personnel rules, but the origins and purposes of rules may vary widely across different types of organizations. Personnel rules in public bureaucracies, as will be shown below, are largely outgrowths of the civil service movement and the press for "merit" standards. In industry, by contrast, many personnel rules evolve through collective bargaining and have less to do with the question of merit than of adjudication of disputes between management and labor. Problems of comparability are even greater when one attempts to measure environments of organizations. To use Emery and Trist's phrase, how does one compare the "causal texture" of diverse sorts of organizational environments? Small businesses, for example, are affected greatly by market fluctuations, whereas public bureaucracies operate in political environments largely devoid of classical market considerations. To compare such disparate environments other than qualitatively is extraordinarily difficult and perhaps beyond the reach of the social sciences at their present stage of development. These considerations, however, were largely overlooked in the work of the Aston group.

Research on organizations, then, is caught between the Scylla of inadequate variation in environments, as occurred in Blau's research, and the Charybdis of inordinate variation in environments whose meaning cannot be captured quantitatively, as occurred in the Aston group studies. Perhaps because of this difficulty, intensive analyses of organizational processes illuminating the effects of complex environments continue to appear in the literature (see Mintzberg, 1973; March and Olsen, 1976). It need hardly be said that this approach is not taken here. Studies of process are little different in form if not in content form the case-study method that was dropped in favor of comparative analysis because inferences drawn from single cases usually do not hold for other organizations. But if one is not to abandon the comparative method of studying organizations, then how could it be extended and yet avoid the pitfalls of either insufficient variation or inordinate variation in environments? Put somewhat differently, must comparative organizational studies choose between examining single types of organizations and the buckshot approach, which captures as many types as organizations studied?

One solution to the dilemma of inadequate versus inordinate variation in the environment is the longitudinal approach, the study of a set of organizations over an extended time period. The longitudinal approach is particularly appealing for public organizations whose functions are routine and whose continued existence can be taken for granted. Routineness of functions means that environments are sufficiently stable to be measured reliably; continuity means that the organizations exist long enough for long-term shifts in administrative patterns to occur and to be noticed. The work of the finance agencies studied here is largely routine, and their continuity is assured; public agencies with short lifespans, such as Model Cities programs, could not be studied in the same way. Some organizational changes caused by variation in the environment, then, will occur in a longitudinal study of finance agencies if only because of the interval between measurements. Variation is limited, however, by the choice of a somewhat, although not wholly, homogeneous set of organizations. Limited variation in the environment allows for understanding and interpretation of environmental effects when they do occur, and it reduces very much noncomparability of indicators. In short, the longitudinal approach offers at least a possibility of bringing theoretically interesting constructs describing environments into empirical research on organizations.

The last point deserves elaboration, for it does not specify what takes place between environments and organizations that one would want to study if he could. "Contingency" theory suggests that the focus should be on the consistency between organizations and environments; and it also suggests, if only indirectly, that mismatches between organizations and environments lower the survival chances of an organization. This is, of course, but a restatement of an evolutionary theory of organizations. But static theorizing in terms of matches or mismatches between organizations and environments leads to circularity, because the degree of match or mismatch can be judged only by an organization's survival or performance. A more dynamic perspective removes the circularity, however. Instead of speaking of consistency or match between organizations and environments, one can describe relations between organizations and environments in terms of measurable variables. Shifts in environments, shifts within organizations, and the replacement of old organizational forms with new ones can be observed. Sometimes, environmental shifts and shifts within organizations coincide in a manner indicative of orderly change. Sometimes drift occurs—environments change but organizations do not, or vice versa—such that correspondences between environment properties and elements of organizations affected by them deteriorate over time. Sometimes there is total rather than incremental change, and old organizations either vanish or are wholly reorganized. Once basic processes taking place between organizations and environments are identified, then attention can shift to the causes of these processes. In this way, empirical research can address directly some of the issues central to organizational theory, and a greater correspondence between the effort expended on empirical-research studies and their theoretical significance becomes possible.

### The problem of causal inferences
Another problem endemic to organizational research is the gap between observation and causal inference. Whereas research of all types is affected by measurement

error as well as error due to omission of variables from statistical models, studies of organizations are affected by ambiguity as to the direction of causality where statistical associations appear. Studies of behavior of individual people are usually not affected by this uncertainty because of known sequences of events in the life cycle: Parents' social class precedes that of their children, education precedes occupational attainment, and political-party affiliation normally precedes actual vote. Organizational properties, by contrast, are not known to precede in orderly sequences, or at least there is little evidence suggesting the existence of such sequences. In the absence of a known time-ordering of organizational variables, this ordering must be assumed, and often without a strong theoretical basis. Environmental properties are usually assumed to take precedence over others, followed by size, technology, structure, and outcomes such as effectiveness measures. The impact of arbitrary assumptions on causal inferences drawn from cross-sectional data is demonstrated in Aldrich's (1972) reanalysis of the Aston group data concerning effects of technology on organizational structure. By assuming that technology precedes size rather than the other way around, Aldrich was able to find causal paths from measures of technology to measures of size and structure. This dependence of substantive results on untestable assumptions concerning causal ordering suggests the need for more robust models of organizational processes.

Aside from the question as to the direction of causation, there is also the issue of whether causality is directional or simultaneous—$x$ causes $y$, but $y$ causes $x$ at the same time. This issue does not normally arise in sociological studies of individual persons; but, again, it does arise when organizations are the subject of research. (Consider again the research on voting behavior and status attainment, as well as numerous attitudinal studies in which assumptions about the time ordering of variables can be made.) There is a much greater likelihood of simultaneity in organizations than for individual persons because of explicit goals and the tendency of organizations to "satisfice" (i.e., to settle for satisfactory levels of performance rather than maximal levels). The relationship between supervision and productivity is illustrative. The more supervision, the more productivity; but the greater the productivity, the less supervisory effort needed to maintain it. (Advocates of soft management may disagree.) If organizations were maximizers, causality would run predominately from supervision to productivity, but because workers can realistically be pushed only so far, productivity will have some effect on the intensity with which they are supervised. The relationship between organizational size and technology may also be simultaneous; larger organizations may be better able to afford advanced technologies, but advanced technologies often promote growth.

An advantage of longitudinal studies is that they usually permit stronger causal inferences than cross-sectional comparative studies; and they offer at least the possibility of testing models involving simultaneous or reciprocal causation, which cross-sectional studies of organizations normally cannot do. Strong causal inferences are possible in longitudinal research because the time ordering of variables is known. All variables measured at an earlier time precede those measured later on. For the same reason, testing for simultaneity is possible. One can ask both whether $x$ at an earlier time affects $y$ later on and whether the earlier measure of $y$ affects the later measurement of $x$. A cautionary note is required, however. Even though longitudinal data permit tests for causality and simultaneity, this does not mean that results of these tests will be conclusive. All statistical models depend upon unproven assumptions, and the assumptions underlying longitudinal analysis are somewhat more restrictive than those necessary for cross-sectional studies. These assumptions will be discussed presently. A further cautionary note has to do with the nature of organizations studied. When the research began, it assumed that public bureaucracies behaved according to stereotypes, that they were relatively closed from the environment, and that questions concerning causal ordering and simultaneity among variables describing organizational properties were of more interest than environmental effects. The results, however, suggest that the initial expectations were inaccurate. Whereas some causal relations among organizational variables were clarified by the longitudinal analysis, the most interesting results showed links between environments and organizations. Indeed, the actual findings were so different from those anticipated that a new imagery was needed to describe the bureaucracies studied. Instead of closed and fairly well coordinated systems, we began to think of public agencies as open to the environment and very loosely coupled. The implications of openness and loose coupling for the administration of public businesswill be discussed in some detail in Chapter 7.

### Some statistical issues in longitudinal analysis

Longitudinal analysis involves statistical estimation from data describing cross sections of units (people, groups, organizations, or other social aggregates) at two or more points in time. It is distinguished from analysis of cross-sectional data collected at a single point by repeated measurements and substantial lags between them. It differs from time-series analysis in that representative cross sections, not single units, are studied repeatedly. The term "time series of cross sections" describes longitudinal analysis most accurately, but it is cumbersome and somewhat misleading in that true time-series usually involve data collection at ten or more points. Sociologists often refer to the longitudinal approach as panel analysis (see, for example, Berelson et al. 1954). The utility of the longitudinal approach is in its ability to test hypotheses that cannot be considered easily when only cross-sectional data are available—especially hypotheses of simultaneous causation, because identification of regression models is not an insurmountable problem. There are some limitations in longitudinal analysis, however, and they should be explored along with its advantages. These limitations arise due to uncertainties as to identification (i.e., what causal paths can be *omitted* from models), lags between cause and effect, and autocorrelated error terms. Problems of identification, lag, and autocorrelated error will be discussed with reference to hypotheses concerning organizations.

### The identification problem

Identification of regression models is not a problem in simple recursive systems where causality is unidirectional, that is, where $x$ causes $y$ which causes $z$, and so forth. For example, in the simplest of regression models, $y$ is a function or follows from $x$, and $y$ is not a cause of $x$.[1] The error term, $e$, is also a cause of $y$, and it is assumed not to be a cause of $x$.

$$y = b_1x + e \tag{1}$$

This assumption permits easy estimation of $b_1$ from the following

$$\Sigma xy = b_1\Sigma x^2 \tag{2}$$

because $\Sigma ex$ is assumed to be zero. Note that this is one equation with one unknown, $b_1$, hence "just identified."

Let us now consider another recursive model where $y$ is a function of both $x$ and $w$, that is,

$$y = b_1x + b_2w + e \tag{3}$$

The following two equations permit estimation of $b_1$ and $b_2$.

$$\Sigma xy = b_1\Sigma x^2 + b_2\Sigma wx$$
$$\Sigma wy = b_1\Sigma wx + b_2\Sigma w^2 \tag{4}$$

Note that we have two equations and two unknowns. Again, the system is "just identified."

Unfortunately, studies of organizations do not lend themselves well to recursive models. An observed correlation between $x$ and $y$ can mean that $x$ causes $y$, $y$ causes $x$, or both, because rarely do there exist strong a priori grounds for believing that either $x$ alone or $y$ alone is the causal variable.

The model one would like to test, then, is

$$y = b_1 x + e \quad \text{and}$$
$$x = b_2 y + e \tag{5}$$

This model cannot be estimated in its present form because it is hopelessly underidentified. The second equation states that $e$ is the cause of $x$, hence $\Sigma ex$ is nonzero, hence $b_1$ cannot be estimated as in Equation 1 above. The same holds for $b_2$. The error term, $e$, is a cause of $y$, hence $\Sigma ey$ is nonzero, hence $b_2$ cannot be estimated from a simple regression of $x$ on $y$. Formally, underidentification occurs because there are two equations but four unknowns, $b_1$, $b_2$, $\Sigma ex$, and $\Sigma ey$. (The reader is reminded that $\Sigma ex$ and $\Sigma ey$ are unknowns because the $e$'s are unmeasured and nonzero.)

The usual procedure for dealing with underidentification is to introduce additional variables into the model. The added variables must be exogenous (i.e., not appear as dependent variables in the system), and there is the additional restriction that the number of exogenous variables *excluded* from each equation equal the number of endogenous variables *included* as independent variables. The just-identified model of a system with two endogenous variables, then, usually takes the following form:

$$y = b_1 x + b_3 w + e$$
$$x = b_2 y + b_4 z + e \tag{6}$$

Here $w$ and $z$ are the exogenous variables. Because $w$ and $z$ are exogenous, $\Sigma ew$ and $\Sigma ez$ can be assumed zero, and estimates of $b_1$, $b_2$, $b_3$, and $b_4$ can be derived from these four equations

$$\Sigma wy = b_1 \Sigma wx + b_2 \Sigma w^2$$
$$\Sigma yz = b_1 \Sigma xz + b_2 \Sigma wz$$
$$\Sigma wx = b_2 \Sigma wy + b_4 \Sigma wz$$
$$\Sigma xz = b_2 \Sigma yz + b_4 \Sigma z^2 \tag{7}$$

The specification of exogenous variables to identify simultaneous models usually creates more problems than it solves for organizational research. Simple recursive models, it will be remembered, may be unsatisfactory because they require a choice as to the direction of causality among variables. A similar choice must be made when specifying exogenous variables in simultaneous models (e.g., following Equation 6, $w$ causes $y$ but not the reverse, and $z$ causes $x$ but not the reverse), and, in addition, there is the further restriction that certain causal links between exogenous and endogenous variables be absent (e.g., between $w$ and $x$, and between $y$ and $z$). The problem of identification, then, leads to the following paradox: The present state of organizational theory makes recursive models unrealistic because assumptions as to the direction of causality cannot be defended on a priori grounds. Underidentification, however, yields biased results in simultaneous models unless additional variables are added to the system. But the requirement that the additional variables be truly exogenous and that each not affect one of the endogenous variables is as restrictive as the assumptions underlying ordinary recursive models. The dilemma for organizational researchers is whether to make arbitrary assumptions concerning causal precedence, hence abandon the possibility of finding simultaneity, or to seek models of reciprocal causation requiring less stringent assumptions. The latter course was taken in our research.

*The use of lagged variables*

One partial solution to the identification problem lies in the use of lagged variables in simultaneous models. A lagged variable is one measured earlier in time than other variables. Our convention will be to denote lagged variables with the subscript $t$-1. Variables without this subscript are by implication measured at time $t$. A longitudinal study generates automatically a number of lagged variables because all items measured in the first wave of data collection are lagged behind the later measurements. Thus, in the study of finance agencies, all of the 1966 data are lagged one interval behind the 1972 data. Lagged variables can be used to identify simultaneous equation systems, and a question to be explored here is the desirability of so using them given the assumptions required. Lagged data also permit estimation of reciprocal effects from recursive models without problems of identification, but again certain assumptions are required. There is also the question of whether measurement intervals need correspond closely to actual causal lags. The design of the research reported here constrains us to a six-year measurement interval even though actual causation may take considerably less time and, in some instances, considerably more.

Identification of simultaneous models with lagged variables is a straightforward matter. Instead of positing $w$ and $z$ as exogenous variables as in Equation 6, one treats lagged values of $y$ and $x$ as exogenous so that the system becomes

$$y = b_1 x + b_3 y_{t-1} + e$$
$$x = b_2 y + b_4 x_{t-1} + e \tag{8}$$

This model is just identified because the following four equations have four unknowns:

$$\Sigma y_{t-1} y = b_1 \Sigma x y_{t-1} + b_3 \Sigma y_{t-1}{}^2$$
$$\Sigma x_{t-1} y = b_1 \Sigma x_{t-1} x + b_3 \Sigma x_{t-1} y_{t-1}$$
$$\Sigma x y_{t-1} = b_2 \Sigma y_{t-1} y + b_4 \Sigma x_{t-1} y_{t-1}$$
$$\Sigma x_{t-1} x = b_2 \Sigma x_{t-1} y + b_4 \Sigma x_{t-1}{}^2 \tag{9}$$

Parallel to Equation 6, Equation 9 involves certain assumptions about the lagged variables that must be made explicit. First, the lagged terms that are used to identify the model must be truly exogenous. This assumption is not problematic because $x_{t-1}$ and $y_{t-1}$ precede in time the other variables in the system and cannot be affected by them. (The parallel assumption in Equation 6 is problematic because there is no way to know that $w$ and $z$ measured at the same time as $x$ and $y$ are truly exogenous.) Second, the lagged variables are assumed to be causally unrelated to the dependent variable in Equation 8. The lagged value of $x$, $x_{t-1}$ is *not* specified as a direct cause of $y$, and $y_{t-1}$ is *not* specified as a direct cause of $x$

in the model. Were the lagged values of independent variables added without this restriction on causal paths, the system would become underidentified, hence unsolvable.

An alternative to treating lagged values as exogenous and assuming that the lagged variables have no causal impact save for stability or autocorrelation is to treat all effects as lagged. The resulting model is

$$y = b_1 x_{t-1} + b_3 y_{t-1} + e$$
$$x = b_2 y_{t-1} + b_4 x_{t-1} + e \tag{10}$$

Note that this is not a simultaneous system. The variable $x$ is explicitly omitted as a cause of $y$, as $y$ is omitted as a cause of $x$ even though their lagged values are assumed to be of causal importance. Because the system in Equation 10 is recursive, or, better, because it involves two recursive equations, identification is not a problem, and variables other than $x$ and $y$ can be added to either equation in the model without limit. The fully lagged model allows estimation of effects of $x$ on $y$ and $y$ on $x$ at the same time, provided that one assumes these effects to be for the most part lagged. If there are substantial instantaneous effects, then the fully lagged model is inappropriate. The investigator's choice is between nonexistence of lagged effects or nonexistence of instantaneous ones. Neither of these assumptions can be entirely accurate, of course. The question is whether one wishes to treat most causal connections as instantaneous in which case lagged values of dependent variables may be included in the models, but not lagged values of other variables, or to treat most causal connections operating over substantial time-intervals in which case all independent variables should be lagged.

There is no simple decision rule for choosing between the two approaches, but statistical considerations together with certain theoretical preconceptions about organizations suggest that fully lagged models are preferable for present purposes. Estimates of causal parameters, it can be shown, are somewhat exaggerated in lagged models where variables have relatively high stability over time and causal paths are small compared to stability coefficients. These estimates, however, are somewhat depressed in lagged models where variables have low temporal stability and true causal paths are large in relation to stability coefficients. The effects of lengthy lags on parameter estimates are illustrated in Figure 3. In the upper panel of Figure 3, causality from $x$ to $y$ is assumed to operate over one interval (e.g., between time zero and time one) but not instantaneously, causal paths are small compared to stability coefficients, and the measurement lag is three intervals. As shown in the upper panel of Figure 3, although the true causal path over one interval is

Figure 3. Effects of lengthy measurement intervals on estimates of causal paths.

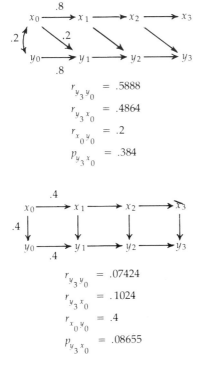

.2, the estimated parameter over three intervals will be .384. Lengthy lags depress rather than enhance regression estimates when causality is instantaneous and true causal paths are about the same as stability coefficients, as the lower panel of Figure 3 shows. Here, the true instantaneous causal path from $x$ to $y$ is .4 as are the stability coefficients in each interval. A measurement lag of three intervals, however, reduces the estimated effect of $x$ on $y$ to .0866, which would be well below statistical significance except for very large samples of organizations. The choice between simultaneous and fully lagged models, then, must rest on substantive assumptions about the nature of organizations. Organizational theory suggests that concern should be focused on enduring rather than labile properties; and theory also suggests that because some inertia is built into organizations of all sorts, short-run effects of causal processes will be relatively weak compared to effects of stability. To be sure, organization theory and this book in particular are concerned with processes of change, but the concept of structure, which is central to thinking about organizations, connotes more stability than change in the short run. In the long run, of course, change is ubiquitous; but, as some of the results discussed below show, the long run may be very long indeed. Our preference, then, is for lagged as opposed to simultaneous models because of the stability assumed to inhere in organizations and because of the focus of organizational theory upon enduring properties.

### Autocorrelated error

A third statistical problem in longitudinal research is the possibility of autocorrelated error terms in regression models. The term *autocorrelation* refers to the correlation of a variable, measured or unmeasured, with itself over time. Autocorrelation does not necessarily bias regression estimates, but it may do so in models with lagged terms, even in simultaneous models where the lagged term is present only as an exogenous variable in order to identify the system. The effects of autocorrelation on possible biases in regression estimates can be seen from the following:

If

$$y = b_1 x_{t-1} + b_2 y_{t-1} + e$$

then

$$y_{t-1} = b_1 x_{t-2} + b_2 y_{t-2} + e_{t-1} \tag{11}$$

In other words, just as $e$ is a cause of $y$, $e_{t-1}$ is a cause of $y_{t-1}$. If $e$ is highly autocorrelated but unmeasured, its stability over time will appear in regression estimates as apparent stability or autocorrelation of the dependent variable and possibly bias downward estimates of effects of the independent variables in the model.

Unfortunately, there is no simple solution to the problem of autocorrelated error in lagged models, and for this reason some statisticians do not recommend their use. But what appears on theoretical grounds to be a significant stumbling block may in practice turn out to be inconsequential or even advantageous. Consider properties of organizations and their environments that are likely to be highly autocorrelated over time but omitted from empirical studies, hence from regression models using data from these studies. For example, characteristics of societal environments in which organizations are embedded are likely to be omitted. The value attached to human life is often used to explain the organization of medical services, but it is rarely introduced as an operational variable in hospital studies. The demand for rational accounting obviously underlies the existence of local-government finance agencies, but it will not appear as an operational variable here. Other autocorrelated but less tangible elements of organizations and their environments include an organization's legitimacy or public support as well as beliefs of members as to the desirability of maintaining existing structures. Again, although important, these things usually go unmeasured in empirical studies, hence, they cannot be incorporated into formal models. It is not accidental that societal values, legitimacy, and member support are not taken into account in most organizational studies. Research on organizations usually proceeds on the assumption that organizational structures are of interest in their own right and that, therefore, the stability of structures over time is also of interest apart from societal values and individual attitudes supporting them. For this reason, one source of autocorrelated error, while of concern, is not controlled explicitly in the analysis below.

Autocorrelated error caused by misspecified regression models cannot be disregarded, however; and theory or common sense must guide one to key causal variables. For example, the size of an organization is in part a function of its scope of activities and the volume of work for which it is responsible. To examine effects of size without controlling volume and scope of responsibilities would probably distort results. Similarly, the range of functions performed by an organization cannot be examined in isolation from measures of the functions performed by other organizations in its immediate environment. For public bureaucracies, a function absent from one agency is usually found in another just as in the private sector, intermediate products not made by a firm are necessarily obtained from suppliers. A difference between cross-sectional and longitudinal analysis is this: Whereas analysis of cross sections can safely ignore causes of dependent variables that do not influence independent variables of interest, no potential causes of dependent variables can be excluded safely from longitudinal models. This limitation would seem to be severe enough to preclude longitudinal analysis in all but exceptional instances. But there is a counterpart to autocorrelated error that limits inferences that can be made from cross-sectional models. The counterpart is in the fact that high autocorrelation among measured variables can produce cross-sectional associations from which spurious causal inferences are likely. Suppose that $x$ caused $y$ in the past but no longer does, and that $x$ and $y$ are now highly although not perfectly autocorrelated. A substantial correlation between $x$ and $y$ will occur whenever they are measured despite the fact that causality no longer operates. In this instance, cross-sectional analysis would lead to a false causal inference, whereas the longitudinal approach, by contrast, would yield the correct inference.[2] Indeed, there are instances in which present causality runs in the opposite direction from effects of past causal processes. In these instances, cross-sectional correlations deteriorate over time, but any one of them alone would yield a misleading causal inference. Precisely this pattern characterizes relations among some key variables describing properties of finance agencies and their environments.

In sum, autocorrelated error is a source of difficulty in longitudinal analysis, but it is sometimes tolerable and sometimes avoidable by including all expected causes of key dependent variables in regression models. The problem of autocorrelated error is not insubstantial, but the potential advantages of the longitudinal approach may outweigh the difficulties.

### The study design and unanticipated consequences of it

A brief description of the study of finance agencies is needed here, for its history parallels some of the development of organizational research. The original survey of finance agencies was conducted in 1966 as part of the Comparative Organizational Research Program (CORP) at the University of Chicago. No longitudinal or time-series study was envisioned at the time. Rather, the intention was to find interrelations among properties that might provide an empirical basis for Weber's theory of bureaucracy. Several reasons prompted the choice of local-government finance agenceis as one of the several CORP studies (the other studies covered employment-security agencies, hospitals, retail stores, and, later, some industrial firms). First of all, finance agencies are ubiquitous. Virtually all government units have finance functions. A second reason for selecting finance agencies was their structural complexity. Compared with other common functions of local government such as police, fire, highways, and the like, finance activities require intensive division of labor; and there is substantial variation in administrative patterns across local-government units. Finally, finance administration seemed to be more bureaucratized than other local-government activities. Rules cover virtually all aspects of the management of local-government finances, and the decision criteria governing lower-level officials in finance agencies leave little room for discretion.

The ubiquity, complexity, and bureaucratization of finance agencies was such that some critical elements received scant attention in the original 1966 study. One absent element was the environment, the importance of which has already been discussed in some detail. Another was descriptive and historical material that usually eludes quantification, but distinguishes finance agencies from other types of organizations. Because finance agencies so closely resembled prototypical bureaucracies, they were treated as representative of all organizations in the 1966 study. Very little attention was devoted to their distinctive properties; and even less consideration was paid to the fact that they are embedded in larger structures of local governments that are, in turn, increasingly constrained by various federal regulations. The 1972 survey of finance agencies was designed to study environment–organization relationships, to bring qualitative considerations peculiar to finance agencies to bear in the interpretation of quantitative data, and, as noted above, to pinpoint the direction of known causal relations among organizational attributes such as size, technology, and structure.

At the time the 1972 survey was planned, the task of ferreting out the direction of causal relationships seemed more important than that of identifying elements in the environment influencing finance agencies or of bringing qualitative considerations to bear in interpreting quantitative results. The results of the 1966 and 1972 surveys together, however did not fit these expectations. Most of the causal links found in the longitudinal study are between the environment and organizational properties, and in all instances but one causality runs unambiguously from the environment to organizations. The richness of environmental effects was surprising; and, more importantly, it quickly became apparent that the interpretation of these effects rested heavily on descriptive and historical information about the agencies studied. The nature of these effects and their interpretations will be outlined in Chapters 3 through 6. For now, it should suffice to note that although a number of general statements about bureaucracies are made in the course of analyzing the data describing finance agencies, there is no reason to expect that the same *empirical* results would hold for different types of organizations. Indeed, there is strong reason to believe that many of the results reported here are time-bound, would not have held for finance agencies in the past, and probably will not hold for them in the future. It is hoped that what has been lost in generality is more than retained in vividness and fidelity allowed by the qualitative materials.

The 1966 survey of finance agencies began with a survey of all U.S. cities with 50,000 or more population in 1960, all counties of over 100,000, the fifty states, and the District of Columbia. The chief financial officer of each jurisdiction was identified, and he was sent a brief questionnaire asking about the department he headed. Two hundred and sixty-three agencies—most of them finance departments, but about a third comptrollers' offices, and a smattering with other names—fit the criteria for the initial study, which were a minimum of twenty full-time employees and two distinct subunits called divisions or bureaus. Interviews were completed in 254 of these agencies in 1966 and 240 in 1972. The interview schedules and instructions were almost identical in the two surveys, as were the coding procedures. Appendix 1 describes the items used in constructing the key variables used in this book.

One innovation in the 1972 study was a screening procedure directing interviewers to the chief financial officers of the local governments studied. (In 1966 we had relied on a list of such persons supplied by the Municipal Finance Officers Association.) In seven instances, the screening procedure led us to a department different from the one surveyed in 1966, and these cases had to be excluded from the longitudinal analysis even though interviews were completed for them. Another four cases were technically completed in 1972, but they yielded such fragmentary or inconsistent data that they had to be dropped. There were, in addition, fourteen cases where complete reorganization had taken place between 1966 and 1972. In these instances, both department names and the assignment of responsibilities among divisions changed so greatly during the six-year interval between the surveys that the new departments showed no similarities to their predecessors. Table 1 displays the classification of cases completed in 1966 and 1972. Of the 263 cases eligible for the 1966 survey, 254 were completed; 240 of the 254 were completed in 1972. Eleven of the 240 were dropped because of errors or omissions, and the 14 reorganized cases, called "name changers" below, were separated from the remaining 215 stable departments that were not reorganized. The bulk of the analysis in this book concerns the 215 stable departments that experienced only incremental change between 1966 and 1972; but in two of the chapters below, data describing the 14 reorganized cases aid greatly in understanding how incremental change occurred in the 215 stable agencies. Comparison of the reorganized departments with others shows that incremental change and total change of public bureaucracies are wholly different processes.

Another innovation in the 1972 survey was the administration of separate questionnaires to units in charge of data processing and budgeting functions regardless of whether or not they were located within the focal finance agencies. The screening procedure was used to identify these units, and some 229 data-processing-unit and 114 budget-unit interviews were completed in 1972. Only 146 of the data-processing units and 95 of the units in charge of budgeting had been in existence since 1966, 89 of the former and 47 of the latter located within finance agencies. Some of the data describing ongoing data-processing and budget units are analyzed in the Chapter 4.

A lengthy description of actual interview procedures is not needed here, but it should be noted that both department heads and division heads were contacted in each agency, the latter mainly for information about their subunits. Since there were, on average, about six divisions in each department, the modal number of respondents or informants in each agency was seven. Department heads' and division heads' responses to key items were checked against each

Table 1. *Disposition of cases, 1966 and 1972*

| | |
|---|---|
| Eligible for 1966 study | 263 |
| Not completed | 9 |
| Cases completed in 1966 | 254 |
| Eligible for 1972 study | 254 |
| Omitted | 5 |
| Not completed | 9 |
| Cases completed in 1972 | 240 |
| Stable departments, 1966–72 | 215 |
| Reorganized departments | 14 |
| Interviewer error[a] | 7 |
| Inadequate data[b] | 4 |
| | 240 |

[a] Cases where 1972 data revealed that wrong department had been interviewed in 1966.
[b] Cases technically complete but fraught with omissions and inconsistencies.

another, and major inconsistencies were resolved before the interview was terminated. Minor inconsistencies were flagged by data-cleaning programs, and telephone calls to informants were often used to resolve them.

### Summary: Intended versus actual consequences of the longitudinal approach

The initial intention of the longitudinal approach to organizations was to sort out the causal direction of relationships among variables describing the environment, technology, size, and various aspects of administrative structure. Its accomplishments, however, were somewhat different, namely capturing greater variation in organizational properties and in environments than normally appears cross-sectionally. More specifically, the unintended outcomes of the longitudinal design were the following:

*Increased variation in the environment.* Elements in the larger social, economic, and political environments may be identical for organizations of a given type but change over time. For this reason, time becomes a surrogate for other variables in longitudinal analysis. The connection between time and environmental shifts, importantly, is derived from descriptive and historical accounts of critical elements in the environment, not from examination of organizations themselves. The effects of such environmental shifts, however, should be evident in organizations. Certain environmental shifts over time are discussed in Chapter 4, 5, and 6.

*Variability of causal processes.* Longitudinal data can reveal increasing, static, or declining correspondences between elements of environments and organizations as well as among organizational properties. Of particular interest are instances where deterioration of correspondences established by past causal processes is observed—for example, deterioration in the positive association between the size of a finance agency and the size of the community it serves (see Chapters 3 and 4). Past and present causality operate differently, suggesting their dependence on environmental elements unlikely to be captured quantitatively in research on organizations but susceptible to qualitative description.

*Variation in rates of organizational change.* Causal inferences drawn from cross-sectional data assume both that static patterns reflect dynamic ones and the uniformity of change processes for all units observed. Longitudinal data can show whether static patterns conceal diverse processes of change, and they can suggest whether markedly different rates of change reflect different causal processes. In particular, longitudinal designs allow separation of ordinary, incremental shifts in organizations from changes so fundamental that they are best described as reorganization or replacement of earlier units. As Chapters 5 and 6 show, incremental and total change are very different processes.

In sum, the longitudinal approach introduces greater variety into organizational analysis through, first, increased variation in properties usually studied in cross-sectional designs and, second, variation in properties that are invariant at any point, hence cannot be considered cross-sectionally. Greater variety was not the intent when this research was designed, but it is its result. Variety, of course, implies complexity, but it also increases the likelihood of more accurate portraits of organizations than conventional research strategies have permitted. It is left for the reader to decide whether this gain in fidelity more than offsets the complexities introduced by the longitudinal approach.

# 3

# The concept of organizational structure

The concept of organizational structure pervades theory and research on organizations. Diverse theoretical works attempt to account for the structure of organizations in terms of size (Blau, 1970), technology (Perrow, 1967), and the degree of certainty or uncertainty arising in the environment (Thompson, 1967). Contemporary research studies comparing organizations have likewise analyzed data describing organizational properties, as opposed to characteristics of individual people, in order to test and refine propositions about structure. Surprisingly, neither these theoretical developments nor research studies comparing organizations have pursued the implications of denoting as structure certain relational properties of organizations such as levels of hierarchy, spans of control, and the like, as well as more global properties of organizations such as their rules and decision-making practices. One implication is that reporting relationships and rules, usually outlined on organization charts and in manuals, reflect actual configurations of behavior in organizations. This raises, of course, the issue of validity; and it is not of central concern here as it can be argued that formal representations of reporting relationships and rules are themselves of interest. A second implication is that configurations of behavior in organizations are in fact recurrent—that, at least for short intervals, there is some stability in allegedly structural features of organizations. In other words, the attribution of structure to organizational characteristics asserts that they change less over time than things not structured.

Concepts describing organizational structures have figured most prominently in so-called closed-system or rational models of organizations. These include Taylor's (1911) prescriptions for scientific management, Gulick and Urwick's (1937) discussion of specialization, unity of command, span of control, and the like, and Weber's (1946) ideal–typical model of bureaucracy. Closed-system models ask what organizational arrangements are most effective for a given organization purpose. The question itself, not any particular answer to it, carries the implication that structure has a reality apart from the individual persons who happen to be in organizations, and that structural arrangements in organizations are as enduring as the purposes for which organizations themselves were created. Structural concepts also abound in recent research studies concerned with the effects of size on other organizational properties; studies of this sort appear with high frequency in *Administrative Science Quarterly*. (See especially Kimberly's [1976] review article on organizational size.) Although not explicitly using the closed-system model of the classical administrative theorists, such research studies are implicitly closed system in that the nexus of causation is within organizations, and variables describing the environment are not usually considered.

It should be noted that the concepts of structure and structured behavior are not monopolized by closed-system theories of organizations. Open-system theories such as Thompson's (1967) treat organizations as intendedly closed, hence intendedly stable and predictable, even though in fact they are open to the environment and hence affected by uncontrollable and unpredictable events. The imagery of intended closedness despite actual openness is very suggestive, for it portrays organizations as essentially stable at their technical cores and somewhat less stable at their peripheries where boundary spanners mediate environmental influences. Organizational structure, then, becomes a means of preserving calculability and rationality despite unpredictable elements in the environment. A tentative hypothesis is generated: Over relatively short intervals, organizational structures will exhibit somewhat more stability than critical elements in their environments, and especially so at their technical cores. No prediction about long-run organizational change is made because organizations remaining stable over long intervals will be rendered inconsistent with their environments and replaced.

Another version of open-system theory views structure very differently. Weick's (1976) discussion of "loose coupling" suggests that organizational activity is much less well coordinated than commonly believed. Lack of coordination occurs in the absence of imperatives preserving organizational structures, and accounts for the relatively low stability of supposedly structural elements. A more radical view elaborated by J. Meyer and Rowan (1977) treats structure as isomorphic to institutionalized myths and intended to satisfy expectations for rational administration but largely decoupled from the actual activities of organizations. Because the larger social environment demands ritual conformity of organizations, but organizations do not similarly constrain their environments, the J. Meyer and Rowan formulation predicts as much or more stability in institutional environments than in organizations—contrasting vividly with Thompson's model of organizational stability in the midst of environmental uncertainty. A hypothesis can be derived from theories of loose coupling and structure as institutionalized myth: Glacial drifts in the environment compel parallel changes in formal representations of organizations, but actual behavior in organizations tend to change somewhat more erratically, resulting in less stability in organizations than in environments surrounding them.

One aim of this chapter is to begin testing open- versus closed-systems theories of organizations and discriminating between the variations of open-systems theory sketched above. The results cannot but have implications for these ideas. But the immediate purpose is to ask whether elements of organization normally labeled as structural have sufficient stability and interrelatedness to be worthy of study by themselves; or whether, contrariwise, there is apparent instability and unconnectedness in organizations such that organizational patterns require explanation primarily in terms of external events. At stake here is not only whether there are environmental effects on organizations. The more fundamental question is whether formal organizational structures are of interest apart from environmental elements in the longitudinal analysis to be undertaken here. Most organizational research, although not theory, has proceeded as if organizational structures were of interest in their own right. This assumption is questioned below. A variety of factors, some intrinsic to the organizations studied and some arising in their immediate environments, combined to produce a pattern of apparent instability in organizational structures and dependence on environmental elements.

### Changes in the environment

Because we are interested in the stability of organizational structures compared with their environments, perhaps it is best to begin by asking how one can describe meaningfully changes in both occurring over the interval between the two surveys of finance agencies. Changes in organizational structures, of course, will be evident from the data describing organizations themselves, but environmental shifts may not be as accessible. This occurs for several reasons. First, environments are likely to be more complex than organizations. Organizations, it will be remembered, cope with and presumably reduce uncertainty (Thompson, 1967) or equivocality (Weick, 1969) in their environments. The clear implication is that greater complexity lies outside organizations than within them. Second, organizations respond to multiple environments, some of which affect all organizations of a given type, some of which do not. This holds even for public agencies, which do not compete openly. All finance agencies, for example, share a common market for local-government securities, and a common environment of federal regulation. Elements of the environment that may not be shared include characteristics of the cities, counties, and states that finance agencies serve. But differences between local environments may not be significant. Some recent research on policy innovations suggest that the intrusiveness of federal programs is such that states can no longer be considered independent entities (see Rose, 1973). The same may now hold for cities where the federal presence is substantial and accelerating.

### Changes in the larger environment

If it is the case that a complex national or societal environment, what was labeled earlier as the larger environment, ultimately governs much of the behavior of local finance agencies, then statements about the stability or variability of the environment over time cannot be made easily over a single interval such as that between the 1966 and 1972 surveys. Two observations of one environment—in this instance, the national environment—cannot yield measures of uncertainty or variability. More observations and, perhaps, more environments are needed. A description of changes in this environment is, however, possible.

The six years from 1966 to 1972 was a period of rapid growth for local government. The scope and scale of local services increased substantially as a result of two factors: The urban crisis in the late 1960s and the proliferation of federal categorical-grant programs funneled mainly through the Department of Housing and Urban Development to cities and the Department of Health, Education, and Welfare to the states. The Department of Housing and Urban Development had been established in 1965, and the Model Cities Program was funded the next year. (Revenue-sharing funds did not reach local government until 1973; and federal block grants to cities, which simplified greatly application and reporting requirements compared to categorical grants, did not appear until 1974.) Widespread rioting in urban areas in the late 1960s signaled discontent of minority populations; the growth of federal aid to local communities was, of course, the tangible expression of President Johnson's Great Society program. Rising unemployment rates after 1969, similarly, triggered passage of the Emergency Employment Act of 1971, which authorized direct federal subsidization of local-government payrolls. The impact of both urban unrest and massive federal funding of local programs is clearly evident in the growth of local-government employment and of budgets, which will be discussed presently.

Aside from these social and political changes in the larger environments of finance agencies, a number of changes occurring between 1966 and 1972 reflect shifting beliefs about appropriate organizational forms for the finance function, in what might be termed the environment of the public-finance profession. These changes included: the emergence of data processing and budgeting as local-government functions in their own right, distinguished from routine fiscal activities; the emergence of new organizational forms for the finance function, especially departments of administration and of management; and the imposition of federal personnel standards upon local governments. The separation of data processing and budgeting functions from finance will be discussed at length in Chapter 4, new administrative forms will be the subject of Chapter 5, and the effects of earlier federal laws affecting personnel matters as well as of the Intergovernmental Personnel Act of 1970 will be covered in Chapter 6. What is important for the present discussion is that beliefs about appropriate administrative forms, like larger social and political environments, shifted with some uniformity. To be sure, only a minority of finance agencies actually lost their data-processing and budgeting functions during the interval between our two surveys, very few were actually transformed into more comprehensive departments of administration or of management, and not all altered their personnel practices toward conformity with federal standards. But, like forces arising in the larger social and political environments, a common professional environment was present for almost all local governments; and when it triggered actual organizational changes, the direction of change was fairly predictable. A high level of uncertainty and turbulence such as that triggered by the 1975 New York City fiscal crisis did not characterize the environments of local-government finance agencies during the 1966−72 interval.

### Changes in the immediate environment

Some quantitative indicators of environmental elements in cities,countries, and states, the immediate environments of finance agencies, also suggest a pattern of fairly uniform change or predictability. Table 2 displays shifts in these indicators for the 215 ongoing finance agencies and the 14 reorganized cases together. Briefly, Table 2 shows that local-government employment in the jurisdictions studied increased about 20 percent in the 1966−1973 interval, from a mean of about 7,300 to about 8,700 full-time equivalent workers. General-fund expenditures covering common services such as police, fire, recreation, and health, *but not federal grants,* increased about 110 percent in the same interval, from 88 to 185 million dollars. Total expenditures, *including federal grants,* jumped some 150 percent, from about 148 to about 359 million dollars for the cities, counties, and states covered in our surveys. Finally, the average population of the cities, counties, and states covered increased about 8 percent over the ten-year interval from 1960 to 1970, from 850,000 to about 920,000.[1]

These four measures—general-fund expenditures, total expenditures, local-government employment, and population—indicate partially the level of demand for services of local-government finance agencies. Although they change considerably over time, the demand measures have high predictability across cities, counties, and states as shown by their autocorrelations. The autocorrelation for general-fund expenditures is .8327; for total funds administered it is .8240; for government employment it is .9602; and the autocorrelation of population over a ten-year (1960—70) interval is .9446. These estimates of predictability, it should be noted, are reduced only slightly by logarithmic transformation, indicating that they are not caused entirely by skew distributions.[2] In summary, measures describing the demand for services of finance agencies in the jurisdictions studied increased subtantially during the 1966—72 interval, but changes in demand were highly predictable. Strong

Table 2. *Means, standard deviations, and autocorrelations of demand variables. (N = 229)*

| Variable | 1966 Mean | 1966 S.D. | 1972 Mean | 1972 S.D. | Auto-correlation |
|---|---|---|---|---|---|
| General Fund [a] | 87,625 | 268,843 | 184,917 | 496,808 | .8327 |
| Total funds administered [a] | 147,880 | 398,712 | 359,016 | 914,044 | .8240 |
| Government employees | 7,342 | 17,256 | 8,718 | 20,461 | .9602 |
| Population [a] | 849.8 [b] | 2,144.7 [b] | 920.4 [c] | 2,286.5 [c] | .9446 |

[a] Figures are in thousands.
[b] 1960 mean and S.D.
[c] 1970 mean and S.D.

trends but high predictability characterized the quantifiable aspects of immediate environments of local-government finance agencies.

### The stability of organizational structures

Given the predictability of change in the immediate environments of finance agencies, it might be expected that organizational structures would also change predictably. Increased demand in the environment might be accompanied by growth of finance agencies, and increased task complexity would be mirrored in organizational complexity as indicated by numbers of subunits, levels of hierarchy, and the like. A close correspondence between environmental changes and organizational adjustments, in other words, would be posited. Indeed, following traditional theories of administration, one might expect more uniformity or predictability in organizations than in their environments due to deliberate efforts to buffer the environment if not due to other forces tending toward inertia.

The alternative model, consistent with the metaphor of loose coupling, portrays organizational changes as somewhat more chaotic. Though possibly counterintuitive, the notion that organizational structures are more variable than environments is appealing on several counts. For one thing, close correspondences between organizational structure and the environment may be required by efficiency considerations or if survival is problematic. But if there is no easy calculus of efficiency, and if survival can be assumed, at least for the short run, then a wide range of organizational structures may be acceptable in a given environment. Second, work is often shifted both within organizations as well as between them, resulting in major changes in structure in response to only incremental changes in the environment. Firms, for example, commonly alternate between contracting for intermediate goods and vertical integration of producers of these goods—a major organizational shift—depending upon market conditions (Williamson, 1975). Public agencies may be grouped together into superagencies (e.g., New York City's garbage is now collected by their Environmental Protection Services Administration) to reduce the number of department heads, or superagencies may be dismantled in order to reduce layers of hierarchy. Finally, the logic of hierarchy is such that small changes in staffing patterns can produce important alterations in quantitative measures of administrative structure. Figure 4 illustrates the variability of hierarchical structures when positions are reordered. The hierarchy at the left has one department head and three division heads with four subordinates each. Should one division head become the department head's deputy, and his subordinates be split between the two remaining division heads, the hierarchy at the right of Figure 4 results. This minor adjustment in reporting relationships yields substantial changes in quantitative measures of structure. The number of divisions decreases from three to two, the number of levels of hierarchy increases from three to four, and the span of control of first-line supervisors also increases from four to six. The sensitivity of quantitative measures of structure to minor changes in reporting relationships, coupled with ab-

Figure 4. Changes in measures of organizational structure.

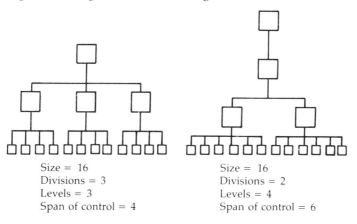

Size = 16
Divisions = 3
Levels = 3
Span of control = 4

Size = 16
Divisions = 2
Levels = 4
Span of control = 6

sence of threats to organizational survival and the ease with which the work can be shifted between units, suggests that some instability in organizational structures should be anticipated.

*Changes in organizational structure*
Table 3 displays means, standard deviations, autocorrelations, autocorrelations net of size (or, technically, autoregression coefficients), and effects of size for eight basic organizational variables used in the study. The construction of these variables is described in Table 4. It should be noted that all the organizational variables are based upon multiple items or redundant responses to the same items from multiple informants. Data describing the 215 ongoing finance agencies are reported in Table 3. The fourteen reorganized agencies are deleted because their organizational structures have, by definition, little temporal stability. I shall discuss first the overall trends in the eight variables describing organizational structures between 1966 and 1972. I shall then turn to predictability of organizational structures over time and then to the effects of size.

Table 3. *Means, standard deviations, autocorrelations, autoregression coefficients net of size, and effects of size for organizational variables (N = 215)*

|  | 1966 Mean (1) | 1966 S.D. (2) | 1972 Mean (3) | 1972 S.D. (4) | Autocor- relation (5) | Autore- gression net of size (6) | Effect of size (7) |
|---|---|---|---|---|---|---|---|
| Size | 102.3 | 167.9 | 126.7 | 212.5 | .9497 | — | — |
| Divisions | 5.730 | 2.767 | 5.623 | 2.440 | .5765 | .5285 | .1194 |
| Levels | 3.945 | .906 | 4.084 | .968 | .5700 | .4290 | .2700 |
| Sections | 11.944 | 9.677 | 12.403 | 8.805 | .6385 | .4147 | .3351 |
| Span of control | 7.135 | 5.293 | 6.833 | 4.325 | .4068 | .2573 | .3091 |
| Formalization | .6403 | .2968 | .6969 | .2816 | .6859 | .6843 | (.0190) |
| Responsibilities | 6.344 | 2.562 | 6.270 | 2.628 | .6642 | .6668 | (.0183) |
| Competitors | 2.595 | 2.304 | 2.479 | 2.267 | .6851 | .6750 | .1293 |

*Note:* Coefficients in parentheses are less than twice standard errors.

*Trends.* Only two of the eight basic variables describing the structure of finance agencies exhibit strong tends between 1966 and 1972. These are size and the index of formalization of personnel procedures. The mean size of finance agencies increased from 102 to 127 full-time employees over the six-year interval between surveys, paralleling the increase in local-government employment generally. It should be noted that some, although not all, of this increase is due directly to positions funded by the Emergency Employment Act.

Table 4. *Variables describing organizational structures of finance agencies*

| | |
|---|---|
| Size | Number of full-time employees. Information given by department head, checked for consistency with information given by division heads. |
| Divisions | Number of subunits whose heads report to department head or his deputy. From organization chart. |
| Levels of supervision | Mean number of levels of hierarchy in divisions, plus one level for department head. Information given by division heads, checked for consistency with total division employees. |
| Sections | Total number of subunits within divisions; divisions without section heads are considered to have one section. Information given by division heads. |
| Span of control | The mean ratio of nonsupervisory employees to first-line supervisors in divisions. Information given by division heads. |
| Formalization | An index of formalization of personnel procedures described fully in Chapter 6. Information given by department head. |
| Responsibilities | The number of finance functions for which a department has full responsibility. Information given by department head. |
| Competitors | The number of *other departments* in a city, county, or state having partial or full responsibility for finance functions. Information given by department head. |

*Note:* Appendix 1 describes the questionnaire items used in constructing these variables.

Whereas no such positions existed in 1966, finance agencies had an average of 4.59 EEA jobs in 1972.

The change in the index of formalization of personnel procedures, a scale running from 0 to 1.0, seems modest at first glance, but the increase from .6403 to .6969 is but part of a very long historical trend toward adoption of "merit" standards in personnel matters that will be described in Chapter 6. Had the interval between the two surveys been longer, the increase in formalization of personnel procedures would, in all likelihood, have been much greater. The marginal change in the index of responsibilities held by a finance agency, which runs from 0 to 13, is surprising. This index encompasses, however, only fiscal responsibilities and does not include the data-processing function. As will be noted in Chapter 4, a substantial number of departments that had the data-processing functions in 1966 lost them by 1972; and many fewer added data processing during this interval.

No discernible trends are evident in the other variables describing the organizational structure of local-government finance agencies. There appear to be slightly fewer divisions in finance departments over time, more levels of hierarchy, more sections, but smaller spans of control at the lowest level of supervision. Interestingly, the number of competitors—other local government agencies having one or more primary financial responsibilities that might have been placed in the focal finance department—does not change much either. Again, the number of competitors does not include units in charge of data processing outside of the finance agencies studied.

*Predictability.* A measure of the predictability of organizational structures over time is provided by the autocorrelations of the various measures of structure. The size of finance agencies has a much higher autocorrelation than other organizational elements, .9497. (Logarithmic transformation of size reduces the autocorrelation to .8371, however.) The autocorrelations of other organizational variables, save for a span of control at the lowest level, are in the range of .6—high enough to indicate a modicum of predictability but low enough to suggest substantial changes over time, and substantially lower than the autocorrelations of the four measures of environmental demand. When size is controlled, however, the autocorrelations—or autoregression coefficients—of the four variables describing formal administrative arrangements in finance agencies drop, and in some instances considerably. Net of size, the autoregression coefficient for divisions is .5765; it is .4290 for levels of supervision, .4147 for sections, and only .2573 for spans of control at the lowest level. By contrast, the zero-order autocorrelations of measures of formalization, responsibilities, and competitors are hardly disturbed when size is controlled. Indeed, size has a statistically significant effect only on the last of these.

*Effects of size.* The right-most column of Table 4 shows cross-lagged path coefficients generated when each of the 1972 measures of organizational structure is regressed on 1966 size, net of the comparable 1966 measures of structure. The column is labeled "Effect of Size." Size has a slight although significant effect on the number of divisions, and substantial effects on numbers of supervisory levels, sections, and first-line spans of control. These results fit exactly the findings from a study of somewhat smaller number of finance agencies over a five-year interval (Meyer, 1972b), and they need not be elaborated here. What is important, aside from autocorrelation, is that formal administrative arrangements of public bureaucracies appear to be caused mostly by size. Of equal interest, and not reported in the earlier study, is the absence of significant effects of size on formalization of personnel procedures and on responsibilities. This runs contrary to results from other research (see especially Pugh et al. 1968) and can be explained by the fact that finance agencies are not wholly autonomous organizations but are instead nested in larger structures of government, which control, among other things, their personnel rules and the range of tasks for which they are responsible. The positive effect of size on competitors occurs partly because the largest agencies—those in the largest jurisdictions—are growing least, and partly because other units with fiscal responsibilities are spawning fastest. This process will be explored in some detail in Chapter 5.

*Summary.* The quantitative results so far can be summarized as follows: Measures of environmental demand for the services of finance agencies as well as the size of these agencies exhibit upward trends but high predictability over time. Measures describing the organizational structures of finance agencies do not exhibit strong trends, and their predictability is substantially less than that of size or environmental demand measures. Importantly, variables describing organizational structure are dependent upon size, and their predictability drops substantially when size is controlled. Like measures of organizational structure, formalization of personnel procedures, responsibilities, and competitors do not exhibit strong trends; although formalization increased somewhat over the six-year interval between the 1966 and 1972 surveys. The predictability of formalization, responsibilities, and competitors was substantially higher than that of the measures describing structure, although their predictability was somewhat lower than measures of environmental demand and size. These results showing, first, environmental demand and size to have the most predictability, second, formalization and responsibilities having intermediate predictability, and, third, traditional measures of organizational structure having least predictability are disturbing to conventional theories, for they suggest one of two things. Either organizational structures truly exhibit more variability than environments—in which case the metaphor of "loose coupling" seems more apt than the conception of organizations as open to the environment but intendedly closed – or organizational stability will have to be sought elsewhere than in measures of predictability of formal administrative arrangements.

### Why structure?

In the absence of high predictability of elements of organizational structure over time, one must ask two questions. First, why has the metaphor of structure been used and why does it persist in describing administrative arrangements in organizations? And, second, why is uncertainty said to characterize environments of organizations? Perhaps the answer lies in the following: The interdependencies among elements of administrative hierarchies in organizations are highly stable over time, even though actual structures consistent with these interdependencies vary considerably. By contrast, causal laws governing environment–organization ties may be variable, creating uncertainty and conditions that, in the long run, trigger fundamental change. We shall examine these possibilities.

### *Interdependencies within organizations*

Representations of organizational structures, at least for public agencies, are almost always hierarchical. Each person, save for the highest official, reports to one, and only one, superior. Classical administrative theory calls this unity of command. The implication of hierarchy for measures of organizational structure is that new positions require new subunits, added levels, or increased supervisory ratios. Within the constraint of hierarchy, there is an upper limit to the number of people who can be monitored effectively by one supervisor. Classical organizational theory calls this span of control. The implication of span of control is an upper bound to the size of work groups, hence that organizational size and the number of work groups present should be highly correlated. Importantly, the rules for representing administrative hierarchies do not specify how work is to be divided among units. Classical theory discussed division of labor by person, process, client, and place, but it never suggested one clearly preferred alternative. The implication here is that within constraints of hierarchy and span of control, variables describing organizational structures need not be causally related to one another.

What evidence we have is consistent with the notion of stable interdependencies within organizational structures but variable outcomes consistent with the principle of hierarchy. The first piece of evidence is that correlations among variables describing size and structure are quite stable over time. Table 5 displays cross-sectional correlations of size, divisions, levels, sections, and spans of control for both the 1966 and 1972 waves. The 1966 correlations are to the left of the solidi, and the 1972 correlations are to their right. Very little change in these correlations occurs between the two surveys. The only noticeable differences are in the correlations of the number of sections with numbers of levels and spans of control. This indicates that roughly the same patterns govern the construction of organizational structures in both years. Second, the effects of size are ubiquitous. This was shown in the longitudinal analysis (the left-most column of Table 3 merely replicates the findings of Meyer, 1972b), and the pervasive effects of size are also evident in the top row of Table 5. Ubiquitous effects of size suggest that the

Table 5. *Correlations between size and measures of organizational structure (1966/1972 correlations)*

|  | Divisions | Levels | Sections | Span of Control |
|---|---|---|---|---|
| Size | .4019/.3882 | .5224/.5160 | .6680/.7208 | .4837/.5034 |
| Divisions | — | .0036/−.0718 | .5304/.4887 | .1319/.1446 |
| Levels | — | — | .2853/.4358 | .3493/.4461 |
| Sections | — | — | — | .3430/.5749 |

principle of hierarchy is operating because new positions require adjustments in spans of control, subunits, or levels. Third, the strongest effect of size in the longitudinal analysis (Table 3) is upon numbers of sections, and the largest cross-sectional correlations (Table 5) are also between size and sectons. Because sections are units in finance agencies most closely resembling work groups, this suggests strongly that span-of-control limitations are operating. Fourth, net of size, most relations among variables describing structure vanish. This was also shown in the earlier study (Meyer, 1972b), and it necessarily occurs in longitudinal analysis of the data presented here because of the low autocorrelations of supposedly structural elements. Importantly, about the same result obtains in cross-sectional analysis of the 1966 and 1972 waves. Net of size, there is a negative association between the number of divisions and of levels of hierarchy; and there is a positive association of divisions with sections in both the 1966 and 1972 data. The latter result, the association between divisions and sections, is at least partly artifactual because all divisions are considered as having at least one section. Otherwise, consistent interrelations among the measures of organizational structure do not appear cross-sectionally, once size is controlled.

Clearly, much more needs to be known about the stability of organizational structures. The need for further investigation is evident in the following: Whereas little stability obtains in measures of organizational structures—divisions, levels, sections, and so forth—the rate at which finance agencies as whole departments were either replaced or totally reorganized between 1966 and 1972 was about 1 percent annually, 14 out of 229 cases in six years. This suggests considerable stability of departments if not of units within them. It may be that entire departments are anchored to stable environmental elements (probably statutes and other institutionalized beliefs about the necessity of certain government function) more closely than their subunits and sections. This explanation of apparent stability of departmental units, it should be noted, is not inconsistent with the explanation of instability of internal structure. To the conventions of hierarchy and span-of-control one need only add the notion that highly institutionalized activities (e.g., accounting and auditing) must be represented visibly at the departmental level. Unfortunately, the time span of the study does not permit further tests of the institutional hypothesis. To test the idea that institutional elements sustain the structures of finance agencies at the departmental level but not below, changes in these elements must be observed and compared with actual organizational shifts occurring over time or across societies. Such shifts can be captured only in historical investigations covering intervals of greater than six years or in comparative, (i.e., cross-national) research.

*Environment—organization linkages.*

Whereas relationships among elements of organizational structure were essentially stable or were enhanced between 1966 and 1972, linkages between quantitative dimensions of the environment and organizational size deteriorated over time. Table 6 shows quite clearly that the rate of growth of finance agencies was much smaller in the largest cities, counties, and states, those over one-million population, than in medium-sized jurisdictions of one-quarter of a million to one-million population. The uneven pattern of

Table 6. *Mean size of finance agencies in 1966 and 1972 by type of jurisdiction and 1970 population*

| 1970 Population | Cities | | | Counties | | | States | | |
|---|---|---|---|---|---|---|---|---|---|
| | 1966 | 1972 | (N) | 1966 | 1972 | (N) | 1966 | 1972 | (N) |
| 50,000–99,999 | 35.9 | 38.2 | (46) | — | — | | — | — | |
| 100,000–249,999 | 55.0 | 62.8 | (51) | 34.0 | 35.7 | (9) | — | — | |
| 250,000–499,999 | 94.5 | 118.6 | (23) | 45.4 | 57.2 | (14) | — | — | |
| 500,000–999,999 | 166.8 | 205.3 | (13) | 79.2 | 128.2 | (19) | 231.5 | 382.3 | (6) |
| 1,000,000+ | 161.0 | 164.3 | (4) | 159.9 | 182.1 | (8) | 338.0 | 398.6 | (22) |

growth results in a slippage in the correlations of the four demand variables with the size of finance agencies. The correlation of general-fund expenditures with size drops from .5592 in 1966 to .4552 in 1972; the correlation of total expenditures with size is .4897 in 1966 and .4887 in 1972; that of the total government employment with size declines from .6894 to .6194; and the association of population served with the size of finance agencies drops from .6686 to .6166. It will be argued in the chapters below that these deteriorating correlations reflect a causal process, namely the absence of growth or actual contraction of finance agencies in the largest cities, counties, and states with shifts of resources and responsibilities to other agencies.

Aside from the question of what causal processes account for these deteriorating correlations, this pattern necessarily triggers uncertainty or instability for finance agencies. Retrospectively, uncertainty is introduced because declining correspondences with the environment either did not hold in the past or could not have held for long. Prospectively, instability is created because, past a point, continued deterioration of correspondence with the environment will not be allowed and fundamental organizational change will ensue. The slippage in environment−organizational correspondence is in contrast to the relative stability of relations among variables describing organizational structure, and in this sense the environment is less certain and stable for finance agencies than are relations among their internal elements.

### Strategic implications

The results sketched above posed a number of questions, indeed puzzles, at the outset of this research. First of all, the low autocorrelations of variables describing organizational structures−divisions, levels, sections, and spans of control−all but foreclosed the possibility of finding causal relations among them over time. Thus what remained was the uncomfortable choice between elaborating a complex, contingent model of change in public bureaucracies, one somewhat idiosyncratic from the perspective of conventional organizational theory, and abandoning altogether the longitudinal study of bureaucracies. Needless to say, the first strategy has been chosen. Secondly, the deteriorating relations between categories describing environments and organizations raised the dilemma of whether or not to introduce descriptive and historical materials that might explain apparent complexity but that do not vary for the set of organizations studied at the time of research, hence cannot be introduced into quantitative models. I have opted for incorporating such materials even though explanations hinging upon them are not strictly verifiable within the confines of this study. The alternative would be a series of empirical generalizations without implications for organizations other than those studied. The reader will note that the amount of descriptive and historical material in the following chapters is somewhat greater than is common in quantitative organizational research.

### Research issues

Aside from these broad questions concerning strategy for this study, a number of implications for research arise from these first empirical results. Some specific research questions include the following:

*Reliability versus stability.* Apparent instability in measures of organizational structure (or anything else) can have its source in random measurement error, which degrades both autocorrelations and path coefficients. Because most attributes of organizations are not manifestations of some underlying construct that is the focus of inquiry (e.g., conservatism), the use of multiple indicators for organizational attributes is normally precluded. The use of multiple informants is not, however, and measures of organizational structure (e.g., levels, sections, and spans of control, for which multiple indicators are not available) were constructed from reports given by several informants, an average of six per organization. Measures of formalization, responsibilities, and competitors are based on multiple indicators. Panel or time-series designs can separate reliability from stability, but only under very stringent conditions. These include the availability of at least three and preferably four waves of data, equal measurement intervals, measurement intervals corresponding to causal lags (i.e., a system in lag-1), and constant causal laws. Clearly, our research design does not permit these criteria to be met or even approached. We do not have three waves of data at equal intervals; there is no guarantee that our measurement interval corresponds even closely to actual causal lags; and there is reason to believe that within the bounds of the systems studied quantitatively—finance departments and their immediate environments—causal laws are anything but constant. Because most of the measures describing formal administrative structures are based on multiple responses, however, there is reason to believe that the reliability of our measures is not unacceptably low.

*Accounting for low autocorrelations.* Assuming the problem of reliability to be manageable, a further question is whether there are identifiable conditions in organizations enhancing or attenuating the stability of organizational structures over time. Research has usually been directed toward explaining organizational structures, but not their temporal stability. The search for factors associated with stability or instability of organizational structures focused first on the effect of leadership change, which is described in detail in Chapter 4.

*Accounting for the declining correspondence of environmental demand with the size of finance agencies.* Another empirical question was why, for the 215 ongoing finance agencies, the correlations between measures of environmental demand and agency size deteriorated over the six-year interval. Importantly, this decline did not occur for the 14 reorganized cases. Quite the opposite, the correlations of environmental demand with size increased markedly for the reorganized units. The search for factors associated with declining (or increasing) associations of size with environmental demand gave rise to Chapter 5, on domains. But as Chapter 5 and Chapter 6 point out, there may be a regular cycle of change in organizations regardless of internal conditions: Correspondences between environment and organization are established at the time of formation or reorganization; the fit between environments and organizations then decreases until replacement or reorganization occurs again.

### Theoretical issues

Some basic questions concerning the direction of thinking about organizations are raised in finding somewhat less predictability in organizational structures than in their environments over time, and in declining correspondences between environments and organizations. These questions include the following:

*Are studies of organizations to be directed toward explaining administrative structures?* The answer will have to remain open for a while, but the preliminary evidence suggests not. It should be remembered that early research on organizational structures assumed implicitly their stability compared to attitudes and predilections of individual people in organizations. This assumption is now in doubt. Abstract categories describing numbers of units, subunits, and levels are mainly functions of size. The *principle* of hierarchy, however, as opposed to the distribution of individuals in offices within hierarchies, holds universally for the agencies studied, hence is invariant across them. It may be that less-abstract categories—those having more organization-specific content, for example, whether or not a finance agency operates its own data-processing unit—will have higher temporal stability, hence yield greater insights, than quantitative measures of administrative structures. The loss in generality in using such organization-specific variables is more apparent than real. To pursue our example for a moment, the presence or absence of data processing from finance determines its position in the information flow of local government. Access to information is as generic an organizational variable as span of control. How this concept is measured will vary across types of organizations, however.

*What remains for closed-systems theories?* If variables describing administrative structures are of little interest in their own right apart from the pervasiveness of hierarchy, then closed-system models of organizations are unlikely to yield many more results than are already in the literature; and they are unlikely to have much applicability to organizations' problems. Because empirical interrelations among elements describing organizational structures are sparse, save for effects of size, no optimal fit among these elements is likely to be found. Hence sociological theories of organizations will focus primarily upon external elements and boundary-spanning relations. This does not preclude developing closed-systems models that are social–psychological in character (e.g., the bulk of the literature on supervisory style does not take into account external conditions). But this does preclude studies of structure without explicit environmental referents. Contingency theories, it should be noted, take a first step in this direction in acknowledging that interrelations among organizational elements depend somewhat upon work technologies and the environment.

*Which version of open-systems theory is to be pursued?* As noted at the outset of this chapter, one version of open-systems theory treats organizations as intendedly closed despite openness, whereas a more radical version finds organizational structures responsive to institutionalized elements and largely decoupled from day-to-day activities. The low predictability of administrative arrangements in finance agencies over time and the much higher predictability of elements in the environment despite strong trends suggest that the more radical version of open systems be given some credence. But the relative stability of interdependencies within organizations compared to deterioration of environment–organization linkages supports the more conventional view. Clearly, research ignoring either perspective is in danger of overlooking critical causal elements in the environment. The problem is how to design research that captures both variation in the immediate environment and variation in larger societal environments from which definitions of appropriate organizational forms for given purposes emanate. The present investigation was not intended originally to take into account the latter sort of variation; but the empirical results could not, in many instances, be generalized beyond the organizations studied without reference to societal and historical processes. As the reader will note, the environments of finance agencies are described in Chapters 4, 5, and 6 as much in qualitative as in quantitative terms. In part, this is due to a measurement problem. What constitutes, for example, stability (or instability), homogeneity (or heterogeneity), placidity (or turbulence) *for finance agencies* is not easily grasped except through the researcher's understanding of the peculiarities of these organizations. But this also reflects invariance in key environmental properties, namely the developments affecting all finance agencies that altered correspondences between quantifiable aspects of environments and organizations. Organizational elements such as leadership, claims to domain or domain consensus, formation, and reorganization mediated effects of these developments on individual agencies. The following chapters will explore environmental shifts and the organizational mechanisms through which processes of change in public bureaucracies are either accelerated or impeded.

# 4

## Some effects of leadership

This chapter is about the effects of leadership on the administrative structure of organizations, but it is broader in scope than the title implies. It is necessarily about the organizations that were surveyed in order to gather data for the research – city, county, and state departments of finance headed by the chief financial officers of their jurisdictions. It also touches on one of the central theoretical issues in the sociology of organizations: the debate between so-called open-system and closed-system approaches. The three strands of argument are inseparable here. The empirical findings cannot be interpreted without an understanding of what finance departments were like in the past, finance officials' beliefs about what their organizations should look like, and the changes in technology and management practices that have forced a different reality on these agencies. The findings suggest that characteristics of leadership positions have a profound impact on organizations, and they call into question the distinction between open and closed systems of which much has been written.

Finance agencies, it will be remembered, are headed by officials who, for the most part, believe that fiscal administration of local government ought to be centralized under their aegis. But finance activities that were once complementary have become inconsistent, largely due to developments in budgeting and data processing. The result has been some contraction and dedifferentiation of finance agencies, especially in the largest cities, counties, and states, and deteriorating correspondences of environmental demand with organizational size. In this chapter, it will be shown that leadership affects this process. Stable leadership and leadership that is autonomous of higher authority block environmental intrusions, whereas leadership turnover and dependence accelerate change.

### Leadership in organizational theory

The literature on leadership in organizations is large, but the findings are few. No simple relationship of leadership style to the performance of workers has been found (see Campbell et al. 1970; Graen et al. 1972). The link between the two is either moderated by other variables or nonexistent. Similarly, the relationship of leadership to overall organizational performance has been found to be tenuous. The effects of business cycles, peculiarities of specific industries, and histories of individual firms account for far more variance in the performance of large businesses than does leadership (Lieberson and O'Connor, 1972). One might conclude that leadership makes no difference to large organizations. But to do so would violate common sense; and, more importantly, it would overlook the connection between leadership and variables describing organizational structure, which we do not normally associate with effectiveness or performance. In this chapter some small but consistent relationships between the stability of leadership and the stability of organizational structures will be shown. I shall also discuss how leadership characteristics affect causal relationships among organizational variables.[1] Such relationships are all but absent among organizations with stable, autonomous, and insular leadership. By contrast, where there is turnover in leadership positions, dependence on higher authority, and frequent communication with immediate superiors, causal relationships abound. The function of leadership, I argue, is to mediate between environmental uncertainties and organizational structure. Where organizations are insulated from uncertainties, variables describing organizational structure are stable over time and do not affect one another. Where uncertainties intrude because of leadership conditions, stability declines; but there are orderly causal links among environmental measures, organizational size, and structure.

Sociological theories of organizations have all but ignored the question of leadership. This tendency, I believe, has several sources. One is the theory of bureaucracy that emphasizes the permanence of the administrative structure of government and its superior competence compared with that of elected officials. As Max Weber wrote, "Once it is fully established, bureaucracy is among those social structures which are hardest to destroy. Bureaucracy is the means of carrying 'community action' over into rationally ordered 'societal action' . . . The power position of the fully developed bureaucracy is always overpowering. The 'political master' finds himself in the position of the 'dilettante' who stands opposite the 'expert,' facing the trained official who stands within the management of administration" (1946: 228,232).

Leadership is overlooked in contemporary organizational theory also. James D. Thompson (1967), for example, argues that technical requirements and environmental uncertainties shape most behavior in organizations. To be sure, Thompson discusses boundary-spanning activities, particularly those involved when environmental contingencies are diverse and uncertain, but he never identifies such activities with leadership. Together, the two theoretical perspectives form a paradox. One overlooks leadership on the grounds that organizations that are rational, hence bureaucratic, are so efficient compared to other forms of administration that changes in leadership cannot affect their stability. The other overlooks leadership because organizations that are rational,

and hence responsive to environmental uncertainties, require considerable boundary-spanning activity, only part of
which can be handled by a single leader. Put somewhat differently, bureaucratic theory de-emphasizes leadership because little changes, and open-system theory de-emphasizes
leadership because everything is in flux.

Another source of sociologists' reluctance to consider
leadership is the discrepancy between the few theories of
leadership we have and the kinds of research studies that
have been conducted. Selznick (1957), for example, speaks of
leadership's responsibility for shaping organizational character, infusing values, and generating a sense of distinctive
competence among members. Much research, by contrast,
has been concerned with dimensions of leadership style,
primarily "initiation of structure" and "consideration" (e.g.,
see Stogdill and Coons, 1957), which seem far removed from
Selznick's discussion of institutionalization. Almost equally
removed from Selznick's theoretical ideas are some studies
of leadership change, or what is called managerial succession
(Gouldner, 1954; Grusky, 1961, 1963; Kriesberg, 1962). Leadership turnover appears to be highest in large organizations
(Grusky, 1961; Kriesberg, 1962), although Grusky's results
have been challenged by Gordon and Becker (1964). Where
change does occur it saps morale, either because of increased
bureaucratization (Gouldner, 1954) or because the departure
of a leader is taken as evidence of organizational failure
(Grusky, 1963). So large is the gap between sociological
theorizing and research on leadership that it is tempting to
dismiss leadership as a sociological variable altogether.

An alternative is to reformulate theories so that sociologi-
cally interesting propositions emerge and can be tested.
There are several possibilities. First, both extreme positions—that organizations are rigid closed systems or that
they are fraught with uncertainty—should be disregarded. A
more appealing notion is that organizations are sometimes
stable and sometimes changing.[2] Second, one should ask

how leadership affects the likelihood of change in organizations. The literature on management succession suggests that shifts in leadership are accompanied by other changes in organizations; hence, a plausible hypothesis is that leadership turnover creates turbulence or uncertainty in organizations. Third, instead of pursuing relationships between social–psychological characteristics of leaders and organizational properties, research should focus on variables describing the larger network of relationships in which leadership roles are embedded. For example, one might hypothesize that to the extent to which leaders are autonomous rather than dependent, they can protect organizations from uncertainties arising in the environment.

In discussing the degree of uncertainty or turbulence within organizations, one must consider the broader question of the "openness" or "closedness" of organizational structures. There has been much discussion of the need for an "open-system" approach to organizations and recognition of the causal primacy of variables describing the environment (e.g., see Katz and Kahn, 1966; Terreberry, 1968). However, many research studies have overlooked environmental variables either because they were not measured in the first place or because they were measured but could not be separated from basic organizational attributes such as size. Some effects of environmental variables on organizational structure will be examined in this chapter, but only after controlling for several variables describing leadership. The basic premise is this: At least for the organizations studied, whether they are more like "open" or "closed" systems is variable. To the extent that leadership is vulnerable to external pressures, it also allows environmental uncertainties to intrude upon organizational structures. And to the extent that leadership characteristics are associated with stability, the impact of environment is diminished.

The analysis of the data describing the 215 departments will proceed as follows: Controlling for leadership conditions we shall first examine autocorrelations between the 1966 and 1972 measures of four basic organizational variables—size, the number of divisions, the number of levels of supervision, and the number of subdivisions or sections. These autocorrelations are measures of the predictability of organizational structure over time. For example, the first column of Table 7 shows autocorrelations of the four variables for 113 departments in which leadership changed between 1966 and 1972, whereas the second column shows the autocorrelations for 102 departments in which there was stable leadership. We shall also look at turnover of control of computing facilities, again grouping the departments according to variables describing leadership. Results of regressions testing for causal relationships among environmental variables, organizational size, and measures of structure will then be examined. Here too, the data will be grouped according to variables describing leadership. Finally, relationships between environmental variables and the size of data-processing and budget units will be reviewed. Needless to say, the effects of environment on the growth of data processing and budgeting are quite different from what they are on whole finance departments.

## Leadership and predictability of organizational structure

### Turnover of leadership

The most reasonable, indeed obvious, hypothesis with which to begin is that change in leadership is associated with change in organizational arrangements and, correspondingly, stability in leadership positions is a concomitant of organizational stability. To test this proposition, departments were grouped according to the length of time their heads had held their offices in 1972. One group consists of 113 departments whose top executives, having held their jobs for less than six years at the time of the 1972 survey, had come into office after the 1966 data were collected. The re-

Table 7. Autocorrelations of structural variables by leadership conditions

| Variables | 1972 Tenure 0–5 years (N = 113) (1) | 1972 Tenure 6+ years (N = 102) (2) | 1966 Tenure 0–5 years (N = 122) (3) | 1966 Tenure 6+ years (N = 93) (4) | Head is political appointee (N = 93) (5) | Head is elected or civil servant (N = 71) (6) | More than 10% of time with head of govt. (N = 65) (7) | Up to 10% of time with head of govt. (N = 150) (8) |
|---|---|---|---|---|---|---|---|---|
| Size | .9380 | .9786 | .8825 | .9789 | .8551 | .9944 | .8196 | .9694 |
| Divisions | .5178 | .6246 | .5032 | .6791 | .5316 | .6152 | .5241 | .5931 |
| Levels of supervision | .6058 | .5747 | .5395 | .6703 | .5225 | .6716 | .4655 | .6460 |
| Sections | .6372 | .7434 | .6320 | .7409 | .6358 | .7726 | .4769 | .7135 |

maining 102 departments had the same leadership in 1972 as in 1966. The autocorrelations in Table 7 generally support the hypothesis that turnover is associated with instability; but the differences are not large, and there is one reversal. The autocorrelation of departmental size – the number of full-time employees – increases from .9380 in agencies with turnover to .9786 where there is stability; the autocorrelation of the number of divisions increases from .5178 to .6246; and for the number of sections there is a similar increase from .6372 to .7434. The autocorrelation of the number of levels of supervision does not follow this pattern; it drops from .6058 to .5747.[3]

Aside from the weakness of the empirical evidence, the hypothesis that stability of leadership is associated with predictability of organizational structure is fraught with other problems. Most important is that where leadership has changed, some, though not all, of our informants have changed.[4] Apparent instability in organizational structures may reflect different perceptions of similar administrative arrangements. Where leadership has not changed, apparent stability may reflect either ignorance of actual change or unwillingness to accept it. A second problem is the causal direction of the association between leadership turnover and organizational stability. I would like to argue that leadership is the causal variable, but there are two other possibilities. One is that leaders quit when their organization are compelled to change; indeed, one might speculate that leadership is often forced out under the cover of reorganization. Another possibility is that a simultaneous relationship holds between stability of leadership and that of organizational structure. More turbulent organizations may have higher rates of turnover, which make them more turbulent, and so forth.

One way of handling both of these problems is to lag the measure of leadership turnover. If changes in leadership engender fluctuations in organizational structure, then leadership at an earlier time should predict organization at a later time as well as or better than leadership turnover occurring at the same time organizational changes are observed. Should the relationship between leadership turnover and structure be simultaneous; or should structural changes affect leadership, the differences revealed by the lagged measure of leadership should be small, if not altogether degenerate. Furthermore, turnover in leadership before 1966 should not greatly affect changes between 1966 and 1972 in informants whom we interviewed.[5] The third and fourth columns of Table 7 show the autocorrelations of structural variables measured in 1966 and 1972 controlling for the tenure of leadership prior to 1966. The differences in the autocorrelations are somewhat greater than those yielded by controlling for leadership turnover between 1966 and 1972. Where leadership changed before 1966, the autocorrelations of size, the number of divisions, levels of supervision, and sections are .8825, .5032, .5395, and .6320; where there was stability the autocorrelations are .9789, .6791, .6703, and .7409, respectively. Continuity of leadership during an earlier interval is associated with predictability of organizational structure later on. These results suggest that leadership is the causal variable, but the other possibilities ought to be examined.

The data do not allow a complete test of the effects of organizational change on leadership turnover rather than the other way around. In part, this is due to the complexity of the problem. Department heads who anticipate reorganization may quit before the actual changes take place; the effect, leadership turnover, may appear before its cause. In part, the design of this research prevents a direct test. I have little information about organizational structure prior to the first wave of interviews; hence, specific changes in structure between 1960 and 1966 are not known. One item that is available, however, concerns whether any major changes in organizational structure occurred in finance agencies during the year preceding the 1966 interviews. About one-third of the departments reported such changes. Lacking better data, we will have to rely on this item. Briefly, the tabulations show that departments experiencing structural change between 1965 and 1966 were much more likely than others to have had leadership turnover between 1960 and 1966. Moreover, organizational change before 1966 does not predict leadership turnover between 1966 and 1972. Departments that have had structural change kept their chiefs slightly (but not significantly) longer than others.[6] Disregarding a possible anticipation effect, then, structural change does not appear to be the source of much leadership turnover.

Testing for simultaneity between turnover and structural change is even more difficult, but not impossible. Although I cannot identify all of the conditions that might cause simultaneous change in both organizational structure and leadership, I do have information on one. The 1972 questionnaire asked whether there had been a major reorganization of local government since 1966. Two effects of governmental reorganization are evident. First, reorganization is significantly associated with leadership turnover. Of the 30 departments that reported reorganization of local government (though not necessarily of the finance agency), twenty-two or 70 percent, changed leaders between 1966 and 1972; whereas only 49 percent of the others did. Second, although the autocorrelations of variables describing organizational structure are weaker where the structure of government has changed — especially with regard to the number of divisions — the effects of leadership turnover remain. Indeed, the impact of leadership is greatest where there has been governmental reorganization.[7]

On balance, it appears that organizational change affects leadership turnover very little and that exogenous forces that disturb organizational structure do so mainly through their impact on leadership, though they do have some direct effect. I have no way of controlling for anticipation effects, nor do I have information on all the factors that might render the association between stability of leadership and organizational stability spurious. With these limitations in mind, it seems appropriate to speak of leadership as the causal variable.

*Autonomy and insularity of leadership*

A second hypothesis is that constraints on leadership affect the stability of organizational structures. One possibility is that minimal external influence allows leaders to change organization at will; hence, autonomy of leadership should be associated with unstable structures. More plausible is the notion that autonomous leadership shields organizations from pressures to change administrative arrangements; this prediction is most consistent with the argument that uncertainty is generated by the environment rather than by internal processes in most organizations. An indicator of department heads' dependence on higher authority is the method of appointment. Finance directors who are appointed by their immediate superiors or otherwise politically appointed are considered to be dependent on higher authority; those who are either elected or appointed through civil service procedures are considered autonomous.

The autocorrelations of variables describing organizational structure suggest that there is greater predictability when leadership has autonomy from higher authority than when it is dependent. In the fifth and sixth columns of Table 7, finance agencies are grouped according to the method of selection of department heads. The fifth column includes departments whose heads are political appointees, hence subject to arbitrary dismissal; whereas the sixth column shows autocorrelations for agencies whose heads are more independent because they are either elected or appointed through civil service procedures. For all four measures of organizational structure, the autocorrelations are higher where department heads are elected officials or civil servants. Where chief financial officers are political appointees, the autocorrelations of size, numbers of divisions, levels of hierarchy, and sections are .8551, .5316, .5225, and .6358, respectively. The autocorrelations increase to .9944, .6152, .6716, and .7726 where department heads are not dependent on the head of government because they have been elected or have civil service protection.

A similar pattern is evident when the insularity of department heads in relation to higher officials is controlled. Presumably, the more time a finance director spends in dealing directly with the head of government, the more he is influenced by him and the more vulnerable to external influence the finance department becomes. In the seventh and eighth columns of Table 7, the proportion of time department heads spend with the head of government is controlled. The seventh column in Table 7 shows autocorrelations of the structural variables for departments whose heads spend more than 10 percent of their time with their nominal superiors; the eighth column shows autocorrelations for the remaining departments, where the head of government takes up to one-tenth of the working hours of his chief financial officer. For the former group of departments, the autocorrelations of size, divisions, levels, and sections are .8196, .5241, .4655, and .4769, respectively. For the latter groups they are somewhat higher: .9694, .5931, .6460, and .7135. For both indicators of department heads autonomy from higher authority, the results are similar and quite consistent. The less dependence and the less interchange, the greater the predictability of organizational structure.

### Control of the computer

Just as leadership affects the predictability of organizational structure, it also influences the likelihood of change in control of the computing facilities used by the finance department. Of the 120 departments that used computers in 1966 (all but a handful do now) 91 ran their own computers;

but only 67 did so in 1972. Thirty-two have given up control of the computer since 1966, whereas 8 have gained it.

Table 8 shows Q-coefficients derived from the cross-tabulation of the finance departments' management of their own computers in 1966 and in 1972. The coefficients show that stability of the location of data-processing facilities in local governments, like the administrative structure of finance departments, depends on leadership conditions. To illustrate, the Q-coefficient of predictability of control of the computer is .5190 for agencies whose leaders changed between 1966 and 1972 and .7576 for departments with stable leadership. Where the department head is a political appointee, the Q-coefficient drops to .1667; it is .8445 where the head is either elected or a civil servant. Other variables describing leadership have similar effects on the stability of control of the computer. This adds to the evidence that organizational properties are affected by the rate of turnover of leaders and their relationships to superiors.

### Causal relationships among organizational variables

In this section, I test the hypothesis that where leadership allows uncertainties to intrude in organizations, causal relationships among organizational variables appear; whereas leadership conditions that minimize uncertainty make causal links vanish. Three sets of variables will be examined. One is measures of environmental demand for the services of finance departments. The demand variables are the total amount of funds a department administers for a city, county, or state; the size of the general or corporate fund that covers common activities such as police and fire protection, debt service, and health and welfare; the number of full-time government employees of the city, county, or state served; and the 1965 population of the jurisdiction served by a finance department. The second, a single variable, is organizational size as measured by the number of

Table 8. Q-coefficients of turnover of operation of computer by leadership conditions (departments that used computers in 1966)

| 1972 Tenure 0–5 years (N = 61) (1) | 1972 Tenure 6+ years (N = 59) (2) | 1966 Tenure 0–5 years (N = 70) (3) | 1966 Tenure 6+ years (N = 50) (4) | Head is political appointee (N = 50) (5) | Head is elected or civil servant (N = 43) (6) | More than 10% of time with head of govt. (N = 27) (7) | Up to 10% of time with head of govt. (N = 93) (8) |
|---|---|---|---|---|---|---|---|
| .5190 | .7576 | .6092 | .7561 | .1667 | .8445 | .4783 | .8109 |

full-time employees of a finance department. The third consists of measures of organizational structure: the numbers of divisions, levels of supervision, and sections in an agency. A causal relationship is said to exist when the value of a variable at a later time is predicted by another variable measured at an earlier time with the dependent variable at the earlier time controlled. For the sake of brevity, full regression models are not presented here; results of some eighty-four regressions are summarized in Tables 9–14. The reader should keep in mind that no causal relationship exists when the only significant predictor of a dependent variable is the same item measured at an earlier time. When other variables at an earlier time predict the dependent variable at a later time net of the dependent variable at an earlier time, we speak of causality.

The specific hypotheses to be tested are the following: (1) where leadership conditions tend toward uncertainty, environmental demand affects organizational size; (2) where leadership conditions tend toward uncertainty, environmental demand affects organizational structure; (3) where leadership conditions tend toward uncertainty, organizational size affects structure; and, (4) where leadership conditions tend toward certainty, environment affects neither size nor structure, and size does not influence structure. The earlier discussion of finance departments suggests that the impact of environment on size and structure should be negative for these agencies, even though positive associations appear cross-sectionally. The effect of size on structure should be positive as in Chapter 3. I deal with these hypotheses seriatim.

### Effects of environment on size

The results of regressions of 1972 size on 1966 size and the four measures of environmental demand are summarized in Table 9. In the first and second rows, 1972 size is regressed on 1966 size and 1966 total funds administered by

Table 9. Regressions of 1972 size on 1966 size and 1966 demand variables, controlling for leadership conditions

| Variables | 1972 Tenure 0–5 years (1) | | 1972 Tenure 6+ years (2) | | 1966 Tenure 0–5 years (3) | | 1966 Tenure 6+ years (4) | |
|---|---|---|---|---|---|---|---|---|
| | Zero order | B* | Zero order | B* | Zero order | B* | Zero order | B* |
| 1966 Size | .9380 | 1.0293 | .9786 | .9873 | .8825 | .9868 | .9789 | 1.0023 |
| 1966 Total funds administered | .2255 | −.2140 | .7035 | (−.0121) | .3033 | −.2032 | .4679 | (.0457) |
| 1966 Size | .9380 | 1.0160 | .9786 | .9779 | .8825 | .9293 | .9789 | 1.1104 |
| 1966 General fund | .2776 | −.1750 | .6765 | (.0010) | .3736 | (.0993) | .6721 | −.1728 |
| 1966 Size | .9380 | 1.0204 | .9786 | .9768 | .8825 | .9518 | .9789 | 1.0367 |
| 1966 Total govt. employees | .5711 | −.1215 | .7076 | (.0025) | .3525 | −.1354 | .8499 | (−.0654) |
| 1966 Size | .9380 | 1.0093 | .9786 | .9933 | .8825 | .9760 | .9789 | .9974 |
| 1965 Population | .5564 | −.1083 | .6977 | (−.0204) | .3804 | −.1670 | .7267 | (−.0245) |

| Variables | Head is political appointee (5) | | Head is elected or civil servant (6) | | More than 10% time with head of govt. (7) | | Up to 10% of time with head of govt. (8) | |
|---|---|---|---|---|---|---|---|---|
| | Zero order | B* | Zero order | B* | Zero order | B* | Zero order | B* |
| 1966 Size | .8552 | .9430 | .9944 | .9982 | .8196 | .9496 | .9694 | 1.0073 |
| 1966 Total funds administered | .2147 | -.1999 | .6976 | (-.0053) | .2057 | -.2633 | .4376 | -.0745 |
| 1966 Size | .8552 | .9229 | .9944 | .9725 | .8196 | .9416 | .9694 | .9838 |
| 1966 General fund | .2617 | -.1514 | .7094 | (.0314) | .2033 | -.2522 | .5894 | (-.0231) |
| 1966 Size | .8552 | .9268 | .9944 | .9578 | .8196 | .9583 | .9694 | .9865 |
| 1966 Total govt. employees | .2442 | -.1630 | .8988 | (.0409) | .2457 | -.2618 | .7535 | (.0218) |
| 1966 Size | .8552 | .9204 | .9944 | .9720 | .8196 | 1.0330 | .9694 | .9751 |
| 1965 Population | .2611 | -.1471 | .9161 | (.0245) | .2138 | -.3747 | .6747 | (-.0082) |

the finance department; in the third and fourth rows, 1972 size is regressed on 1966 size and 1966 general fund; and in the remaining rows, the environmental variables are 1966 total government employees and 1965 population, respectively. The columns represent different leadership conditions. For example, the first column shows results of regressions for departments whose heads had been in office for less than six years before 1972, whereas the second column represents results for agencies where the 1972 tenure of the head was six or more years. Each column shows the zero-order correlation of each independent variable with 1972 size as well as the standardized regression coefficient (B*). Coefficients less than twice their standard errors are in parentheses.

The odd-numbered columns in Table 9 report regressions for departments where leadership conditions tend toward uncertainty—1972 tenure of department head less than 6 years, 1966 tenure less than 6 years, political appointment of department head, and more than 10 percent of department head's time spent with the head of government. In these columns, the environmental measures of demand have almost consistent negative effects on 1972 size of finance departments. (One of the sixteen coefficients is not significant.) By contrast, in the even-numbered columns—where leadership conditions would tend to limit the impact of external uncertainties because of long tenure of the department head, election or civil service appointment, and insularity from the head of government—the coefficients of the environmental variables are almost consistently zero. (Two of the sixteen are significant.) Environmental demands appears to have a negative effect on the size of finance departments where leadership introduces uncertainty or unpredictability but no effect at all under other leadership conditions. Leadership thus mediates or filters the effect of environment on organizational size.

*Effects of environment on structure*

The effects of environmental demand on organiza-tional structure are not so clear-cut as they are on size. To begin, there are some null findings. Neither the total funds administered by a department, the size of the general fund, total government employment, nor the population served predicts the number of levels of supervision in a finance agency under any conditions. The vertical structure of bureaucracies is apparently unresponsive to these environ-mental fluctuations. Whether an organization has an elabo-rated or a truncated hierarchy is determined by internal ad-ministrative needs. In addition, when the tenure of leader-ship *in 1972* is controlled, there are very few significant ef-fects of the demand variables on organizational structure, and the few that appear are inconsistent. Similarly, control-ling for the amount of time department heads spend with the head of government yields only sparse and inconsistent ef-fects of demand on structure. The null effects that appear when finance agencies are grouped according to the 1972 tenure of the department head reflect very long lags between changes in leadership and their impact on organizational structure. The null effects of demand when time spent with the head of government is controlled may be due to poor measurement—it is an estimate—but are otherwise not easily explained.

Two measures of organizational structure that do respond to environmental pressures are the number of divisions and the number of sections or subunits within divisions. The effects of environment on the number of divisions, control-ling for leadership conditions, are shown in Table 10; Table 11 shows relationships of measures of environmental de-mand on the count of sections. The findings can be sum-marized as follows: Even when 1966 size is included in the regressions (the effects of size will be discussed below), en-vironmental demand contracts the horizontal structure of fi-

Table 10. Regressions of 1972 divisions on 1966 size, 1966 divisions, and 1966 demand variables, controlling for leadership conditions

| Variables | 1966 Tenure 0–5 years (1) | | 1966 Tenure 6+ years (2) | | Head is political appointee (3) | | Head is elected or civil servant (4) | |
|---|---|---|---|---|---|---|---|---|
| | Zero order | B* | Zero order | B* | Zero order | B* | Zero order | B* |
| 1966 Size | .3318 | .2172 | .3695 | (.0302) | .3977 | .3001 | .3122 | (−.1428) |
| 1966 Divisions | .5032 | .4253 | .6791 | .6347 | .5316 | .4146 | .6152 | .5387 |
| 1966 Total funds administered | −.0329 | (−.1229) | .3003 | (.1213) | −.0226 | (−.1793) | .4523 | .3500 |
| 1966 Size | .3318 | .3113 | .3695 | (−.1886) | .3977 | .3420 | .3122 | (.1255) |
| 1966 Divisions | .5032 | .4921 | .6791 | .5064 | .5316 | .4232 | .6152 | .6126 |
| 1966 General fund | −.5032 | −.3685 | .5910 | .4428 | −.0683 | −.2780 | .4045 | (−.0724) |
| 1966 Size | .3318 | .3220 | .3695 | (.0972) | .3977 | .3442 | .3122 | (.3803) |
| 1966 Divisions | .5032 | .4356 | .6791 | .6387 | .5316 | .4044 | .6152 | .5873 |
| 1966 Total govt. employees | −.0843 | −.3360 | .2617 | (−.0076) | −.0896 | −.2698 | .2232 | (−.3299) |
| 1966 Size | .3318 | .2861 | .3695 | (.1256) | .3977 | .3188 | .3122 | (.1891) |
| 1966 Divisions | .5032 | .4345 | .6791 | .6362 | .5316 | .4140 | .6152 | .5834 |
| 1965 Population | .0095 | −.2422 | .2179 | (−.0450) | −.0438 | −.2194 | .2771 | (−.1121) |

Table 11. *Regressions of 1972 sections on 1966 size, 1966 sections, and 1966 demand variables, controlling for leadership conditions*

| Variables | 1966 Tenure 0–5 years (1) | | 1966 Tenure 6+ years (2) | | Head is political appointee (3) | | Head is elected or civil servant (4) | |
|---|---|---|---|---|---|---|---|---|
| | Zero order | B* | Zero order | B* | Zero order | B* | Zero order | B* |
| 1966 Size | .7019 | .6165 | .6220 | (.1101) | .7184 | .6110 | .3122 | (−.1428) |
| 1966 Sections | .6320 | .3418 | .7409 | .6485 | .6358 | .2983 | .6152 | .5387 |
| 1966 Total funds administered | .1901 | −.2713 | .3623 | (.0151) | .1439 | −.2569 | .4523 | .3500 |
| 1966 Size | .7019 | .5774 | .6220 | .2580 | .7184 | .5707 | .3122 | (.1255) |
| 1966 Sections | .6320 | .3802 | .7409 | .8484 | .6358 | .3988 | .6152 | .6126 |
| 1966 General fund | .2349 | −.2497 | .4809 | −.3884 | .1514 | −.3283 | .4045 | (−.0724) |
| 1966 Size | .7019 | .6124 | .6220 | (.2900) | .7184 | .5999 | .3122 | (.3804) |
| 1966 Sections | .6320 | .3722 | .7409 | .6193 | .6358 | .3277 | .6152 | .5873 |
| 1966 Total govt. employees | .1867 | −.3027 | .4667 | (−.1692) | .1399 | −.2811 | .2232 | (−.3299) |
| 1966 Size | .7019 | .5839 | .6220 | (.1657) | .7184 | .5850 | .3122 | (.1819) |
| 1966 Sections | .6320 | .2495 | .7409 | .6435 | .6358 | .2710 | .6152 | .5834 |
| 1965 Population | .3060 | −.1993 | .4130 | (−.0583) | .2299 | (−.1506) | .2772 | (−.1121) |

nance departments where leadership conditions contribute to uncertainty; but the environment has no effect where leadership conditions tend toward certainty. In Table 10, the four demand variables have negative effects on 1972 divisions when the 1966 tenure of leadership was less than six years and the department head is politically appointed. (Two of the eight coefficients are not significant, however.) In six out of eight instances, environment has no effect on the number of divisions where leadership had six or more years' tenure prior to 1966 and where it is either elected or appointed through civil service procedures. And the two significant coefficients that appear under these leadership conditions are positive. The safest conclusion seems to be that environmental demand decreases the number of divisions in finance departments where leadership has been unstable in the past or is politically appointed, but that under other conditions demand has no effects on the number of subunits reporting to the head of the department.

A similar pattern appears in Table 11, where the number of sections is regressed on 1966 size, 1966 sections, and the four demand variables. Where leadership creates uncertainty, demand variables are negatively related to the number of sections, though one of the eight coefficients is not significant. Where leadership has long tenure and is autonomous of higher authority, six of the eight coefficients of the environmental measures are not significantly different from zero, one is positive, and one is negative. The same leadership conditions that allow the environment to erode the number of divisions also allow contraction of subunits within divisions; and conditions that protect the number of divisions also maintain the horizontal structure of finance departments at the third level of hierarchy. All other things being equal, including size, environmental demand leads to loss of functionally specialized subunits from finance departments, just as demand impedes growth. Leadership mediates the effects of environment on organizational size and structure: Continuity and autonomy of leadership shield finance departments from environmental pressures; whereas turnover and dependent allow outside forces to take their toll.

*Effects of size on structure*

Here I wish to show that the causal relationship between organizational size and measures of structure that was shown in Chapter 3 is contingent on leadership characteristics. The reader is directed again to Tables 10 and 11 as well as to Table 12. In Table 10, we are now interested in the coefficients of 1966 size net of 1966 divisions and the environmental variables. Similarly, in Table 11 we are interested in effects of 1966 size net of 1966 sections and environment. The effects of 1966 size on 1972 divisions when other variables are controlled are unambiguous. Under leadership conditions tending toward instability—short tenure of department head and dependence on higher authority—the causal impact of size is evident. All eight coefficients are positive and significant. Where leadership aids stability— where the department head has six or more years' tenure and where he is either elected or a civil servant—no significant effects of size on the number of divisions appear in

Table 12. *Regressions of 1972 levels of supervision on 1966 size and 1966 levels of supervision, controlling for leadership conditions*

| | 1966 Tenure 0–5 years (1) | | 1966 Tenure 6+ years (2) | | Head is political appointee (3) | | Head is elected or civil servant (4) | |
|---|---|---|---|---|---|---|---|---|
| Variables | Zero order | B* | Zero order | B* | Zero order | B* | Zero order | B* |
| 1966 Size | .5646 | .3969 | .4646 | (.1595) | .5264 | .3321 | .4924 | (.2460) |
| 1966 Levels | .5395 | .3485 | .6703 | .5875 | .5859 | .3225 | .6716 | .5641 |

Table 10. Much the same pattern is in evidence in Table 11, where 1972 sections are regressed on other variables. Where department heads had held office less than six years prior to 1966 and where they are politically appointed, all eight coefficients of size are positive and significant. Where they had lengthy tenure and were autonomous of higher authority, seven of the eight coefficients of 1966 size are not significantly different from zero.

Regressions of 1972 levels of supervision on 1966 levels and 1966 size are shown in Table 12. Variables describing environmental demand, it will be recalled, had no effect on the vertical structure of finance departments; hence, they are not included in the regressions. As before, size has a significant effect on organizational structure only where there is turnover in leadership positions and where dependence on or vulnerability to superior officials reduces department heads' autonomy. Where there was no turnover, and where department heads have the security of a civil service appointment or an elected office, the causal link between size and the number of levels of hierarchy vanishes.

### Recapitulation

The hypothesis that leadership conditions affect causal relationships among organizational variables is for the most part confirmed. Effects of environment on size and structure and effects of size on structure are contingent on leadership's allowing external uncertainties to intrude upon organizations. Two comments are in order. First, these findings suggest that one should be cautious in elaborating deterministic theories of relationships among abstract categories describing organizations. Change occurs in organizations when causal relations operate; and change can be resisted, hence causal relations rendered inoperative, by firmly entrenched leadership. Change is also promoted, sometimes by replacing leadership, sometimes by making leaders more directly accountable for their organizations' activities. Organizational change is the consequence, whether intended or unintended, of choices made by people; it does not occur either automatically or necessarily. This reality is not captured by deterministic theories. Second, the leadership conditions associated with high predictability or stability of organizational structures are also those from which causal relationships are absent. Contrariwise, leadership conditions associated with instability or unpredictability are also those where causal relationships abound. These correspondences suggest that the most fundamental difference between organizations is whether they are stable or changing, not whether they are "open" or "closed" to the environment.

### Closing the circle

Early in this book, it was noted that contraction and dedifferentiation of finance departments are accompanied by expansion of other agencies. Before summarizing the findings, I wish to present data indicating that this latter process indeed takes place. The interviews with finance-department officials were supplemented with questionnaires administered to heads of units responsible for data processing and for budgeting regardless of whether or not these units were part of the finance department. Interviews with heads of 146 data-processing units organized in 1966 or before were completed. Eighty-nine of the units are divisions or bureaus of finance departments; 57 are either departments in their own right or divisions of other departments. Ninety-five interviews with heads of budget units formed in 1966 or before were also completed. Forty-seven of these units are within finance departments, and the remainder are elsewhere.[8]

Whereas environmental demands impede the growth of finance departments, we would expect data-processing units to increase their size over time in response to external pressures. A further expectation is that the impact of demand on growth should be greatest for data-processing units located outside focal finance departments. The data describing units that do computing work for finance departments bear out these expectations very nicely. In Table 13, 1972 size of data-processing units is regressed on their 1966 size and the four measures of environmental demand, controlling for the location of data processing. The regressions can be summarized simply: Data-processing units within finance departments are unaffected by the environment; but data-processing units outside finance departments grow in response to environmental demands. For example, the coefficient linking 1965 population with 1972 size of data-processing unit net of its 1966 size is not different from zero for units in the finance department but is .1314 where data processing does not report to the director of finance. The same effects appear for the other measures of environmental demand.

The pattern of growth in budget units is similar to that in

Table 13. *Regressions of 1972 size of data-processing unit on 1966 size of data-processing unit and 1966 demand variables, controlling for location of data processing*

| Variables | D.-p. unit in finance department (N = 89) (1) | | D.-p. unit outside finance department (N = 57) (2) | |
|---|---|---|---|---|
| | Zero order | B* | Zero order | B* |
| 1966 Size of d.-p. unit | .6984 | .7004 | .9006 | .9041 |
| 1966 Total funds administered | .1614 | (−.0081) | .0899 | .1176 |
| 1966 Size of d.-p. unit | .6984 | .7118 | .9006 | .8759 |
| 1966 General fund | .1783 | (−.0430) | .2948 | .1377 |
| 1966 Size of d.-p. unit | .6984 | .7156 | .9006 | .8661 |
| 1966 Total government employees | .2490 | (−.0421) | .3569 | .1337 |
| 1966 Size of d.-p. unit | .6984 | .6910 | .9006 | .8633 |
| 1965 Population | .1899 | (.0325) | .3764 | .1314 |

data-processing. Briefly, Table 14 shows that for budget units located within finance departments, the four measures of environmental demand do not affect 1972 size significantly, net of 1966 size. (Fairly sizable coefficients are not significant for these units because 1966 size and the environmental variables are nearly collinear. In any case, the coefficients are all negative.) Budget units unattached to finance departments appear to grow in response to environmental demand, however. For these organizations total funds administered, size of the general fund, and government employment are positively related to 1972 size. Only 1965 population does not significantly affect 1972 size.

Unfortunately, there are no data about leadership of data-processing and budget units with which to test other propositions developed in this chapter. One would want to know whether the rate of growth of units outside the finance department is greatest where leadership is unstable, dependent on higher authority, and in close contact with super-

Table 14. *Regressions of 1972 size of budget unit on 1966 size of budget unit and 1966 demand variables, controlling for location of budget unit*

| Variables | Budget unit in finance department (N = 47) (1) | | Budget unit outside finance department (N = 48) (2) | |
|---|---|---|---|---|
| | Zero order | B* | Zero order | B* |
| 1966 Size of budget unit | .8996 | 1.1251 | .9635 | .9487 |
| 1966 Total funds administered | .7691 | (−.2491) | .2690 | .1980 |
| 1966 Size of budget unit | .8996 | 1.1114 | .9635 | .9395 |
| 1966 General fund | .8053 | (−.2278) | .3008 | .1494 |
| 1966 Size of budget unit | .8996 | 1.0034 | .9635 | .8587 |
| 1966 Total government employees | .8208 | (−.1117) | .8219 | .1302 |
| 1966 Size of budget unit | .8996 | .8353 | .9635 | .9198 |
| 1965 Population | .8337 | (−.0703) | .6596 | (.0681) |

visors. Despite this, the findings do suggest that finance officials' worries about "the status of the profession," as they are sometimes expressed, are justified. Environmental conditions that impede growth and contract the structures of finance departments promote expansion of other agencies of local governments. For the larger cities, counties, and states, the centralized model of finance administration has lost viability if the experience of the recent past predicts the future.

### Summary

Clearly, leadership is an important element mediating between environmental uncertainty and organizational change. Three variables describing leadership—turnover, dependence on higher authority, and insularity—predict fundamental differences in organizations. Where leadership is stable, autonomous of higher authority, and insular from it, organizational structures have high predictability over time. More important, where leadership is stable and autonomous, causal relationships among organizational variables are remarkably absent. Variables describing the environment affect neither the size nor the structures of finance agencies, and causal relationships between organizational size and structure are attenuated. By contrast, where leadership has changed in the past, and where it is dependent on higher authority and in close contact with superiors, organizational structures have less stability. Environmental variables indicating demand for the work of finance departments have significant effects on size, and they influence measures of horizontal differentiation when leadership has changed and is dependent. Only the number of supervisory levels is unaffected by demand characteristics. Finally, causal relationships between size and measures of structure abound when leadership conditions introduce uncertainty into organizations. The fact that variables describing leadership positions, not individual leaders, predict fundamental differences in organizations suggests several things.

First, more detailed information on leadership than was sought in these surveys of finance departments might reveal even greater differences among organizations. For example, it would be useful to have information about the social groups from which leaders are recruited and the ways in which informal networks intersect with organizational structures. A rich tradition in political sociology treats leadership as representative of constituencies (e.g., see Dahl, 1961). There is no reason why studies of public bureaucracies or even, for that matter, large business firms should overlook characteristics of the groups from which leaders are drawn. Organizational structures may reflect the values operating in other social structures more than theories of rational bureaucracy have led us to believe. Second, the results of this research, together with the null or inconsistent fundings in the social–psychological literature, suggest that the focus should be on leadership positions as well as on the people who happen to be leaders. Whether a leader shows consideration to subordinates may be no more important than his autonomy in hiring and rewarding employees and in setting the policy goals of his organization. Until many of the influences affecting leadership positions have been identified and controlled statistically, it would be premature to expect to find consistent effects of individual leaders' characteristics. Third, attempts to evaluate the effectiveness of organizations will have to consider attributes of leadership positions if the kinds of basic differences in causal patterns revealed here bear any relationship to performance. Again, a focus on individual leaders is not likely to be fruitful, as Lieberson and O'Connor (1972) have shown. Rather, characteristics of the social networks—both organizational and extraorganizational—in which leadership roles are embedded will have to be examined.

Another implication of these findings is that the polarity between open-system and closed-system approaches to organizations in the theoretical literature may be misleading.

Proponents of the open-system perspective argue that organizations' attributes are largely determined by the environment. The closed-system approach treats organizational variables as interdependent and the environment as a residual category. The findings suggest, however, that where organizations are affected by environmental contingencies, orderly causal relationships between variables describing size and structure appear. But where the environment has no impact, organizational variables do not affect one another either. A more complex model of organizational processes than the open-system/closed-system dichotomy is indicated. Environmental pressures impinge on all organizations, but their impact is mediated by characteristics of leadership positions. To the extent that leaders are vulnerable to external pressures, changes in the environment lead to changes in organizations that are followed by other organizational changes. A chain of causal relationships is evident. Invulnerable leadership, in contrast, blocks outside pressures, with the result that causal links vanish. Stability of organizations, then, is contingent upon the capacity of leaders to stave off environmental demands. In public administration, the formal authority structure as well as the prestige or "clout" of an official determines tenure in office and capacity to resist superiors' wishes. In business, growth and profitability may similarly insulate organizations. Contingencies of this sort must be built into organization theory. Perhaps it would be best for researchers to retreat from the position that organizations are either open or closed and ask, open-mindedly, when organizations are affected by their environments and when they do not respond. Answers to this dual question have obvious policy implications that need not be elaborated here.

Finally, the results reported here also point to the importance of qualitative materials in quantitative organizational research. The central assertion in this chapter—that leadership mediates environmental pressures on organizations—is framed so as to apply to organizations generally. But the evidence adduced in support of it is somewhat specific to finance agencies. In particular, the interpretation of environmental effects depended heavily on the description of what finance agencies were like in the past and of current trends affecting them—in other words, developments in the larger social and political environment. Contraction of the finance function with environmental demand together with growth of budgeting and data-processing activities outside of finance departments could not have been understood without a qualitative account of the nature of this environment. The need for description of the larger environment in interpreting quantitative effects of the immediate environment carries the implication that specific empirical results concerning organizations are likely to be both time bound and contingent. The former occurs because elements in the larger environment of organizations may shift fundamentally, hence create strains between what were once compatible activities, and the latter because divergent responses to immediate environmental shifts may be expected from different kinds of organizations. (The temptation to point out that nursery schools and nursing homes respond quite differently to demographic changes is irresistible.) The underlying laws driving organizations may be constant, but the empirical manifestations of these laws are in all likelihood much less orderly. This theme will be pursued in Chapter 5, where I shall discuss how the environment impinges on different types of finance agencies.

# 5

## Organizational domains

The study of organizational domains is an important yet elusive subject. Conventionally, domain is defined as the technology employed, population served, and services rendered by an organization. The task environment is the obverse of domain—literally everything else. Domain consensus is a "set of expectations both for members of an organization and for others with whom they interact, about what the organization will and will not do" (Thompson, 1967: 26–29). These definitions, although an improvement over simplistic notions of organizational goals, leave considerable ambiguity; and the range of organizations to which they apply is also unclear. The ambiguity occurs because domains and domain consensus are not static. An organization's products and clientele may change over time, and these changes may occur due to organizational action or shifts in the environment. In other words, domains may be either independent or dependent variables. Concern as to whether concept of domain applies to all organizations arises because some, especially administrative bureaus, do not have tangible products. Instead, they make decisions. One can easily speak of a firm's share of the market, but the arena of action reserved to a public bureaucracy is not so easily determined. Indeed, statutes establishing administrative bureaus can be deliberately vague.

In this chapter, organizational domains will be investigated by studying patterns of change among departments of finance, comptrollers' offices, departments of administration, and the like. The analysis hinges on some assumptions about the behavior of public bureaus such as finance agencies that require elaboration and justification. The first assumption is that because the concept of domain is ambiguous in several respects for these agencies, only the effects of claims to domain can be examined. The second is that organizational names often embody their claims. The first assumption can be defended on theoretical grounds, but the second requires some historical and anecdotal information about the agencies studied.

### Domains of public bureaucracies

The distinction between bureaucratic and non-bureaucratic organizations has all but disappeared from contemporary organization theory. Weber's (1946) classic essay on bureaucracy, of course, denies fundamental differences between business firms and public agencies. The modern forms of both—the capitalist enterprise and large-scale public administration—are seen as similarly organized, hence similarly bureaucratic. Other theorists, neoclassical economists and political scientists whose work has not been considered carefully by sociologists, disagree strongly. The differences between profit and nonprofit organizations, those that enter into voluntary quid pro quo transactions and those that do not, are regarded as basic (Von Mises, 1944; Downs, 1967: 25). The former can evaluate their performance, whereas the latter cannot, it is claimed; hence, profit organizations will always be more efficient than other types. Attempts to synthesize bureaucratic theory with the theory of the firm have only buried the issue further. Thompson (1967), for example, treats all "instrumental" organizations, bureaucratic and nonbureaucratic alike, as if they were equally constrained to minimize uncertainty and coordination costs. These needs account for behavior aimed at insulating "core technologies" from the environment and for the development of organizational hierarchies.

Recent research on organizations has hardly improved matters. To be sure, there is agreement that the structural features of organizations are not as consistent as a misreading of Weber's ideal−typical model of bureaucracy might suggest they should be (Udy, 1959; Stinchcombe, 1959; Hall, 1963). But few investigators have been concerned with differences between bureaucratic and profit organizations hypothesized by the neoclassical theorists. (An important exception is Niskanen, 1971.) Most research studies treat only single types of organizations whether bureaucracies or firms (see, for example, Blau, 1970; Blau and Schoenherr, 1971; Hall et al. 1967; Hage and Aiken, 1967a; 1967b; Pondy, 1969) or do not discuss systematically differences between the two types (see Pugh et al. 1969a; Hickson et al. 1969; and Blau, 1972 for example).

The inattention to possible differences between bureaus and firms is unfortunate for several reasons. First, it leads to overgeneralization. Concepts from one type of organization are extended to other types with wholly different purposes. Second, important nuances of organizational behavior are overlooked because they are peculiar to one type. Just as firms operate in markets, bureaus are embedded in larger governmental structures; one would expect the relevant dimensions and effects of the environment to be dissimilar. Third, some questions bearing on public policy cannot even be asked if differences in type are ignored. Of particular importance is whether certain services are best provided by firms or bureaus. The present research does not speak directly to this question, but it suggests strongly that the behavior of bureaus is affected by intangible factors that would not influence firms.

Differences between firms and public bureaucracies are especially salient when one considers the concept of organizational domains. For firms, domains can be quite precarious. A fickle clientele and uncontrollable market conditions are sources of uncertainty that demand organizational responses. One would want to study firms' strategies for stabilizing domains and establishing domain consensus. For bureaus providing public goods, there is less uncertainty. The clientele is fixed—the citizens of the jurisdiction served (or sixth graders, or the indigent, etc.). Because there is no market for public goods, it is difficult to prove inefficiency, and relatively few bureaus may be put out of business for this reason (see Kaufman, 1976). The absence of a market does not mean that bureaus lack competitors, however. Though the clientele is assured, the right to monopolize certain programs and activities of government is not. Bureaus compete with one another•for "turf" or domain through a political rather than through a market process. A key element in this competition is the way programs are articulated or claims to domain asserted. The outcome of competition is allocation of functions and resources among bureaus. The crucial difference between firms and bureaus is this: Whereas firms strive to maintain or expand domains by competing successfully in the market, bureaus use claims to domain that cannot be tested in the market to maintain or expand their activities. One would thus want to study the effects of different claims to domain on the distribution of activities and programs among public bureaucracies.

The argument that bureaus use claims to domain to maintain or expand resources acquires more force if we examine the history of the Municipal Finance Officers Association of the United States and Canada, the professional association to which most of the agencies studied here belong. MFOA was established in 1906 as the National Association of Comptrollers and Accounting Officers. In 1927, the association's name became the International Association of Comptrollers and Accounting Officers in recognition of Canadian members. A permanent secretariat and headquarters were established in Chicago in 1932, and the name was changed to the Municipal Finance Officers Association of the United States and Canada. The 1906 constitution of the National Association of Comptrollers and Accounting Officers described its purposes as follows:

> The object of this Association shall be the consideration of improved methods of public finance and the extension of the movement for the installation of a uniform system of state and municipal accounting and reporting throughout the United States, and the promotion of legislation toward these ends.

The bylaws MFOA adopted in 1932 list many more purposes:

> Its object shall be to improve methods of public finance, including: to extend the movement for adequate procedures of accounting, budgeting and financial reporting by state, provincial and local government; to encourage the use of common terminology, classifications and principles relating to these subjects; to develop general principles of economy and efficiency in state, provincial, and local government administration; and to bring about the enlistment and training of qualified public officials and employees.

Other changes occurred when the association changed its name. Membership classes were added, and the association's quarterly publication, *The Comptroller*, adopted the title of *Municipal Finance*. It is now *Government Finance*.

Documentary evidence offers little explanation for the switch from the old International Association of Comptrollers and Accounting Officers to the Municipal Finance Officers Association. No doubt, the original objectives of the association, accuracy and uniformity of accounting, had been achieved to some extent by the early 1930s. The problems of local-government administration were perceived as broader, not limited to accounting but also including revenue collection and budgeting. A parallel situation existed recently. The concern for local-government finance triggered by the New York City fiscal crisis sparked active discussion of rewriting the bylaws of the MFOA and changing the association's name. This process is by no means complete, but the objectives of the MFOA have been broadened to encompass improvement of information systems for local governments and implementation of modern budgeting techniques that take account of policy outputs as well as fiscal inputs. New bylaws, which were approved by the membership in 1975, revise the objectives of the association to include:

1 To identify principles of economy and efficiency in state, provincial and local government.
2 To develop and encourage the use of uniform standards and procedures of public finance management.
3 To provide for the professional development of public finance managers and to assist individuals in seeking a public finance career.
4 To resolve issues of public fiscal policy and to inform those persons interested in such issues.
5 To develop, improve and publish a body of knowledge in public finance management.
6 To extend cooperation and assistance to other associations and professional organizations concerned with public finance management.

The last three are new. No new name was agreed upon by the membership. Of the alternatives to MFOA, Government Finance Management Association received the widest support, but less than a majority.

The changes in MFOA's bylaws and proposed name change are by no means accidental. They are intended as a response to the removal of resources and responsibilities from finance departments, which is widely felt by the membership and was discussed earlier. By changing the bylaws, the leadership of the association hoped to redefine the functions of local-government finance officers and prevent further contraction of the finance officer's role. The hope is not without foundation. In the past, changes in the MFOA have anticipated changes in finance agencies. Indeed, there is a striking parallel between the various names of the association since 1906 and the evolution of forms of finance administration. Just as the association has moved from one of comptrollers and accounting officers to finance officers and may eventually become one of finance managers, the dominant organizational forms for the finance function have been comptrollers' offices, finance departments, and departments of administration. The simplest form is the comptroller's, (or auditor's, or accountant's) office, which used to be universal; the most common pattern is the finance department, which nowadays is also the most precarious; and a relatively new but rapidly spreading model of organization is the department of administration. As noted in the Introduction, the comptroller's function is primarily regulatory, and his domain is narrow but well defined. The finance director is meant to manage all fiscal activities; his objectives are broader, less well defined, and his domain is subject to erosion as the separation of financial from nonfinancial administration crumbles. The director of administration links financial with other administrative activities. What he does is not much different from what many finance directors would like to do, but he has established a claim to do much more; hence, administration departments are now expanding.

Perhaps several observations about the link between organizational names and claims to domain are in order. First, finance agencies do not change their names casually. A legal action, usually enactment of an ordinance or statute, is required to name a new agency or change the name of an existing one. This means that organizational purposes will be scrutinized and some consistency between names and the scope of responsibilities claimed will be expected.Second, organizational names may affect the range of decisions in which a department head participates. A comptroller is asked to certify whether a proposed expenditure is allowed by the budget; a finance director's responsibility is to raise the money if it is not available; and a director of administration may be consulted to determine whether the project is the most cost-effective means of attaining long-run objectives. In other words, people outside an agency will associate a name with a domain. Third, certain names and labels also reflect commitments to modern administration, which is presumed to be able to accomplish things old-fashioned organizations cannot. "Administration" is the most contemporary label. What is modern at one point in time may be eclipsed later on, however. A final observation is that direct measurement of claims to domain would require intensive case studies of individual organizations, which would exhaust most researchers and research budgets. Names are only imperfect indicators of claims to domain, but they are accessible and unambiguous.

Some broad hypotheses to be explored here include the following:

1 Because the outputs of bureaucratic organizations, especially administrative agencies, are ill defined, intangible claims to domain may have definite consequences. It is especially important to examine the relationship of domains claimed by bureaus to their success in holding or expanding resources.

2 Whether a bureau's domain is held, contracts, or expands depends on its claim, technological advancement, and newness:

a. Bureaus claiming narrow domains and performing essential services remain stable over time.

b. Bureaus making broad but inconsistent claims contract over time.

c. Bureaus making broad claims, using advanced technologies, and having the temporary advantages of newness expand their domains over time.[1]

3 Despite erosion of resources, bureaus rarely contract their claims to domain. The inflation of claims may lead to increased conflict among bureaus over time.

### Domain and organizational structure

The surface characteristics of comptrollers' offices, finance departments, and departments of administration should be compared at this point. Table 15 displays some of the major structural attributes of these bureaus in 1966. Finance departments, on the average, were somewhat smaller than comptrollers' offices—the mean numbers of full-time employees are 85.1 and 118.2, respectively—and departments of administration were considerably larger. A relatively small proportion of employees of finance departments—less than one-fifth—were expected to have col-

Table 15. *1966 structural characteristics of departments by name*

|  | Comptrollers' offices[a] | Finance departments | Administration departments |
|---|---|---|---|
| Mean size | 118.2 | 85.1 | 294.0 |
| Mean proportion expected to have college degree | .230 | .184 | .256 |
| Percent using computer | 63% | 53% | 86% |
| Of those using computer, percent operating own computer | 69% | 74% | 100% |
| Mean index of automation[b] | .527 | .403 | .869 |
| Mean number of financial responsibilities | 4.41 | 7.37 | 6.29 |
| (N) | (71) | (135) | (7) |

[a] Includes auditors' and accounting offices.
[b] Of those accounting activities for which a department is responsible, the proportion done on a computer.

lege degrees compared to comptrollers' offices and departments of administration. About half the finance departments, three-fifths of comptrollers' offices, and all but one of the seven administration departments used computers in 1966. About 70 percent of finance departments and comptrollers' offices that used computers in 1966 had their own data-processing equipment; all six of the automated administration departments did. An index of automation reflects the same pattern as the percentages of agencies using computers; finance departments were least likely and departments of administration most likely to have computerized their major accounting activities. Finally, and not surprisingly, comptrollers' offices had considerably fewer responsibilities than either finance departments or departments of administration in 1966. Comptrollers' offices had a mean of 4.41 major fiscal functions; finance and administration departments had 7.37 and 6.29, respectively. These data describing 1966 structure indicate quantitatively some of the differences in organizational patterns sketched above. More important, however, they allow examination of the impact of claims to domain. If, on the one hand, causal processes among comptrollers' offices, finance departments, and departments of administration are similar once measures describing organizational structure are controlled, then names that reflect claims to domain are unimportant. If, on the other hand, differences remain or are accentuated after surface characteristics are taken into account, then claims to domain must be understood as central to the behavior of bureaus. My data show the latter to be the case. Indeed, it will be argued that some of the differences revealed in Table 15, especially differences in size and scope of responsibilities, are effects of claims to domain rather than causes.

**Environmental demand and domain**

One way of testing the importance of a bureau's claim to domain is to ask how it mediates external pressures influencing organizations. A narrow claim is easily protected because it identifies a bureau's outputs and services that would have to be reduced should resources decline. The obverse does not necessarily hold, however; a narrow claim can be enlarged. A broader claim to domain is more volatile. The broader the claim, the greater the diversity of clientele, hence the greater the likelihood of dissatisfaction. Bureaus that are new and technologically sophisticated can use broad claims to augment their resources, but over time broad claims may become inconsistent and clients disenchanted so that resources are shifted elsewhere. All three patterns – stability, growth, and contraction – are evident among the agencies administering local-government finances we have studied.

One element of the environment to which administrative agencies may respond is demand for their services. For bureaus in charge of the finance function, the size of the budget, the size of the government, and the size of the population served can create demand but need not do so. The limited domains claimed by comptrollers' offices may make them insensitive to such pressures because budgets and disbursements can increase without affecting the number of accounts maintained or checks written. The broader domains claimed by finance departments and departments of administration render them more vulnerable, however. The management of investments, purchasing, and especially data processing are sensitive to scale factors. One would expect finance departments to contract somewhat with environmental demand as their functions are shifted to other agencies, and administration departments to grow with demand as they accumulate responsibilities. My data are consistent with these expectations.

Table 16 shows regressions of 1972 size as measured by the number of full-time employees on 1966 size and measures of environmental demand for agencies administering local-government finance. Twelve separate regressions are displayed in the table. Each panel includes one of the four measures of demand. The four are the size of the general fund that covers common services such as police, fire protection, health and highways; the total funds administered by a department; the number of government employees; and the population served. The effects of environmental demand on 1972 size are estimated by standard regression coefficients net of 1966 size.[2] Briefly, for comptrollers' offices, there are no effects of environmental demand on 1972 size when the earlier measure of size is controlled. None of the four coefficients is significant. For finance departments, the impact of environmental demand is consistently negative,[3] and for departments of administration three out of four coefficients of the demand variables are significantly positive despite the small number of cases. (The number of cases does suggest caution in interpreting this finding, however.)

It is important to note that the same data can be presented descriptively rather than as causal statements. Comptrollers'

Table 16. *Regressions of 1972 size on 1966 size and 1966 demand variables by name*

| Variables | Comptrollers' offices | | Finance departments | | Administration departments | |
|---|---|---|---|---|---|---|
| | Zero order | B* | Zero order | B* | Zero order | B* |
| 1966 Size | .9879 | .9908 | .8142 | .9085 | .9717 | .8174 |
| 1966 General fund | .6816 | (−.0042) | .1766 | −.2174 | .7376 | .2692 |
| 1966 Size | .9879 | 1.0038 | .8142 | .9464 | .9717 | .9231 |
| 1966 Total funds administered | .4943 | (−.0305) | .0397 | −.2392 | .4381 | (.1631) |
| 1966 Size | .9879 | .9816 | .8142 | .9291 | .9717 | .8526 |
| 1966 Government employees | .8320 | (.0074) | .2676 | −.2192 | .6628 | .2403 |
| 1966 Size | .9879 | .9935 | .8142 | .9864 | .9717 | .8482 |
| 1965 Population | .7244 | (.0077) | .2742 | −.2972 | .6675 | .2524 |

offices in 1966 had a mean of 2.3 percent of local-government employees and 2.1 percent of employees in 1972, an insignificant change. Finance departments dropped from 6.4 to 4.0 percent of employees, whereas departments of administration grew from 3.3 to 4.4 percent. The causal statements about effects of environmental demand are preferred to the descriptive ones because, as will be shown later, demand is the exogenous variable driving a set of relationships among environmental and organizational variables.

The domains claimed by bureaus administering local-government finances, then, influence patterns of growth. Environmental demand appears not to affect comptrollers' offices and similar agencies claiming narrow domains, contracts finance departments, and spurs growth of departments of administration. An important question, however, is whether the apparent effects of domain are due to identifiable structural attributes of these bureaus.

### An effect of automation

To check the possibility that the effects of environmental demand are spurious, each of the variables listed in Table 15 was controlled in additional regressions.[4] Neither size, the proportion of college-trained employees, nor operation of data-processing facilities made any difference. The scope of activities of a department yielded an anomolous result: Finance departments least like comptrollers' offices, those with most responsibilities, were least likely to be influenced by environmental demand. But even this effect disappeared when departments were grouped by whether or not they used computers in 1966. Computerization had no impact on comptrollers' offices; but finance departments that were automated in 1966 did not contract with environmental demand, whereas those not computerized were strongly affected. The regressions are shown in Table 17. As before, each of the four panels includes 1966 size and one of the measures of environmental demand; the left columns display regressions for departments that were computerized in 1966, and nonautomated departments appear at the right. Among finance departments that did their accounting work on computers, no significant effects of the demand variables appear. Finance agencies that were not computerized are affected by demand. The coefficients of all four demand variables are significantly negative. Again, these data can be presented descriptively. Using a computer had no effect on the relative size of finance departments in 1966 – 6.4 percent of government employees. But those that were computerized in 1966 dropped only to 4.9 percent of employees in 1972 whereas those not computerized dropped to 3.1 percent.

Several explanations for this pattern can be imagined. One is that technological advance of any kind has the element of novelty that helps a bureau expand or at least maintain its resources. No doubt there is some truth to this, but the explanation cannot be tested easily. And there is no evidence

Table 17. *Finance departments only: regressions of 1972 size on 1966 size and 1966 demand variables controlling for use of computer in 1966*

| Variables | Used computer | | Did not use computer | |
|---|---|---|---|---|
| | Zero order | B* | Zero order | B* |
| 1966 Size | .8340 | .8236 | .8212 | 1.1227 |
| 1966 General fund | .6162 | (.0089) | .2124 | −.3393 |
| 1966 Size | .8340 | .8135 | .8212 | 1.4418 |
| 1966 Total funds administered | .6628 | (.0151) | .4299 | −.6616 |
| 1966 Size | .8340 | .8101 | .8212 | 1.1969 |
| 1966 Government employees | .6587 | (.0272) | .4170 | −.4074 |
| 1966 Size | .8340 | .9273 | .8212 | 1.4808 |
| 1965 Population | .6719 | (−.1513) | .4987 | −.6988 |

that computerization has augmented the size of comptrollers' offices. Another possibility is that resources lost from finance functions are balanced by growth in data processing whether or not a department actually operates a computer. Some of the data support this interpretation. Automated finance departments are losing fiscal functions as rapidly as others; I shall deal with this presently. Finally, automation may redefine a department's tasks somewhat so that its claims becomes less precarious. The availability of a computer may allow a shift of emphasis away from disparate, even antagonistic responsibilities (for example, budgeting and purchasing) and toward machine processing of fiscal data regardless of their purpose. Centralization of control of finance functions may give way to centralization of fiscal data together with decentralization or even loss of specific functions, minimizing the contradictions in the finance-department model of organization.

The data show some evidence of a trend toward decentralization of substantive decisions in automated finance departments that is not present in either nonautomated finance agencies or comptrollers' offices. Table 18 displays percentages of departments where decisions of various kinds are delegated to division heads or below. Several patterns are evident in the table even though most of the percentage differences are not statistically significant. First, regardless of name, agencies that were automated in 1966 tend to be less centralized than those that did not use computers. This is partly, but not entirely, a function of size and is not of major concern here. Second, there is little overall change in decision-making practices among comptrollers' offices. If anything, the trend is toward centralization of authority. Among automated comptrollers' offices, 54 percent delegated budgeting and accounting decisions in 1966, but 42 percent did in 1972; 47 percent of department heads had a policy of delegating other than routine decisions in 1966, but only 40 percent did this in 1972. Third, there is a trend toward decentralization of automated finance departments. Only 36 percent delegated budgeting and accounting decisions at the time of the earlier study, but 56 percent did in 1972. Finally, 41 percent of finance-department heads had a policy of decentralization of substantive decisions in 1966; 58 percent did in 1972. The trend toward delegation of authority in automated finance departments makes them now less centralized than automated comptrollers' offices, even though they were more centralized in 1966. The interaction of domain and automation may have shifted subtly but importantly the actual functions of finance departments.

In sum, the domains claimed by bureaus administering finance mediate the effects of environmental demand on size. Comptrollers' offices that claim the narrowest domains are least affected; finance departments whose domains are broad but uncertain contract with demand if they were not

Table 18. *Delegation of substantive decisions by name, 1966 use of computer, and year*

|  | Comptrollers' offices | | Finance departments | |
| --- | --- | --- | --- | --- |
|  | Used computer | Did not use computer | Used computer | Did not use computer |
| *Percent of departments where head delegates authority to set budgets or accounting procedures* | | | | |
| 1966 | 54% | 39% | 36% | 44% |
| 1972 | 42% | 39% | 56% | 49% |
| *(N)* | (43) | (26) | (72) | (63) |
| *Percent of departments where head's policy is to delegate decisions* | | | | |
| 1966 | 47% | 39% | 41% | 27% |
| 1972 | 40% | 31% | 58% | 39% |
| *(N)* | (43) | (26) | (71) | (62) |

automated or remain stable but decentralized if they were; and departments of administration claiming broad domains and having the at least temporary advantage of newness increase their resources with demand.

### Competition in the immediate environment

Another way to determine whether the domains claimed by public organizations affect their behavior is to examine the impact of the competition in their environments. Competition is the obverse of a bureau's scope of responsibilities: The former is the number of other agencies in the same unit of government that either share or have fully some of the responsibilities one might expect to find in a finance department; the latter is the number of major finance activities for which a department has full responsibility. My hypothesis is that just as environmental demand shifts resources away from bureaus with precarious claims to domain, competition leads to a loss of functions. Contrariwise, bureaus that are new, have expansive claims to domain, and grow with demand for their services should be able to reduce the competition in their environments as their functions enlarge. In other words, the direction of causality between the number of competitors and the scope of responsibilities depends on the nature of the domain claimed. The weaker the claim, the greater the likelihood that the environment contracts organizations; the more expansive and compelling the claim, the more easily organizations reduce competition from other agencies.

The data generally support these hypotheses, but with some qualifications. Table 19 displays regressions indicating the direction of causality between the number of competitors in the environment and the scope of responsibilities of the agencies studied. The number of responsibilities a department had in 1972 is regressed on 1966 responsibilities and 1966 competitors in the upper panel of the table; 1972 competitors is regressed on 1966 competitors and 1966 responsibilities in the lower panel. From the regressions in the upper panel, it can be seen that the number of competing agencies in the immediate environment reduces responsibilities for all types of finance agencies. The coefficients of 1966 competitors are significantly negative for comptrollers' offices, finance departments, and departments of administration. However, for comptrollers' offices and finance departments, scope of responsibilities has no impact on the number of competitors. But this is not the case for the seven departments of administration. As the righthand columns in the lower panel of Table 19 show, the number of responsibilities departments of administration had in 1966 is negatively related to competitors later on. The more functions they had, the fewer competitors they now have. Departments of administration, unlike the others, are managing their environments to some extent. (Again, given the small number of cases, the results for administration departments should be interpreted cautiously.)

That competition contracts the responsibilities of finance departments is not surprising. It is consistent with the over-

Table 19. *Relationship of number of competitors to scope of responsibilities by name*

|  | Comptrollers' offices | | Finance departments | | Administration departments | |
|---|---|---|---|---|---|---|
|  | Zero order | B* | Zero order | B* | Zero order | B* |
| *Regression of 1972 responsibilities on 1966 responsibilities and 1966 competitors* | | | | | | |
| Variables: | | | | | | |
| 1966 Responsibilities | .5470 | .3229 | .4179 | .4213 | .3489 | (−.2436) |
| 1966 Competitors | −.5463 | −.3205 | −.2057 | −.1767 | −.8185 | −.9677 |
| *Regression of 1972 competitors on 1966 competitors and 1966 responsibilities* | | | | | | |
| Variables: | | | | | | |
| 1966 Competitors | .6562 | .6526 | .4844 | .4505 | .5269 | (−.5230) |
| 1966 Responsibilities | −.2792 | (−.0089) | −.3415 | (−.0524) | −.8545 | −1.2826 |

all pattern of decline of these agencies. The same effect was not anticipated for comptrollers' offices or administration departments. Indeed, the negative effect of competitors on scope of responsibilities persisted when other variables such as size and use of computers were controlled. And, save for the seven departments of administration, no variable other than the number of competitors directly affected an agency's scope of responsibilities. These results suggest that the antecedents of competition in the environment should be traced in order to understand how these bureaus gain or lose functions.

### Sources of competition

If competitors in the immediate environment reduce an agency's scope of responsibilities regardless of other conditions, then some of the conditions creating competition should be identified. In particular, possible effects of environmental demand as well as of organizational size should be examined. My expectation is that for finance departments, environmental demand increases competition, which in turn limits scope of responsibilities. Size may have the same effect; the domains of finance departments may be so precarious that past a point growth ceases and functions are dispersed to other agencies. For comptrollers' offices, a different pattern is anticipated. It may be that their environments were essentially stable between 1966 and 1972 so that neither size nor demand increased the number of competing agencies. My data indicate that this was the case.

Table 20 shows regressions of 1972 competitors on 1966 competitors, responsibilities, size, and the four measures of environmental demand. For comptrollers' offices, no significant predictors of 1972 competitors other than level of competition in 1966 appear; their environments are stable. The regressions for finance departments are quite different. The amount of competition in 1972 is a positive function of 1966 competitors, 1966 size, and the demand variables. Only 1966 responsibilities have no effect. Environmental demand and size contribute separately to the number of competitors, and their independent effects are significant. For finance departments, then, demand and size lead to proliferation of other agencies with fiscal responsibilities; as the number of competing agencies increases, the range of responsibilities of finance departments declines. Again, the broad but inconsistent domains of finance departments are buffeted by the environment.

Because of the small number of cases, regressions for departments of administration were limited to a single independent variable and the lagged dependent variable. This limitation means that estimates of regression coefficients may be quite biased and should be taken as only suggestive.

Table 20. *Regressions of 1972 number of competitors on 1966 competitors, 1966 responsibilities, 1966 size, and 1966 demand variables by name*

| Variables | Comptrollers' offices | | Finance departments | |
|---|---|---|---|---|
| | Zero order | B* | Zero order | B* |
| 1966 Competitors | .6561 | .7513 | .4844 | .4211 |
| 1966 Responsibilities | −.2692 | (−.0022) | −.3145 | (.0504) |
| 1966 Size | .0085 | (.2298) | .4156 | .2576 |
| 1966 General fund | .1492 | (−.2478) | .3669 | .1736 |
| 1966 Competitors | .6561 | .6392 | .4844 | .4311 |
| 1966 Responsibilities | −.2692 | (.0965) | −.3145 | (.0748) |
| 1966 Size | .0085 | (.0125) | .4156 | .2008 |
| 1966 Total funds administered | .2666 | (.0732) | .4301 | .2413 |
| 1966 Competitors | .6561 | .6719 | .4844 | .4135 |
| 1966 Responsibilities | .2692 | (−.0174) | −.3145 | (.0492) |
| 1966 Size | .0085 | (.1505) | .4156 | .2345 |
| 1966 Government employees | .0749 | (−.1188) | .4102 | .1905 |
| 1966 Competitors | .6561 | .6591 | .4844 | .4247 |
| 1966 Responsibilities | −.2692 | (−.0006) | −.3145 | (.0694) |
| 1966 Size | .0085 | (.0477) | .4156 | .1971 |
| 1965 Population | .1143 | (.0049) | .4383 | .2377 |

With this understanding, it appears that size has no impact on the number of competitors for administration departments—the regression is shown in the upper panel of Table 21—and the effects of environmental demand are inconsistent. One interesting effect of size emerged. For departments of administration, size increases scope of responsibilities as is shown in the lower panel of Table 21. This was not the case for comptrollers' offices and finance departments. The link completes the causal path between demand and competitors for departments of administration. Demand increases size, size increases responsibilities; and as responsibilities increase, competitors decrease. For finance departments, demand had a direct and positive effect on competitors; for comptrollers' offices, the link was nonexistent.

### Summary

At this point, the findings presented so far should be reviewed. Taken together, they indicate that the causal structures of variables describing comptrollers' offices, finance departments, and departments of administration are quite different. Figure 5a shows the causal structure for comptrollers' offices; Figures 5b and 5c describe finance departments and departments of administration, respectively. Among comptrollers' offices, practically no causal links can be

Table 21. *Administration departments only: effects of size on number of competitors and scope of responsibilities*

| Variables | Zero order | B* |
|---|---|---|
| *Regression of 1972 competitors on 1966 competitors and 1966 size:* | | |
| 1966 Competitors | .5269 | .5268 |
| 1966 Size | .0153 | (.0067) |
| *Regression of 1972 responsibilities on 1966 responsibilities and 1966 size:* | | |
| 1966 Responsibilities | .3489 | .5854 |
| 1966 Size | .1964 | .4831 |

found. As Figure 5a indicates, competition tends to reduce the scope of functions of comptrollers' offices, but there are no other connections among the four variables. Finance departments are replete with causal paths. Environmental demand decreases size; both size and demand increase competition; and competition contracts the scope of responsibilities of finance departments. The effect of demand on size holds only for finance departments that did not use computers in 1966. (This is indicated in Figure 5b, but not shown is the trend toward decentralization among automated finance departments.) Departments of administration are also replete with causal paths, but they are quite different from finance departments. Environmental demand increases size; size increases the scope of responsibilities; increased responsibilities reduce competition. (At the same time, as Figure 5c shows, competition in environment reduces respon-

Figure 5. Causal relationships among organizational variables.

a. Comptrollers' offices

b. Finance departments

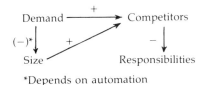

*Depends on automation

c. Departments of administration

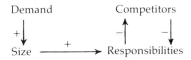

sibilities.) In a sentence, comptrollers' offices are essentially stable over time, finance departments are being contracted by their environments, whereas departments of administration are growing, adding functions, and to some extent, shaping their environments.

### Changing domains

Here I wish to test the proposition that when bureaus reorganize and change their names, they usually expand their claims to domain. The data are straightforward and nearly overwhelming. Some fourteen departments interviewed in 1966 did not exist in 1972. They were replaced by or subsumed under new agencies with new names whose heads became the chief financial officers fo their jurisdictions. Table 22 shows the cross-tabulation of 1972 name by 1966 name for the fourteen departments. Eleven of the fourteen were comptrollers' offices and the like in 1966; of the eleven, four became departments of administration, six changed to finance departments, and one that had combined the county clerk's and auditor's functions became a separate accounting office. Two finance departments changed names. One became a department of administration, whereas the other was split into several offices leaving the comptroller as the chief fiscal officer. One administration department be-

Table 22. *Name changers only: 1972 department name by 1966 name*

| 1972 Name | 1966 Name | | |
|---|---|---|---|
| | Comptroller's office | Finance department | Administration department |
| Comptroller's office | 1[a] | 1 | 0 |
| Finance department | 6 | 0 | 1 |
| Administration department | 4 | 1 | 0 |

[a] Clerk–auditor to accounting office

came a department of finance, but the new name in this case was inappropriate because the new finance department incorporated all of the functions of the former department of administration and added to them. In short, in only two instances out of fourteen did bureaus split and domains claimed by the agency with primary financial responsibility contract. In one case, a name changed was patently misleading, and in eleven others claims to domain expanded.

That a number of comptrollers' offices changed to finance and administration is not surprising, though it is striking that there were about as many new administration as finance departments. More important is the near absence of change among finance departments. One might have expected declining resources and responsibilities to have forced more of them to revert to the comptroller's model of organization. No doubt, this occurred in fact if not in name for a number of departments of finance, especially those not computerized in 1966. But the name "finance" and the claims accompanying it persisted for most. Evidently, there is reluctance to contract claims to domain despite loss of responsibilities. Perhaps the title of finance director is needed to justify the department head's salary; perhaps jobs can be preserved if obsolete claims can be maintained. Whichever is the case, fundamental change among the agencies studied here is a one-way process. Claims to domain expand, but they rarely contract. If this is true for most bureaus, then one would predict increasingly overlapping jurisdictions, hence greater conflict and proliferation of coordinating bodies over time.

### Antecedents of change

A brief comment on the antecedents of change among the fourteen name changers is required. Their surface characteristics in 1966 were unremarkable. Indeed, the eleven comptrollers' offices replaced by other agencies between 1966 and 1972 were of the same size and had on average the same structural features as the seventy-one comptroller's offices that did not change. The lack of consistency with environmental demand for their services among the fourteen name changers in 1966 does draw attention, however. As the right-most columns in Table 23 show, the correlations between the four measures of environmental demand and size were little different from zero in 1966. After reorganization and change of name, the correspondence between demand and size increased markedly. The correlations of the demand variables with size range from .66 to .84 in 1972. These data suggest that, among other things, a source of fundamental change in organization is inconsistency with environmental demand.

Whether inconsistency with the environment is a sufficient condition for change is another matter. Departments of finance were less likely than others to undergo reorganization; yet, as is evident in Table 23, their consistency with environmental demand dropped substantially between 1966 and 1972. Comptrollers' offices remained highly consistent with demand during this interval, and the correspondence between demand and size actually increased for departments of administration. My best guess is that change will

Table 23. *Correlations of size with demand variables by name and year*

|  | Comptrollers' offices | | Finance departments | | Administration departments | | Name changers | |
|---|---|---|---|---|---|---|---|---|
|  | 1966 | 1972 | 1966 | 1972 | 1966 | 1972 | 1966 | 1972 |
| General fund | .6922 | .5723 | .4337 | .2528 | .5730 | .6981 | .0477 | .6599 |
| Total funds administered | .5228 | .6041 | .5526 | .2423 | .2978 | .6707 | .1433 | .5989 |
| Government employees | .8400 | .8256 | .5239 | .3133 | .4956 | .6198 | −.0074 | .8423 |
| Population [a] | .7368 | .8498 | .5793 | .2547 | .4894 | .6627 | −.0370 | .7713 |

[a] 1960 and 1970 population figures are used.

take place eventually among finance departments, but the process will be delayed because of internal opposition to contracting claims to domain.

## Conclusions

*A cycle of change in public bureaucracies?*

Some effects of organizational claims to domain embodied in names were explored in this chapter. The conventional view of domain – technology, population served, and services rendered – was not applied to public bureaucracies because the population served is fixed and the services rendered are intangible for administrative agencies. In its place, the notion of claim to domain was developed, and it was argued that the kind of claims made by public agencies strongly affect their behavior. Differing claims to domain were illustrated by the recent experience of agencies administering finances of city, county, and state governments. Comptrollers', auditors', and accountants' offices make the narrowest claims to domain; the claims made by departments of finance are broad but inconsistent; and the claims of departments of administration are broad and expanding at the present time. It was hypothesized that bureaucracies claiming narrow domains but performing essential services remain stable over time; bureaus claiming broad but inconsistent domains decline over time; and bureaus claiming broad domains that are consistent have the advantage of newness, and utilize advanced technologies tend to grow and expand their responsibilities.

The data show these hypotheses to be essentially correct. Causal links were sparse among comptrollers' offices. Environmental demand reduced size, and competition reduced responsibilities among finance departments. For departments of administration, demand increased size, which increased responsibilities, which in turn reduced competition.

It was also hypothesized that the domains claimed by

bureaus may expand but tend not to contract over time. Data describing fourteen agencies that were reorganized and changed their names between 1966 and 1972 support this notion. They also suggest that inconsistency with environmental demand is one source of fundamental change.

The findings underscore the importance of unprovable claims made by administrative bureaus. Unlike firms operating in competitive markets whose clientele is not fixed by jurisdiction, bureaus can justify expansion only by increasing their functions. And as the neoclassical critics note, the outputs of bureaus are often ill defined and not subject to quantitative measurement. Under these circumstances, what a bureau claims to be doing may be more important than anything else in augmenting its size and responsibilities. The broader the claim, the greater the growth; but claims rendered inconsistent by either technological change or changing beliefs about administrative organization render a bureau vulnerable to the environment as new agencies take over its functions. The findings also underscore the need for research comparing bureaus and firms (or segments of firms) performing similar functions. If the results reported here are not unique to agencies administering local government finances, then the distinction between bureaus and firms may be important. One must ask not only whether differences exist between bureaus and firms, but also whether the differences can be explained in terms of generic organizational variables. My own inclination is to believe that the distinction drawn by the neoclassical economists and political scientists is probably right, but for the wrong reason. Rather than the absence of a market as such, the structure of whole local governments that embeds bureaus within one another and removes them, organizationally if not physically, from their constituents may account for the patterns observed here. Finance agencies not nested in larger bureaucratic structures (for example, accounting firms) would perhaps respond differently to their environments.

An overriding question is whether a predictable cycle of change occurs among public bureaucracies, and if so, whether the pattern contributes to the inefficiencies for which bureaus are often criticized. Among agencies administering the finances of city, county, and state governments, there appears to be a pattern. Claims to domain expand, and increases in size and scope of responsibilities follow. After some time broad claims are rendered either inconsistent or obsolete by technological change and new management concepts, and either stability or decline sets in. Some agencies expand their claims further so as to encompass new technologies and beliefs, and their growth resumes. Claims to domain are rarely revised downward, however, even when key functions are lost. It could be that the constant inflation of claims gives rise to jurisdictional disputes and interagency wrangling, which consume much time and manpower. If so, this is an important dysfunction of bureaucratic organization.

*Reprise: contingencies and time boundedness in empirical results*

In Chapter 4, environmental effects were shown to be contingent on characteristics of leadership positions; and these effects were quite different for finance agencies compared to budgeting and data-processing units. Here, additional contingencies were shown to operate among finance agencies. Relations between environmental and organizational elements differ for departments of finance, comptrollers' offices, and departments of administration. Finance departments decline with demand and lose responsibilities with competition in the immediate environment; comptrollers' offices are essentially stable over time; and departments of administration grow with environmental demand and eliminate competitors with increased responsibilities. Furthermore, the fourteen reorganized agencies behaved differently from others, moving from very low to very high correspondence between environmental demand and size, and changing their names predictably in the direction of broader claims to domain.

These empirical results, like those reported in the earlier chapters, are necessarily time-bound, for there is little likelihood that they merely reproduce patterns of change among finance agencies occurring at earlier periods, especially before departments of finance and of administration were invented. Certainly, not all organizations, not even all public bureaucracies, are now declining like departments of finance or growing like departments of administration and agencies experiencing reorganization. A mixture of growth and decline is more likely. Indeed, it might be hypothesized that most populations of organizations contain relatively small numbers of rapidly growing units and relatively large numbers of stagnant or declining ones, because growth occurs mainly at the time of formation and shortly thereafter, and stability or contraction prevails otherwise. If this is the case, then the contingencies used in the empirical analysis may have helped illustrate regular rather than idiosyncratic patterns of behavior, albeit somewhat indirectly. More importantly, growth and decline are not the only organizational processes governed by environmental elements, mediated through contingencies such as claims to domain, newness, and total reorganization. Chapter 6 will explore the origins and development of formal personnel regulations in finance agencies rather than their size and responsibilities. Some of the results bear striking parallels to those we have already encountered. In particular, they reinforce the impression that routine change in ongoing bureaucracies is wholly different from change occurring during periods of formation or total reorganization.

# 6

# The process of bureaucratization

Max Weber's classic essay "Bureaucracy" (1946) delineates some of the characteristics of modern organizations that distinguish them from traditional forms of administration. These characteristics include division of labor, hierarchy of authority, written rules and regulations, and the like. The surface attributes of bureaucracy identified by Weber are not to be confused with its causes, however. In comparing traditional with bureaucratic means of administration, the latter based on belief in rational−legal authority, Weber was clearly suggesting that bureaucratization is but one aspect of the historical trend toward rationalization in the development of all institutional forms in modern societies. The substitution of authority based on rules for authority based arbitrarily on persons is central to the development of bureaucracy. Weber identifies other preconditions of bureaucratization, including a money economy that allows calculability of results and widespread literacy. To this list one might add such possible causes of bureaucratization as urbanization, mobility of resources, and religious beliefs permitting trust among strangers (see Stinchcombe 1965). The relative importance of these causes of bureaucratization is perhaps of less significance than the fact that they are external to organizations and arise largely as a result of historical processes. Rational−legal authority, cash economies, widespread literacy, and other conditions contributing to the development of bureaucratic forms are characteristics of whole societies that may change over time but need not vary from organization to organization in a society at any one point.

Contemporary research on organizations has apparently overlooked this fact in seeking to explain characteristics of bureaucracies in terms of internal characteristics while ignoring the changes in the larger social and political environments that Weber thought central to the growth of modern organizations. The reasons for concentrating on internal organizational characteristics as opposed to external ones are not difficult to identify. Quantitative research studies can take into account tangible aspects of organizational structures—size, job titles, levels of supervision, spans of control, and the like—much more easily than the less quantifiable elements of the environment, which, although amorphous, may be exceedingly important. The work of Blau (1970) and his colleagues (see also Meyer 1972b) exemplifies the tendency to overlook qualitative elements of organizations in focusing almost exclusively on the implications of organizational size for structural differentiation and of differentiation for administrative overhead. What is disputed is not the accuracy of the results but their importance for understanding the development of bureaucratization. A theory that explains bureaucratic structures solely in terms of size runs afoul of the fact that large organizations existed well before bureaucratization became widespread (see, e.g., Dibble, 1965). A second factor limiting the usefulness of most such studies is that they present data from one point only and thus overlook the possible effects of history. Current trends in research have precluded the possibility that the greatest variations occur over time and are due to environmental shifts affecting organizations of a given type almost uniformly. Given this inattention to qualitative historical aspects of organizational environments, it is not surprising that empirical research has not addressed the question Weber raised in his essay: How does one explain the development of large-scale, hierarchical, and rule-bound bureaucracies?

Only a partial answer can be attempted here. The research is limited to city, county, and state finance agencies and to a time span of six years. The attempt to explain bureaucratization is concerned with only causes and consequences of formalized personnel procedures, because the origins of these rules can be identified easily and because rules vary somewhat across the agencies studied. The results of this limited inquiry are quite suggestive, however. They indicate that the extensiveness of formal procedures in bureaucracies is due in part to the historical era in which organizations were founded and in part to the subsequent effects of the environment. Formalization in turn gives rise to hierarchical differentiation and differentiation to delegation of decision-making authority. The effects of origins are shown to be results of openness to environment at the time of formation. In short, the process of bureaucratization begins with environmental pressures—in this instance the civil service movement—and proceeds by developing rules to accommodate these pressures, elaborating organizational structures consistent with the rules, and delegating authority as necessitated by structure. The primacy of the environment as a determining factor of bureaucratization and the dependence of organizational structure on rules embodying external demands are emphasized here.

Though centrally concerned with the process of bureaucratization, this chapter touches on several other topics. Its method is necessarily intertwined with its substance. A key question to be considered is how history can be incorporated in organizational analysis. An understanding of history requires separating the effects of time of origin from the effects of changes in organizational environments that occurred in the past and could not be observed. Origins and environments are likely to have had opposite effects and to obscure each other, but estimates of the magnitude of the impact of each are important to understanding how bureaucratization or any other organizational process takes place over a lengthy period. The substantive findings developed here are also linked closely to the types of organizations studied, all of which are administrative units of local governments. Because they are government organizations, finance departments are bound by certain federal statutes that do not affect the private sector so directly. These statutes are crucial environmental elements, and it is unlikely that they have affected private organizations similarly. Whether the process of bureaucratization is similar for public- and private-sector organizations cannot be determined until there is comparable research on the latter. In all likelihood, similar patterns of behavior hold for both public and private organizations, but their histories and relevant environments may be so different that they do not behave in the same way at any given point.

We shall proceed by first outlining the development of some federal and local regulations affecting personnel matters. A complete history of civil service legislation is not possible, but important developments in it can be noted. The next section develops a model showing why effects of origins and of the environment are often confounded in organizational research, and it suggests a procedure for distinguishing between them. This procedure is then applied to data on the formalization of personnel procedures in finance agencies. In the following section, we examine relationships among formalization of personnel procedures, multi-tier hierarchies, and decision making. The last substantive section returns to the question of the effects of origins on organizations by examining the formalization of personnel practices in a small number of agencies that reorganized completely during the interval between the two surveys reported here. The implications of the empirical results are discussed in the concluding section.

### Civil service and formalization of the personnel process

The history of the civil service movement in the United States is complex, and only the highlights can be touched on here. But one pattern is unmistakable: There has been increasing federal intervention in local-government personnel practices. Of the three most significant federal acts establishing merit procedures for appointment to public office in place of the spoils system, the first, the Pendleton Act of 1882, which created the U.S. Civil Service Commission, did not mention state or local government at all. State governments fell under the purview of the 1939 amendments to the Social Security Act; and both state and local governments were subject to provisions of the Intergovernmental Personnel Act of 1970. Each of these laws was aimed at removing politics from administration by requiring impersonal procedures for the selection and the advancement of employees. The provisions of these acts should be reviewed in some detail.

The first U.S. Civil Service Act was approved by Congress in 1882 and went into effect the next year. In addition to creating a three-man Civil Service Commission, it required the president, under the advice of the commission, to "provide suitable rules for carrying this act into effect . . . , as nearly as the conditions of good administration will warrant, as follows: first, . . . open, competitive examinations . . . second . . . selection according to grade from those graded highest . . . fourth, . . . a period of probation before any absolute appointment . . . fifth, . . . no person in the public service is . . . under any obligation to contribute to any political fund or to render any political service . . ." (U.S. Congress 1881–83: 403–4). The essence of a merit system of appointment for civil servants, as opposed to the old-fashioned political spoils systems, lay in the use of written examinations and the insulation of officials from electoral politics—two of the characteristics Weber thought common to modern bureaucracy.

It is interesting that the Pendleton Act was much more specific in its provisions than later statutes imposing merit requirements on state and local governments. The Social Security Act amendments of 1939, for example, made repeated mention of "such methods of administration (including after January 1, 1940, methods relating to the establishment and maintenance of personnel standards on a merit basis . . .) as are found . . . to be necessary" (U.S. Congress 1939: 1360), but the amendments did not specify what those merit personnel standards were. They did, however, direct the states to use merit standards in administering old-age assistance, unemployment compensation, aid to dependent children, and grants for the blind. The Intergovernmental Personnel Act of 1970 was aimed at extending merit standards to all government units. It created an advisory council charged with determining, among other things, "(1) The feasibility and desirability of extending merit policies and standards to additional federal-state grant-in-aid programs; (2) the feasibility and desirability of extending merit policies and standards to grant-in-aid programs of a federal–local character; (3) appropriate standards for merit personnel administration . . . [and] (4) the feasibility and desirability of financial and other incentives to encourage State and local governments in the development of comprehensive systems of personnel administration based on merit principles" (U.S. Congress 1970–71: 1911). The 1970 act also provided for grants-in-aid to states and local governments for the development of merit systems and the training of employees. But, like the 1939 Social Security Act amendments, the legislation did not specify the means to be used in enforcing merit principles.[1]

A number of states followed the federal lead in removing partisan pressures from civil servants. New York adopted a merit system in 1883, and Massachusetts did so a year later. Other states lagged considerably. Article XXIV of the

California constitution, which established the state civil service, was not approved until 1934. As late as 1960, eighteen of the fifty states had extended civil service coverage only to employees in agencies receiving federal grants (Mitau, 1966: 154). Generally, permissive legislation allowing counties and municipalities to establish merit personnel systems were enacted. New York State had a permissive statute for cities and counties in 1909; California cities in 1935 and counties in 1939 were authorized to enact their own merit systems. By 1960, thirty-nine of the forty largest cities in the United States and three-quarters of all cities with populations over 10,000 had legal provisions for civil service systems of some sort. Whether these systems were equally effective in enforcing merit practices is another matter, however. As Phillips (1960: 387) notes, "The record, of course, shows wide variation in merit system efficiency . . . merit systems of some cities are sorry exhibits of personnel administration."

Apart from prompting federal acts affecting civil service procedures, the movement to reform local administration that peaked in the early 1900s also gave impetus to the formalization of personnel procedures. Cities suffered recurrent fiscal crises throughout the last third of the nineteenth century, immigration swelled urban populations hence the demand for reliable services, and political spoils were rampant. Among other innovations, the reformers demanded expertise in place of political reliability as the criterion for appointment. As Griffith (1974: 15) notes, one asset of the Progressive movement was the precepts of scientific management, which strengthened the demand for fundamental structural reform in local government. The Taylorites and the Progressives were not always the same people, but they aided each other in municipal affairs.

Despite the trend toward merit personnel standards at all levels of government, there are now some pressures in the opposite direction. Cities and counties have come to rely somewhat on temporary employees whose positions are exempted from normal civil service procedures. Salaries for those positions are often funded out of federal subventions, particularly the Emergency Employment Act (EEA) of 1971, which has since expired. As noted in Chapter 3, EEA grants were funding a number of positions in finance departments at the time of the 1972 survey. In addition, there has been recognition that inflexible merit principles should not extend to policymaking positions. The 1970 Model Public Personnel Administration Law as well as the report of the Advisory Council on Intergovernmental Personnel Policy took cognizance of this. An introductory comment to the 1970 Model Public Personnel Administration Law stated that,

> in order for the spirit of a merit system to be realized, it is essential that a majority of the positions in the public service be classified. Conversely, it is equally important that certain positions be exempted from the provisions of this act. Key policy-determining officials such as department heads and agency heads must be acutely sensitive to the program objectives of the chief elected official. As a result, those persons should serve at the pleasure of the chief executive rather than be under the provisions of the merit system.
>
> The selection of key policy-determining officials by the chief executive does not constitute spoils . . .
> [National Civil Service League, 1970: 6]

In this respect, the 1970 Model Law is a substantial departure from earlier versions.

Several broad conclusions can be drawn from the brief review of civil service legislation in the United States. First, most state and local governments have adopted merit personnel policies in place of either patronage appointments or the spoils system. The only exceptions to this pattern are the more frequent use of temporary employees and the removal of policymaking officials from civil service protection. The historical trend toward the imposition of merit personnel standards constitutes an important alteration in the political environments of local-government agencies. Second, effective merit standards usually entail substitution of impersonal procedures such as written job descriptions and fixed probationary periods for personal and political criteria for appointment. In other words, merit standards promote the formalization of the personnel process. Third, despite the ascendancy of merit principles, their application has been somewhat uneven. For this reason, an exact correspondence between federal legislation and the actions of state and local governments cannot be expected. Instead, considerable variation remains, and the actual procedures adopted by local agencies in conformity with requirements for merit personnel administration are themselves of interest. An important question is whether local-government units have responded uniformly and fully to the demand for personnel standards consistent with merit principles or whether their personnel procedures have remained essentially unchanged over time. If the former, one would conclude that local-government units are vulnerable to certain environmental pressures; if the latter, one would think them resistant to environments and hence bound by their origins. A fundamental sociological question is whether origins or environments dominate organizations. Only an approximate answer can be developed here. The research on finance agencies suggests, however, that both have substantial effects, even though environmental shifts may in the long run have greater impact than origins.

## Origins, the environment, and formalization of the personnel process

*A model of effects of origins and the environment*

A problem in assessing effects of origins and environment is the lack of complete data tracing organizations from their beginnings to the present. Usually data from only one point are available, and inferences about the effects of history or age are made on the basis of contemporary differences between organizations with diverse origins. Exactly this procedure is followed by Stinchcombe (1965) in his analysis of stability of organizational types over time. Stinchcombe found small but consistent effects of era of origin of some characteristics of the labor force in several industries. The correlation between age and labor-force (or organizational) structure, he surmises, can be accounted for by "the postulate that economic and technical conditions determine the appropriate organizational form for a given organizational purpose and the postulate that certain kinds of organizations . . . could not be invented before the social structure was appropriate to them" (p. 160).

This approach to the effects of age on organizations has several limitations, and we shall seek to overcome them here. One problem is that organizations are portrayed as essentially unchanging. The possibility that substantial differences due to origins are reduced over time by the environment is not considered. The source of this difficulty can be seen quite easily in Figure 6, which displays values of a hypothetical index of bureaucratization $(b)$ for three organizations at three points. Organization 1, which was founded in era 1, has index values of $b_{11}$, $b_{12}$, $b_{13}$ at times 1, 2, and 3, respectively; for organization 3, only $b_{33}$ is displayed, because it did not exist in eras 1 and 2. Ignoring organization 2 for the present, Figure 6 shows the effects of origins on the index to be $b_{33} - b_{11}$. The effect of time, which is in fact a surrogate for the environment, is $b_{13} - b_{11}$ for organization 1. There is no effect of time for organization 3, because it was only recently founded. Cross-sectional data do not permit separate estimates of effects of origins and of the environment as suggested by Figure 6. Instead, only the difference, $b_{33} - b_{13}$, can be estimated. But this difference corresponds exactly to the difference between effects of origins and of the environment, $(b_{33} - b_{11}) - (b_{13} - b_{11})$, thereby confounding the two hopelessly. Because environmental effects often diminish differences due to origins,[2] Stinchcombe's data in all likelihood underestimate both the effects of origins on organizations and the amount of change occurring over time.

Another problem with Stinchcombe's approach to the effects of history on organizations is its inability to link specified historical changes to enduring properties of organizations. This derives from his use of census data that do not reveal organizational characteristics other than labor-force composition. The importance of history for organizations can be demonstrated best if certain organizational properties varying with time of origin can be linked to specific historical developments. Showing differences between old and new organizations does not limit possible explanations for observed effects of age; but both by showing that old organizations differ from new ones in some respects but not others and by specifying historical changes that correspond to these differences, the range of possible explanations is narrowed considerably, and hence greater credence is given to the historical argument. Indeed it may be that age does not affect organizations much in comparison with the impact of identifiable historical events.[3]

Figure 6. Hypothetical values of bureaucratization ($b$) for three organizations formed in different eras.

|  |  | Era | | |
|---|---|---|---|---|
|  |  | 1 | 2 | 3 |
|  | 1 | $b_{11}$ | $b_{12}$ | $b_{13}$ |
| Organizations | 2 | — | $b_{22}$ | $b_{23}$ |
|  | 3 | — | — | $b_{33}$ |

Effects of origins $= b_{33} - b_{11}$

Effects of environment $= b_{13} - b_{11}$

Difference $= b_{33} - b_{13}$

The data available from the study of finance agencies allow us to begin to distinguish effects of origins from those of the environment, although they do not permit precise estimates. They are sufficiently detailed to allow separation of organizational properties that should have been affected by historical changes from properties for which no such effects are anticipated. For 215 departments of finance, comptrollers' offices, and the like, we have information on the year in which they were founded, formalization of personnel procedures, and organizational structure for both 1966 and 1972. These agencies existed continuously over the six-year interval between the two studies; hence changes during this time cannot be due to origins. (The fourteen departments that reorganized between 1966 and 1972 will be discussed later.) The finance agencies were classified according to the era of formation – nineteenth century, 1901 – 39, and 1940 and later – so that the breaks between periods correspond closely to the dates of two major federal acts affecting personnel matters and the movement to reform city administration. It should also be noted that the third important piece of legislation – the 1970 Intergovernmental Personnel Act – became law in the interval between the 1966 and 1972 studies.

The kinds of comparisons allowed by the study design are illustrated in Figure 7. Differences appearing within the columns displayed here occurred between 1966 and 1972 and may be due to environmental shifts, although we must consider the possibility that they are due to other factors. The differences appearing across the rows are, as we have shown, due to differences between organizations at the time of their formation, less subsequent effects of the environment. If there were environmental effects between 1966 and 1972, then in all likelihood much greater effects of the environment occurred between the late nineteenth century and 1966, because the interval was longer and the impact of the federal legislation probably greater.

Before turning to the data, one further question, that of the appropriateness of finance agencies for the research on personnel procedures, should be discussed. Two considerations should be kept in mind. First, whereas entire local governments as wholes would seem to be the natural unit of analysis in a study of effects of federal legislation and the reform movement, this approach would pose some difficulties. In particular, identifying a single time of formation of administrative agencies employing civil servants would be impossible, because local agencies are typically founded and reorganized one at a time. One could of course find times during which reorganization of offices of elected officials occurred, but these offices are usually not affected by civil service laws, and reorganization of them does not necessarily generate reorganization of administrative agencies. Second, finance agencies are not atypical of administrative bureaus of local governments, and results concerning them may be treated as representative of local administrative agencies generally. Clearly it would be desirable to have information on other types of government bureaus, but these data are not at hand.

Figure 7. Study design for research on finance departments.

|  | | Era of origin | | |
|---|---|---|---|---|
|  | | 19th century | 1901–1939 | 1940–1965 |
| Year | 1966 | 19th-century organizations in 1966 | Early 20th-century organizations in 1966 | Late 20th-century organizations in 1966 |
|  | 1972 | 19th-century organizations in 1972 | Early 20th-century organizations in 1972 | Late 20th-century organizations in 1972 |

Intergovernmental Personnel Act (1970)

Pendleton Act (1883)  Social Security Act Amendments (1939)

*Origins and formalization in finance agencies*

The information collected from finance agencies included extensive data describing procedures for hiring and evaluating personnel. We have information about whether entry-level employees are usually placed through civil service or equivalent uniform personnel codes; whether written regulations govern the criteria used in promotion decisions; the length of the probationary period, if any, for new employees; whether the department head is appointed or elected; and the number of employees covered by civil service or similar merit systems. Civil service coverage for employees, written promotion regulations, and a meaningful probationary period suggest merit personnel administration of the sort envisioned by federal and state civil service statutes. Their absence and the presence of an elected department head are indicative of the old-fashioned patronage or spoils system. These items were included in both the 1966 and 1972 surveys. In Table 24, they are cross-tabulated by the era when a department was founded. The tabulations show effects of both era of formation and time of measurement, suggesting that the cross-sectional results in fact understate the true effects of origins. The tables should be reviewed in detail.

Section A of Table 24 displays percentages of departments where entry-level employees are placed through civil service or an equivalent merit personnel code. As shown, in 1966, 55 percent of nineteenth-century finance agencies, 71 percent of early-twentieth-century agencies, and 73 percent of those founded after 1940 hired newcomers through civil service. By 1972 these percentages had increased to 65, 72, and 84, respectively. Overall, the proportion of finance agencies placing entry-level employees through civil service increased by about 6 percent between 1966 and 1972. And in both 1966 and 1972, approximately 18 percent more of post-1940 than of nineteenth-century agencies had such civil service arrangements. The same pattern obtains for the use of written regulations governing promotion criteria. There is about a 6 percent increase between 1966 and 1972 and a nearly 16 percent spread between nineteenth-century and post-1940 agencies. Differences due to time of measurement are somewhat smaller in sections C and D of Table 24, where data on the length of the probationary period for new employees and the method of selection of department head are

Table 24. *Measures of formalization in 1966 and 1972 by era when departments were founded*

|  | Pre–1900 | 1901–39 | Post–1940 |
|---|---|---|---|
| A. % *Departments where entry-level employees are placed through civil service or equivalent uniform personnel code (EMPLACE)* | | | |
| 1966 | 55 | 71 | 73 |
| (N) | (49) | (72) | (90) |
| 1972 | 65 | 72 | 84 |
| (N) | (49) | (72) | (90) |
| B. % *Departments where written regulations govern promotions criteria (PROMO)* | | | |
| 1966 | 49 | 68 | 67 |
| (N) | (49) | (71) | (90) |
| 1972 | 59 | 72 | 73 |
| (N) | (49) | (72) | (90) |
| C. % *Departments where probationary period is six months or longer (PROBAT)* | | | |
| 1966 | 65 | 72 | 88 |
| (N) | (49) | (69) | (89) |
| 1972 | 69 | 75 | 89 |
| (N) | (49) | (71) | (90) |
| D. % *Departments where head is elected (HEDEL)* | | | |
| 1966 | 74 | 24 | 7 |
| (N) | (49) | (71) | (90) |
| 1972 | 69 | 22 | 6 |
| (N) | (49) | (72) | (90) |
| E. *Mean proportion of positions covered by civil service (PSCE)* | | | |
| 1966 | .607 | .767 | .746 |
| (N) | (47) | (70) | (88) |
| 1972 | .582 | .691 | .785 |
| (N) | (48) | (72) | (89) |

presented. Between 1966 and 1972, there was but a 3 percent increase in the proportion of departments with lengthy probationary periods and a 2 percent decrease in elected agency heads. The differences associated with era of origin are more prominent in section D, however. Indeed practically all of the variance in whether or not a department head is elected—though not, if he is appointed, in whether such appointment is at the discretion of the head of government or through civil service—can be explained by era of origin.[4] Finally, section E of Table 24 displays mean proportions of positions in finance agencies covered by civil service in both 1966 and 1972. Whereas time of formation is positively associated with civil service coverage—newer agencies have more employees under merit systems—somewhat fewer positions were covered in 1972 than in 1966. The reasons for this contraction of civil service have already been noted and need not be pursued further.

Because the first four items describing finance agencies' hiring and evaluation procedures are dichotomies, they were combined in an index of formalization of the personnel process. Correlations among the four items between 1966 and 1972 and their autocorrelations over time are displayed in Table 25. Generally the correlations are modest and in the expected direction, but there are some exceptions. For example, the correlation of placement of new employees through civil service with written promotion criteria is .6136

Table 25. *Correlations of items in index of formalization (1966/1972 correlations)*

|  | EMPLACE | PROMO | PROBAT | HEDEL |
|---|---|---|---|---|
| EMPLACE | .6321 | .6136/.3989 | .2568/.2884 | −.2376/−.2015 |
| PROMO | — | .4348 | .2683/.1828 | −.1628/−.2093 |
| PROBAT | — | — | .5278 | −.1217/−.0319 |
| HEDEL | — | — | — | .8489 |

*Note:* Autocorrelations on major diagonal.

in 1966 but plummets to .3989 in 1972. And the correlations of whether department heads are elected with length of the probationary period are not very different from zero, −.1217 and −.0319 in 1972. The autocorrelations are also of interest. For the first three items, they range from .4348 to .6321, but for election of department heads the autocorrelation is .8489. The index of formalization ranges from zero to one; its value is the proportion of the four elements of an agency's personnel procedures consistent with merit principles—entry-level placement through civil service, written regulations governing promotions, a probationary period of six months or longer, and an appointed department head. The index had mean values of .640 in 1966 and .697 in 1972.

In order to estimate effects of era of origin and year of measurement more precisely than the cross tabulations in Table 24 allow, the index of formalization was regressed on era of origin. Six cross-sectional regressions are displayed in Table 26, three each for 1966 and 1972. In these regressions, the 1966 and 1972 indexes of formalization are regressed separately on era of origin. In the first two regressions, no additional variables are controlled. Each increment of era—there are two increments, because we have three eras—adds 148 to the index in 1966 and .142 in 1972. The difference between the constants in the first pair of equations, .0622, is a rough estimate of the effects of year of measurement on the index of formalization. In the third and fourth equations in Table 26, a dummy variable coded one for state finance agencies covered in the surveys and zero for others is added; in the fifth and sixth equations, a dummy variable coded one for nonsouthern states and zero otherwise is included. Neither of the added variables significantly predicts formalization of personnel practices, whereas the effects of era of origin remain. The time at which an agency was founded and subsequent environmental shifts account for formalization much better than either level of government or geographic location.

In the last entry of Table 26, the 1966 and 1972 data are pooled, and year of measurement is added to the model as a dummy variable coded zero for 1966 and one for 1972. The pooled regression allows estimates of the statistical significance of year of measurement and comparisons of effects of era and year on formalization. As can be seen from the error terms, the effects of era are far greater than might have occurred by chance, but the significance of year of measurement is uncertain in the pooled regression – the coefficient of year is 1.75 times its error. But the coefficient is in the expected direction; and more important, because the six-year interval between measurements is considerably shorter than the intervals between eras, which are twenty-seven and thirty-nine years, one would expect time of measurement to have considerably less impact than era of origin. Had the

Table 26. *Regressions of indexes of formalization on era of origin and other environmental variables*

---

*Cross-sectional regressions*
1966 formalization = .3712 +  .1484 × era
                             (.0255)

1972 formalization = .4334 +  .1422 × era
                             (.0225)

1966 formalization = .3057 +  .1539 × era −  .0226 × state
                             (.0238)          (.0557)

1972 formalization = .4095 +  .1286 × era +  .0399 × state
                             (.0231)          (.0540)

1966 formalization = .3021 +  .1542 × era +  .0003 × nonsouthern
                             (.0241)          (.0431)

1972 formalization = .4135 +  .1281 × era +  .0030 × nonsouthern
                             (.0234)          (.0418)

*Pooled regression*
Formalization = .3625 +  .1328 × era +  .0485 × year
                        (.0160)          (.0277)

---

*Note:* Errors in parentheses.

measurement interval been longer, the effects of year in all likelihood would have attained significance. Although one cannot legitimately project recent trends backward to the nineteenth century, it may be reasonable to assume that the rate at which personnel procedures in local-government agencies have been formalized since the turn of the century is such that changes in these procedures over time have been greater than differences occurring across organizations at any one point due to persistent effects of origins. To speak of stability of personnel procedures in finance agencies would be accurate for short intervals only. The long-range effects of environmental shifts are in all likelihood far greater than differences due to origins.

### Origins and organizational structure

Although era of origin shapes the personnel procedures used by local-government finance agencies, it does not affect their organizational structures significantly. Table 27 displays mean size and number of divisions, sections (i.e., subunits of divisions), and levels of supervision for the 254 departments studied in 1966 and 1972. The largest agencies are the oldest ones, but early-twentieth-century departments are the smallest; even this difference is not statistically significant because of the large variance in size. Differences in numbers of operating divisions and sections are entirely artifacts of size; and the greatest level of numbers occurred, in 1966, among the early-twentieth-century agencies, which are on the average the smallest. Overall, then, the organizational structure of finance agencies bears no direct relationship to the era in which they were founded. This is not surprising, given that there is no reason to anticipate such a relationship. Organizational structures, unlike personnel procedures, have not been the subject of federal legislation; and they are not directly linked to cultural and political preferences of different historical periods.

## Formalization, hierarchy, and delegation of authority

If origins and subsequent effects of political and social environments account for the extent of formal personnel processes but not for administrative structure in local agencies, one would expect variables describing organizational structure to have little or no effect on formalization. This expectation, however, runs counter to inferences drawn from the results of several research studies, including some publications from the 1966 survey of finance agencies. Correlations between the extensiveness of hierarchy and delegation have been observed in several studies (see Blau, 1968; Meyer, 1968; Pugh, et al. 1968; Blau and Schoenherr, 1971;

Table 27. *Measures of organizational structure in 1966 and 1972 by era when departments were founded*

|  | Pre–1900 | 1901–39 | Post–1940 |
|---|---|---|---|
| *Mean size:* | | | |
| 1966 | 136.96 | 89.31 | 95.16 |
| *(N)* | (49) | (72) | (90) |
| 1972 | 163.35 | 106.78 | 123.28 |
| *(N)* | (49) | (72) | (90) |
| *Mean number of operating divisions:* | | | |
| 1966 | 6.20 | 5.33 | 5.52 |
| *(N)* | (49) | (72) | (90) |
| 1972 | 6.04 | 5.40 | 5.52 |
| *(N)* | (49) | (72) | (90) |
| *Mean number of sections:* | | | |
| 1966 | 12.90 | 10.14 | 11.40 |
| *(N)* | (49) | (72) | (90) |
| 1972 | 12.48 | 11.37 | 13.17 |
| *(N)* | (48) | (71) | (90) |
| *Mean number of levels of supervision:* | | | |
| 1966 | 3.84 | 4.02 | 3.93 |
| *(N)* | (45) | (71) | (90) |
| 1972 | 4.03 | 4.08 | 4.13 |
| *(N)* | (49) | (71) | (90) |

Meyer, 1972a), and they are replicated here. Table 28 displays the zero-order correlations of the index of formalization, the number of hierarchical levels in finance agencies, and two indicators of delegation of authority *in personnel matters*. The indicators of decentralization are (1) whether the department head or someone below him, such as a division head, formally recommends promotions and dismissals and (2) the relative influence of division heads in promotion decisions.[5] The 1966 and 1972 correlations are displayed to the left and right of the solidi, respectively. There are modest but positive associations of levels of supervision with decentralization in both 1966 and 1972. The correlations of levels with delegation of formal authority to recommend promotion and dismissal are .1814 in 1966 and .2326 in 1972; the correlations of levels with division heads' influence are .2645 and .3107, respectively. In contrast, the associations of formalization with delegation of authority in 1966 and 1972 are virtually zero. Of the four correlations of formalization with delegation in Table 28, only one is significantly larger than zero, and, as can readily be seen from the table, this zero-order correlation drops to nonsignificance when the number of levels is controlled.

The minuscule correlations of formalization with decentralization and the small though significant links between era and formalization and between formalization and levels of supervision suggest that formalization precedes proliferation of hierarchical levels rather than the other way around.

Table 28. *Correlations of index of formalization, levels of supervision, and delegation of decision-making authority (1966/1972 correlations)*

|  | Levels | Delegation 1 | Delegation 2 |
|---|---|---|---|
| Formalization | .2338/.2338 | .0716/.1405 | .0600/.0563 |
| Levels | — | .1814/.2326 | .2645/.3107 |

Cross-lagged path analysis shows that neither size nor levels affect formalization over time, whereas the 1966 measure of formalization affects 1972 levels net of 1966 levels, albeit slightly. The regressions are displayed in Table 29. Unfortunately the link between levels and delegation of decision-making authority cannot be confirmed in the longitudinal analysis. Lagged regressions show no significant links between the extensiveness of hierarchy and decentralization. Decision-making practices can change rapidly, and the six-year interval between measurements may be far too long for meaningful results to appear. In sum, the cross-sectional analysis suggests links between formalization and hierarchy and between hierarchy and delegation; no direct relationship between formalization and decentralization was shown. The longitudinal analysis indicates that causality runs from formalization to hierarchy, not the reverse. Although these results are not wholly conclusive, they are consistent with our

Table 29. *Lagged regressions of formalization, size, and levels*

|  | Zero order | B* |
| --- | --- | --- |
| *Regressions of 1972 formalization on 1966 formalization, 1966 size, and 1966 levels of supervision* | | |
| 1966 Formalization | .7802 | .7820 |
| 1966 Size | .0603 | (−.0182) |
| 1966 Formalization | .7802 | .7651 |
| 1966 Levels | .2433 | (.0644) |
| *Regressions of 1972 size and levels of supervision on 1966 formalization and 1966 size and levels* | | |
| Regressions of 1972 size: | | |
| 1966 Size | .9497 | .9492 |
| 1966 Formalization | .1005 | (.0052) |
| Regressions of 1972 levels: | | |
| 1966 Levels | .5700 | .5432 |
| 1966 Formalization | .2419 | .1149 |

expectations: Hierarchy follows from extensive personnel procedures and decentralized decision making from hierarchical differentiation.

### Openness to the environment at the time of formation

One final question remains: How does one account for the persistent though modest effects of era of formation on personnel procedures in finance agencies? Effects of origins, though diminished by environmental forces, do not disappear altogether; and it is not clear from the data describing modifications in ongoing organizations why this should be so. Put somewhat differently, the problem is to identify what takes place at the time an organization is formed that continues to influence it throughout its existence.

A partial solution is suggested by data describing a small number of finance agencies that reorganized totally between 1966 and 1972. All changed their names and altered administrative arrangements so fully that the autocorrelations of variables describing organizational structure between 1966 and 1972 were zero. One other interesting property of these 14 agencies was noted in Chapter 5: The correlations of size with environmental demands for their services were zero in 1966 and much higher in 1972. Not examined were changes in formalization of personnel procedures. A reasonable expectation is that, just as their size moved from inconsistency to consistency with environmental demands as a result of organization, so did their personnel procedures. The amount of this change is critical, however. As will be remembered from Table 26, there was only a slight increase in formalization, .0622 on a 1.0 point scale, for the 215 ongoing organizations between 1966 and 1972. For agencies that reorganized totally, a somewhat greater increase in formalization was anticipated, if only because of the extent of other changes. We had not expected, however, to find that the environment had ten times as much impact on this small group of agencies as it had on ongoing organizations in the six-year interval.

Following is the pooled regression of the two indexes of formalization on era of origin and year for the 14 reorganized finance agencies. Errors are in parentheses.

$$\text{Formalization} = .2977 + .0320 \times \text{era} + .5411 \times \text{year}$$
$$(.0512) \quad\quad (.0936)$$

The regression model is the same as that at the bottom of Table 26; only the estimated parameters differ. Causal inspection of these pooled regressions reveals, first, that the constant terms are somewhat lower for the reorganized cases than for the others, indicating that formalized personnel procedures were nearly absent from the former in 1966. Era of origin has minuscule and nonsignificant effects for the reorganized cases, but this was expected because era describes the period during which the old organizations—those obliterated between 1966 and 1972—were formed. In contrast, year of measurement, which for the reorganized cases indicates whether they were formed before or after 1966, has very large effects on formalization; the metric coefficient of year is .5411. The coefficient of year is an order of magnitude larger for the 14 reorganized departments than for the 215 ongoing finance agencies. This suggests that the environment is much more intrusive when reorganization takes place than otherwise. And it helps explain why effects of era of origin appear and persist over time despite environmental forces that affect all organizations.

In brief, we would argue that the effects of origins (or what Stinchcombe [1965] calls the correlation of age with structure) are but artifacts of the discontinuous nature of change in organizations. Organizational change involves two types of effects of the environment: gradual alterations in the internal structure of ongoing organizations and replacement of organizations that were inconsistent with external demands by new ones highly consistent with the environment. The model in Figure 8 depicts this process graphically. A hypothetical measure of bureaucratization is plotted as a function of time for a set of organizations, most of which continue but some of which are replaced at each time point. A trend toward bureaucratization is assumed due to environmental forces; and some of the organizations that are least bureaucratic, hence least consistent with the environment, reorganize at a level of bureaucratization higher than the others. The implications of this pattern are easily described. First, the association between age and structure can be explained entirely as the replacement of existing organizations with new ones. Second, the effects of era of origin on organizational properties increase over time and are limited only by whatever upper bound may exist for organizational age. The second implication follows directly from the first and can be easily shown by combining data from the 215 continuing finance agencies with data from the 14 reorganized cases and treating the post-1966 years as a fourth era of origin. For the 229 cases in 1966, the correlation of era with formalization of personnel procedures was .3487. In 1972—it

Figure 8. Discontinuous change in organizations.

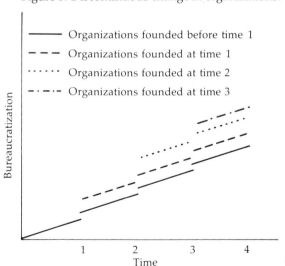

should be noted again that the post-1966 agencies are treated as founded in a fourth era – the correlation was .4264.

The ultimate explanation for the discontinuous pattern of change in organizations lies in the nature of organization itself. At the time of formation, the elements of organizations are not separable from the larger social structures in which they are embedded and thus are wholly dependent on their environments. Once organizations are founded, however, they must remain essentially stable, if only to satisfy the expectations of members and clients. These expectations may change gradually over time, but they are revised substantially when reorganization occurs and the environment intrudes. What has not been explained is why some anachronistic organizations manage to survive whereas others do not. Myriad hypotheses could be put forward, but this is not the place either to propound or to explore them.

### Conclusions

A number of ideas about organizations have been developed in this chapter. We began by pointing out that Weber's theory of bureaucracy emphasizes the primacy of historical forces and in particular the influence of rational–legal authority as causes of bureaucratization. Most researchers acknowledge this but have been unable to grapple with the problem empirically. We took the civil service movement in the United States as an illustration of historical change and the ascendance of rational–legal over traditional standards of authority. The history of federal civil service legislation was reviewed briefly in terms of its effects on state and local governments, and it was hypothesized that the extent of formal personnel procedures in local-government finance agencies would reflect both the historical period in which they were founded and the subsequent effects of the environment. Older agencies were less formalized than the newer ones, but over time all adopted procedures more in keeping with the idea of merit personnel administration and less conducive to the political spoils system. An increase in formalization, it was shown, gives rise to multi-tier hierarchies; and hierarchical differentiation in turn gives rise to the delegation of personnel decisions to lower levels. A causal chain from origins and the environment to formalization to hierarchy to decentralization was thus posited.

A small number of agencies that changed their names and reorganized totally between the two surveys of finance agencies was examined to determine whether the effects of origins could be due to extreme susceptibility to environmental pressures at the time of formation. Environmental effects on personnel procedures are almost an order of magnitude greater in the reorganized agencies than in the ongoing ones. The discontinuous pattern of change explains the observed correlation between age and certain organizational properties, and we predicted that this correlation would increase over time. Our prediction was substantiated by the 1966 and 1972 data describing finance agencies.

Several implications arise from these results. First, the patterns described here need not be peculiar to finance agencies or to the history of the civil service movement in the United States. Effects of origins and the environment and the discontinuous pattern of change should be evident for diverse institutional sectors. Second, if some of the key questions in organization theory concern the effects of societal forces on organizations over time, organizational research ought to be directed toward answering these questions. Historical and longitudinal studies are required, and they must take explicit account of qualitative as well as quantitative elements of environments that have heretofore been neglected. In all likelihood, research will have to be larger in scope and longer in duration than has been usual until now. Third, the results presented here, together with those in earlier chapters, suggest means for stimulating change in organizations. Chapter 4 suggested that change in leadership and dependence of leaders on higher authority open organizations to environmental influences. Here it has been shown that total reorganization speeds the process of accommodation to environmental pressures. These results are not surprising; but they do call into question the efficacy of attempting incremental change, the results of which are at best uncertain, compared with that of changing leaders or the total reorganization of agencies. Our results do not speak to the desirability of reorganization. For some organizations, particularly those performing mediating functions, continuity is essential. But our research suggests that, when shifts in administrative patterns are sought, they are obtained most efficiently through changes in leadership and fundamental alterations in organizational structures.

# 7

## Implications

This chapter summarizes and draws some implications from the study of finance agencies. The first section is a recapitulation of key empirical results. The bearing of these results on organizational theory is discussed in the second section; some implications for the management of public agencies are drawn in the third section; and directions for sociological research are sketched in conclusion.

### Recapitulation of empirical results

*Causal patterns in ongoing agencies*

A number of empirical results have been presented so far, and a summary of them might help buttress the argument developed in Chapter 1, namely that public bureaucracies are considerably more open to their environments than stereotypes would suggest. Figure 9 depicts relations among variables describing finance agencies and quantifiable elements in their environments for the jurisdictions where reorganization of the finance function did *not* occur. The causal relations among these variables can be described as follows:

*Effects of demand.* As Figure 9 indicates, the measures of environmental demand often have a negative effect on the size of finance agencies and on the number of divisions and sections in them. The effects of environmental demand are greatest under conditions of leadership turnover and dependence on higher authority; and they are nearly absent where leadership has been stable in the past and has autonomy. At the same time, demand stimulates formation of agencies with fiscal functions outside of the focal finance departments studied. It should be noted that the negative effect of demand on size (and structure) of finance agencies over time is generated by deteriorating positive correlations of size with demand. The declining fit between environment and organizational patterns in this respect is a historical anomoly and reflects the peculiar circumstances of the city finance profession at the time the research was undertaken. In this sense, then, forces in the larger social environment account for the direction of effects of demand in the immediate environment of finance agencies.

*Effects of competition.* Figure 9 also shows that, generally, the more agencies with fiscal functions in the same jurisdiction as finance departments studied, the fewer the respon-

Figure 9. Causal relations in ongoing organizations.

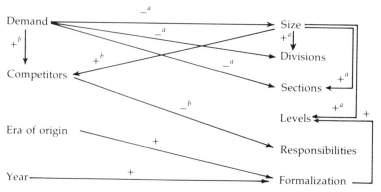

[a] Depends on leadership conditions
[b] Depends on domain

sibilities accruing to, or the greater the loss of responsibilities of finance departments over time. Comptrollers' offices whose responsibilities are quite limited to begin with did not suffer this erosion of responsibilities with competition; and departments of administration reversed the process wholly, discarding competitors as they increased responsibilities.

*Effects of era of origin.* Older agencies, it was shown in Chapter 6, had fewer personnel rules consistent with civil service or merit standards of administration. This pattern held in both the 1966 and 1972 studies and was attributed to civil service laws in effect at the time agencies were founded.

*Effects of time.* Over time, all agencies moved toward imposition of formalized merit personnel standards but, at the same time, added temporary employees. The 1970 Intergovernmental Personnel Act, the Emergency Employment Act of 1971, and other forces in the larger environment account for these results.

*Effects of size.* Two effects of organizational size were discernible. First, size led to elaboration of organizational structure. Greater size was associated with more divisions, levels of supervision, and sections over time. The effects of size, it was shown, were greatest under conditions of leadership instability and dependence on higher authority and were minimal otherwise. These effects of size on structure are consistent with results already in the literature. Second, for finance departments, greater size led to increasing competition in the immediate environment. Past a point, it appears, increases in demand for fiscal services leads to creation of new agencies, and diminution of responsibilities of existing ones, rather than growth of finance departments.

*Effects of formalization.* The data suggest, although not conclusively, that formalization of personnel procedures leads to elaboration of organizational hierarchies, rather than the other way around as has been suggested in the literature.

*Effects of divisions, levels, sections, and responsibilities.* No effects of variables describing numbers of divisions, levels, or sections, or of the range of fiscal responsibilities of a finance agency (save for departments of administration) could be found in the longitudinal analysis. Formal administrative structure, it was surmised, is largely a result of size; the extent of responsibilities in public agencies in all likelihood shows no effects because augmentation of resources with increased responsibilities is offset by the tendency to create new agencies, hence contract resources, with greater demand for services.

*Summary of direct effects.* Save for effects of size upon structure and of formalization upon levels of hierarchy, all causal links in Figure 9 are between environments and organizations; and all but one of the latter run from the environment to the organization rather than the other way around. Openness to the environment rather than closedness, then, characterizes the ongoing finance agencies. The negative signs of environmental effects, it should be noted, suggests that the causal structure sketched in Figure 9 is very much time bound. The erosion of finance departments with demand for their services cannot continue indefinitely. Either these agencies will vanish, a new equilibrium will be reached, or events occurring in the larger environment will restore the correspondence of organizational patterns with elements in their immediate environments. Some attention to variables mediating the causal relations depicted above is therefore in order, for it may be that these mediating mechanisms have greater constancy both over time and across different kinds of organizations than the causal relations just reviewed.

*Intervening mechanisms*

Three key mechanisms mediating environment–organization relations have been identified. They are leadership conditions, an organization's name or claim to domain, and its era of formation. Stable and autonomous leadership limits erosion of finance agencies occurring with environmental demand; leadership turnover and dependence on higher authority opens an organization to external forces. Whether agencies administering local-government finances decline, remain stable, or grow with their environments, and whether competition erodes them or they erode competition are also functions of their domain claims. Finance departments, agencies with the most precarious domains, were most vulnerable to forces in the immediate environment; comptrollers' offices were most stable; and departments of administration were most successful in growing with external demand and eliminating potential competitors. Finally, events occurring in the environment at the time an agency is formed affect it more than external conditions later on. Personnel regulations in finance agencies were affected by both time of origin and the environment, the persistent effects of the former occurring due to extreme openness at the point of formation.

*The process of reorganization*

Reorganization of finance agencies renders them extremely open to the environment, upsetting the pattern of causal relations characterizing ongoing agencies. Correspondences between environmental demand and organizational size increase substantially as a result of reorganization, and the extent to which an agency's personnel regulations fit federal "merit" standards also increases by an order of magnitude more than would be expected otherwise. Reorganization is also accompanied by expanded claims to domain. Rarely do agencies claim less "turf" after reorganization than before.

The rate of reorganization among finance agencies over the 1966–72 interval, it should be noted, was quite low–14 out of 229 cases, or about 1 percent per year. This can be explained as in part an artifact of the stringent definition of reorganization, fundamental structural alteration *and* name change, but it raises the question of why reorganizing activity is not more frequent at the departmental level given the apparent instability of organizational structures below. No single answer can be wholly adequate. Clearly, one explanation lies in institutional mechanisms sustaining whole departments of local governments, such as the statutes that established them. A corollary explanation is possible: Because institutional ties rendered departmental structures almost invariant, processes of organizational selection as well as adaptation are shifted to the subunit level. These explanations, it should be noted, can be tested in empirical research and they should be pursued.[1]

### Implications for the theory of organizations

The empirical results do not fit a simple model of organizational behavior. Concretely, they suggest the following: that formal administrative structure does not have a great deal of temporal stability, hence openness to the environment characterizes public bureaucracies; that leadership mediates forces arising in the larger environment; that the legitimation of claims to domain made by bureaus may be more important then their actual activities in determining their resources and growth or decline; and that despite openness to the environment, residual effects of origins persist because of extreme openness at the time of formation compared to later on. These findings are in some sense disparate, for they do not derive from a consistent set of assumptions or postulates about organizations but instead are the results of empirical research, which can tap only fragments of the complex and varied events occurring in organizations. At this point, then, some attempt should be made to organize these results into a theoretical framework broader than the ideas discussed in Chapter 1. Whereas Weberian and open-systems theory in some sense anticipated our results, the theory now sought would synthesize them.

### Implications for internal organization

We begin from a premise accepted by neoclassical economists and political scientists but not widely acknowledged in the sociological literature:

*1. Bureaucracies do work for which there is no market alternative.* In other words, public agencies exist because voluntary quid pro quo transactions will not suffice (Downs, 1967) or because contracts cannot be relied upon (Williamson, 1975). This point is fundamental; the lack of a market alternative is due to either the inability of public authorities to specify the goods, services, or results for which they are contracting, or their inability to trust others to deliver the goods, services, or results contracted for. With regard to the former, it is difficult to specify in advance what outcomes are expected of systems of education, public welfare, and the like; with regard to the latter, it would be foolhardy to expect private fire departments, police forces, and armies to always act in the public interest. It could be argued—although this is not the place to pursue the point—that the growth of public-sector services nowadays is due largely to complexity with the rise of the welfare state (Wilensky, 1975), whereas local-government services had their origins in failures in the private sector.

*2. Quasi-market organizational alternatives are generally unavailable to public agencies.* Although distrust can be overcome within the boundaries of organizations, complex or vague objectives cannot be. Shadow pricing, profit centers, and the like cannot be implemented in public organizations, and measures linking activities with expenditures rarely convey sufficient information to managers. The inappropriateness of shadow pricing and profit centers is self-evident; the in-adequacy of most performance measures is suggested by the failure of cost-benefit analysis, PPBS, and similar innovations to bring about fundamental economies or efficiencies in government. For these reasons, decentralized multiunit organizational structures cannot be implemented in public agencies.

*3. The only organizational form available to public bureaucracies, then, is simple hierarchy.* Lacking market alternatives that would permit contracting for necessary services and quasi-market alternatives that would permit decentralized administration, simple hierarchy is the only possibility for public agencies. This is, of course, the Weberian model of bureaucracy, which emphasizes strict super- and subordination and a high degree of centralization. The implications of the absence of alternative organizational forms for the public sector are as follows:

3a  Organizational structure proliferates with size. This has been abundantly demonstrated in the literature: What is important here is that mechanisms available to firms that partially overcome the diseconomies of size are not available to bureaucracies.

3b  Performance is measured in terms of conformity with higher authority. Normally, officials in public bureaucracies are bound by rules that formalize wishes of both immediate and distant superiors. Even when distant superiors write the rules, immediate superiors enforce conformity to them, as their performance is assessed in terms of subordinates' conformity.

*4. Criteria of conformity as opposed to efficiency or effectiveness criteria render public bureaucracies highly vulnerable to shifts in the environment.* In one sense, of course, all assessment of organizations is socially rather than organizationally determined, whether assessment is in terms of efficiency, effectiveness, or conformity criteria. An important difference, however, is that the ideals of efficiency and effectiveness are much better institutionalized in the larger social structure than are the kinds of standards to which public bureaucracies must conform. Widespread acceptance of ideals of efficiency and effectiveness allows firms to respond to fluctuations in the environment with short-run adaptations rather than by disrupting objectives; such adaptations are accomplished by mechanisms designed to absorb environmental shocks while leaving the technical cores of organizations intact (Thompson, 1967). Organizations whose performance is measured in terms of conformity rather than efficiency or effectiveness are potentially more disrupted by changes in the environment, because their core activities are directly invaded by rule changes arising externally.

4a *Ceteris paribus,* there will be a closer correspondence between shifts in the environment and shifts in core activities in public agencies than in firms.

4b Buffering mechanisms in public agencies attempt to block, distort, or redirect environmental inputs rather than absorbing them. What are perceived usually as dysfunctions of bureaucracy due to closedness to the environment (Merton, 1940) may in fact be responses to extreme openness.

*5. Leadership, claims to domain, and institutionalization of organizations function as buffering mechanisms for public bureaucracies.*

5a Entrenched leadership blocks the environment, whereas leadership change allows the environment ot intrude. Autonomous leadership blocks the environment, whereas heteronomous leadership also allows environmental intrusions (Chapter 4). Politically and interpersonally skillful leadership distorts or redirects environmental pressures, whereas inept leadership is trapped by environmental demands. In general, leadership positions and personality assume greater salience to the extent that norms of conformity rather than those of efficiency or effectiveness prevail; they are especially important in public bureaucracies.

5b The more expansive an agency's claim to domain, the more easily it can redirect demands for conformity made by other agencies, and the more easily it can impose conformity demands on other agencies. The more ambiguous the claim to domain, the greater the difficulty of redirecting external demands and of imposing conformity demands on others (Chapter 5). Expansive claims to domain in bureaucracies, then, are to be interpreted as means of legitimating one's own activities and rules and delegitimating those of others.

5c Older agencies with more institutional supports than new units can block or redirect the environment most effectively (Chapter 6). Agencies most institutionalized due to extensive networks of extraorganizational ties block or redirect the environment most easily. Survival and anachronism, then, are associated in public agencies, whereas the opposite prediction would be made for firms. Innovative programs create multi-tier public bureaucracies because the establishment of new agencies typically subordinates old institutionalized functions to newer and more inclusive ones.

*Comment.* In the context of the propositions developed so far, the empirical results in the earlier chapters can be reinterpreted as illustrative of buffering mechanisms operating in public bureaucracies. Leadership, claims to domain, and origins influence public organizations because of their roles as intermediaries between environments and organizations. The question that should now be addressed is whether the same principles used to account for specific empirical results—the lack of market and quasi-market alternatives, the dominance of hierarchy, and reliance on conformity as opposed to efficiency or effectiveness criteria—can generate predictions about both the growth of public-sector organizations and their intrusion into the private sector.

### *Implications for growth of the public sector*

*6. In the absence of market or quasi-market alternatives, activities once initiated in public bureaucracies tend to persist* (See Kaufman, 1976). Save for exceptional instances, outputs of public organizations are not comparable. For this reason, resources are not easily shifted from less efficient to more efficient uses. In addition, public agencies once formed tend to elaborate ideologies justifying their existence (in Meyer, 1977, I treat ideologies as "invented environments") and constituents or beneficiaries of programs often form interest groups that defend ongoing programs.

*7. Openness to the environment due to pervasive conformity criteria results in creation of new public-sector organizations.* As the societal or institutional environment (see Meyer and Rowan, 1977) deems new nonmarket activities desirable, they are incorporated into public agencies. It is important to note that new activities are signified only when new organizational units with distinctive identities are formed. The following effects obtain:

> 7a The greater the extent to which nonmarket activities are institutionalized in the societal environment, the greater the number of distinctive organizational units in public bureaucracies. Periodic reorganization does not obliterate the identity of these distinctive units but subordinates them to more inclusive units.

7b The greater the restraints on conduct institutionalized in the societal environment, the greater the extent of rules in public bureaucracies, and the greater the number of rule-making agencies. Because external conformity can be monitored much more easily than internal efficiency and is more consequential, attention is directed away from inconsistent regulations and the costs of administering them. When inconsistencies are officially recognized, second-order rules, that is, rules allowing exceptions, are elaborated.

*8. The absence of alternatives to hierarchy together with persistence of old and formation of new organizational units imply a continued elaboration of structure in public bureaucracies.* New units are usually placed alongside existing units, but span-of-control considerations eventually dictate additional layers of hierarchy. The closer association of size with levels than of size with numbers of subunits found here (Chapter 3) and replicated elsewhere is evidence of vertical elaboration.

8a Control loss in vertically elaborated structures and diseconomies of scale compel decentralization of decisions that can be preformed in rules (Chapter 6) and decoupling of activities from formal structures in situations where rules cannot govern actual conduct (Weick, 1976).

8b When loose coupling in bureaucracies is officially recognized, it is followed by more rules, more rule-enforcing agencies, and greater vertical elaboration (Chapter 6). A vicious cycle (Crozier, 1964) of bureaucratization thus ensues.

*Comments.* Propositions 6, 7, and 8 suggest a model of public-sector growth that is quite different from results of research studies not taking account of forces in societal environments affecting organizations. Whereas conventional research treats size as exogenous and is concerned with its effects (e.g., on structure and administrative overhead), size and structure are viewed here as dependent upon institutionalization of nonmarket activities and the formation of distinctive organizational units responsible for them.

Figure 10 illustrates the relationships implicit in the propositions developed so far. Several observations are in order:

a. The direction of the relationship between institutional and societal environments and the formation of distinctive organizational units is indeterminate because of the tendency of organizations to create environments or pseudo-environments favorable to their continued existence. Causation runs mainly from the larger environment to organizations rather than the other way around, but not entirely so. ·For this reason, separating elements of institutional and societal environments from the process of formation of distinctive organizational units may be difficult given the types of historical and comparative (cross-national) data that are usually available. The one concrete prediction is that made by Stinchcombe (1965): Formation of organizational units of a given type will occur in noticeable waves.

b. The relationship between size and measures describing organizational structures are due, in part, to their mutual dependence on formation of distinctive organizational units. Adjustments in structure follow almost immediately from formation of new units (Proposition 8), and augmentation of size follows soon thereafter. The relationship between formation of distinctive units and elaboration of structure is partly tautologous but not entirely so. New organizational units can be placed at any level in existing organizational structures. An important question, then, is what kinds of activities are placed at what organizational levels. The relationship between formation of new units and size is all but taken for granted nowadays, but it is not tautologous because it arises from the inability of bureaus to substitute new programs for existing ones.

c. The immediate environment appears as a variable in Figure 10 because its carrying capacity (Hannan and Freeman, 1977) or munificence determines in many instances whether new organizational units will be formed in response to external forces. Whether other elements in the immediate environment (e.g., homogeneity versus heterogeneity, stability versus instability, and the like) affect size and structure directly is questionable, because of the likelihood that they are generated by definitions arising in the larger social and institutional environment. In other words, consensus on the meaning of local events hence the appropriate organizational response to them usually arises at the societal level.

d. Various buffering mechanisms discussed above (Proposition 5) intervene between both immediate and societal environments and organizational patterns.

e. The model in Figure 10 may be applicable with equal force to public bureaucracies and firms, provided that two considerations are kept in mind. First, the munificence or carrying capacity of immediate environments may be all but decisive for private firms, whereas it is much less so for public agencies. Second, buffering mechanisms used by firms may be quite different from those employed in the public sector, for example, forecasting, stockpiling, ration-

Figure 10. Hypothesized relationships among variables.

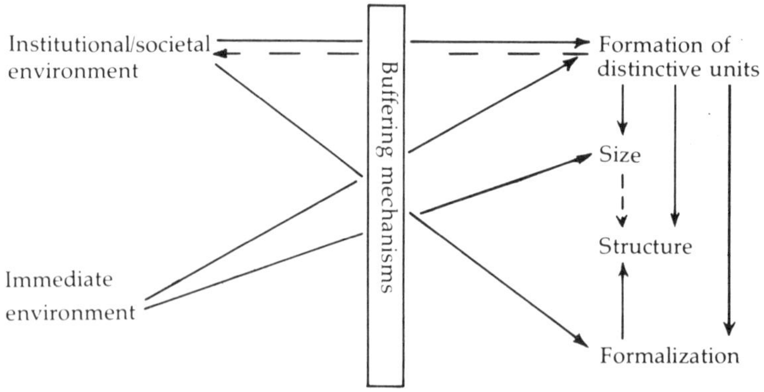

ing, and so forth (Thompson, 1967). Institutional and societal factors, then, will affect formation and formalization in the private sector somewhat less than in public organizations. This does not mean that there are no effects of institutional and societal forces on firms and private, not-for-profit agencies. Quite the contrary, such effects exist and are becoming more intense over time.

### Implications for relations among organizations

If hierarchy, conformity, persistence of old units, and elaboration of structure as new units form characterize public bureaucracies, then one should ask what implications this has for relations among organizations. A basic assumption is that with extension of the nation-state, there is greater penetration of all organizations by the national bureaucracy. This development is illustrated, in part, in Chapter 6. I use the term *societal determination of organizations* to denote this process.

The following propositions, which go somewhat beyond the empirical research reported above, are intended mainly to stimulate research into interorganizational relations.

9. *Societal determination of organizations affects peripheral elements first and the technical core last.* Following Thompson (1967), the technical core consists of areas of organizations protected from the environment by buffering mechanisms, where cause-and-effect relations operate and are understood, and where efficiency tests are possible. The periphery, by implication, is everything else.

   9a  Societal determination of the technical core is resisted on grounds of impaired efficiency.
   9b  Boundary-spanning elements at the periphery of organizations proliferate with increased societal determination. The principle of isomorphism between boundary-spanning elements and environments pre-

dicts that the structure of peripheral elements of private organizations and of state and local agencies will increasingly resemble the structure of national bureaucracies penetrating them.

*10. Conformity criteria displace efficiency criteria with increased societal determination.*

10a Organizational survival is increasingly based on conformity to externally imposed rules, especially if there is demonstrable inefficiency.

10b Administrative overhead, and units with purely administrative functions whose outputs cannot be assessed in efficiency terms, proliferate with conformity criteria.

10c Conformity criteria render quasi-market alternatives to hierarchy increasingly risky for private organizations. Conformity criteria generally detract from efficiency, and managers responsible for profit in decentralized firms have strong incentives to behave opportunistically with respect to these criteria. Because such opportunism can, if detected, imperil an entire organization, recentralization and reimposition of hierarchy occur. Put in somewhat different terms, private organizations become more like public bureaucracies as externally imposed conformity criteria proliferate.

*11. Ambiguity and indeterminateness in decision making increase with greater societal determination of organizations.* (See March and Olsen, 1976.) Increased ambiguity and indeterminateness occur for two reasons, First, aside from impeding efficiency, conformity criteria themselves can be inconsistent hence introduce ambiguity into decisions. Second, changing conformity criteria disrupt cause-and-effect relations upon which organizations rely to maximize efficiency, adding to uncertainty.

*Comment.* If true, the propositions developed immediately above suggest that debureaucratization of both public and private-sector organizations is an unlikely prospect. Rule boundedness and hierarchy are expected responses to the imposition of conformity criteria on organizations of all kinds, and they will decrease only when conformity criteria promulgated centrally are withdrawn. Whether or not even incremental contraction of the nation-state is possible remains an open question. It may be that political and social change of the most fundamental sort are required to reverse societal penetration of organizations.

Two lines of research are suggested. Studies of organizational change over lengthy intervals within a single society can illuminate the effects of increased societal determination. An explanation of why some societies are more intrusive than others requires comparative (cross-national) research. Such studies may have to be more historical than contemporary because of erosion of differences across societies due to increased communication and mobility as well as the emergence of multi-national corporations and agencies.

*Organizational structure and effectiveness*[2]

The possible relationship of organizational structure to effectiveness in public bureaucracies should be examined in light of the research results and theoretical analysis above. The research results suggest that when structure is treated as administrative arrangements linking individual people and organizational subunits together, it is an outcome of size, formalization, and the level of demand in the immediate environment. Delegation of decision-making authority is affected by hierarchical differentiation, but aside from this effect, the consequences of structure are quite sparse. Additionally, the low temporal stability of measures of organizational structure suggest that administrative arrangements are more outcome than cause. All of this is not to say that administrative patterns are inconsequential for people in organizations, but the empirical results suggest that any causal connection running from structure to organizational effectiveness is likely to be either spurious or dependent on a host of intervening mechanisms.

Furthermore, the theoretical analysis above suggests that, for public bureaucracies, the range of available organizational forms is limited. Whereas firms have market and quasi-market alternatives to hierarchy, bureaus generally do not. To be sure, hierarchies can be tall, flat, or ballooned at intermediate levels. But whatever the distribution of individual people and subunits within the structure of public bureaucracies are, all are bound together by relationships of super- and subordination in which conformity to rules and to wishes of superiors is expected.

Also limited is the variability of effectiveness outcomes for public bureaucracies. This is not self-evident but is often the case for several reasons. First of all, most public agencies are *potentially* very effective (if not efficient). Not only is their legitimacy taken for granted by most people, but they can draw upon enormous resources at the disposal of public bodies that are unavailable to private organizations. Secondly, because the openness of public bureaucracies renders them vulnerable to environmental shifts, new effectiveness criteria arising externally are quickly transformed into conformity criteria enforced internally. For this reason, attempts to impose objective performance criteria on public bureaucracies may have only marginal impact and can be self-defeating. Some almost commonplace examples illustrate the inadequacy of many performance criteria: The per-unit cost of maintaining public property is held constant by either decreasing or abandoning maintenance altogether; student−faculty ratios are maintained by admitting inferior students; and a city's operating budget remains balanced by treating certain routine activities as capital improvements and borrowing for them. Managers of public agencies typically understand the circularity of performance evaluation better than politicians and the public, and they therefore resist evaluation by using buffering mechanisms like those outlined above.

Even though variations in structure and effectiveness outcomes are limited for public bureaucracies, it is true that certain administrative arrangements can seriously impede effectiveness. For example, wheel structures (everyone reporting to the boss) and chain structures (everyone, save at the lowest level, having one subordinate) are clearly cumbersome. Placing activities that must be closely coordinated proximate to one another is preferable to separating them widely. Subordinating unimportant functions to critical ones is also preferable to the opposite. It should be noted, however, that the required level of coordination between activities, their relative importance, and their compatibility are not immutable states. New technologies eliminate some problems of coordination and create other problems; shifts in the larger environment render some problems moot and others more salient; learning and personnel turnover can shift attitudes in organizations so that formerly incompatible activities become compatible.

For public bureaucracies, then, organizational structure is to be viewed as, at best, a temporary accommodation to a confluence of events. Wholly inappropriate structures will, of course, detract from effectiveness. But the range of organizational forms and of effectiveness outcomes is quite limited in public agencies, hence any rationale for a particular organizational structure becomes transient. Simple relations between structure and effectiveness holding for diverse public agencies over time are not likely to be found.

*A note on size.* Even though organizational structure may be unrelated in any simple way to the effectiveness of public agencies, save for extreme instances, it has been argued elsewhere that increasing size may impede effectiveness. Control loss (Tullock, 1965), communication distortion (Halberstam, 1972), and subgoal pursuit (Williamson, 1975) are thought to be consequences of large size and extended hierarchies. Despite these diseconomies associated with size, however, there may be economies of scale in administration (Blau, 1970). Furthermore, if structure and size are outcomes of the formation of organizational units with distinct functions, then the complexity or range of activities undertaken by public agencies must be considered before conclusions about possible adverse effects of size are drawn.

In all likelihood, the impact of size on effectiveness is, like the impact of structure, a function of many variables. What constitutes an adequate but not excessive work force depends upon the importance of the task and the available technologies. The absence of alternatives to hierarchy, however, compels either proliferation of levels or inadequate supervision with increased size. Gains in effectiveness resulting from additional workers may be offset partially by losses in control. Variations in tasks and in technologies should lead to variations in organizational size. The size of an effective public bureaucracy, then, might be as much of a temporary accommodation to external events as is structure. But in actuality, as the data in Chapter 3 show, organizational size is anything but temporary and variable – due partially to effects of civil service tenure arrangements intended to minimize political spoils, also due in part to "rollover" budgeting. A ratchet or bumperjack effect thus results. The public work force can be increased easily, but shrunk only with great difficulty and persistence. Indeed, one should entertain the possibility that variability of public-sector organizational structures over time is in part an effect of invariant size: Reorganization and shuffling of offices may be used in some instances to shift surplus personnel into units removed from public view.

*Effectiveness as a source of structure.* Even though causal paths running from structure to effectiveness and from size to effectiveness may be indeterminate or nonexistent, there is a distinct possibility that assessment of organizations influences structure and size. The transformation of external effectiveness criteria into internal conformity standards and the necessity of erecting offices and assigning personnel for evaluation purposes suggests the following:

12. *The greater the number of effectiveness criteria, the greater the number of organizational units and of positions assigned to assessment purposes.* Organization proliferates with effectiveness criteria for several reasons. First, there is the tendency to construct organization charts so that alleged outputs and names of organizational units correspond. The more of the former, the more of the latter. (This correspondence is made exact in program budget documents that substitute terms such as *program, subprogram, program element,* and *subelement* for *department, division, section,* and *subsection.*) Second, the more effectiveness criteria, the greater the effort devoted to evaluation hence the more personnel required.

*Organizational structure as an impediment to change*

Despite the openness and variability of bureaucratic structures, there is also evidence that organizational change does not occur as rapidly as do shifts in the environment. As a result, the fit between organizations and enviornments is greatest at the time of formation and declines gradually thereafter until reorganization or replacement of existing units becomes necessary. Structure, which is initially an accommodation to the environment, eventually becomes an impediment to change and must be altered fundamentally.

An important question is why these inertial processes pervade organizations, and whether they operate in bureaus and businesses alike. Inertia occurs, in part, because of widely shared expectations about organizations and expectations of permanence and stability. Concepts such as careers within organizations and the relative hierarchy of prestige and power among organizations of different types are deeply embedded in our culture and are not easily changed. Socialization into the skills and attitudes demanded by any particular organization can be costly and time consuming, and it is not easily undone. Additionally, people become attached to organizational symbols, rules, and accustomed ways of doing things. In the short run, therefore, it is easiest to leave routines undisturbed rather than to upset them, and routines are formalized as organizational structure. Structure provides for continuity, for anticipation that rewards proffered for dedicated service will in fact be forthcoming, and for an unambiguous definition of a person's position if not his exact responsibilities. But structure also impedes responsiveness and can, eventually, undo an organization's ability to perform effectively.

Research needs to be directed to the question of whether many types of organizations exhibit the same cycle of change we have observed in public finance agencies. If extreme openness to the environment at the time of formation together with deteriorating fits between organizations and environments over time are observed for diverse organizations, then inquiry into the further question—what rates of change best balance internal organizational efficiency with accommodation to external exigencies—is warranted. This requires designs that can take into account both varying rates of organizational change and variations in organizational outputs—something not easily accomplished within the confines of a cross-sectional study or even panel research on organizations over limited intervals. Almost by definition, organizational structure and responsiveness are opposed to each other. Whether optimal rates at which organizations should accommodate their environments can be identified, and whether there are optimal rates of reorganization or replacement of existing structures should be the subject of sustained research.

## Implications for the management of public organizations

*Paradoxes*

The study of finance agencies reported here was planned as basic research on organizations, aimed at testing theories concerning relations among properties of organizational structures and between environments and organizations. The results, however, cannot but have implications for the management of public organizations, especially in light of evidence showing openness and variability in them that does not fit stereotypes. It should be emphasized that no nostrums are advocated here. The complexity of public agencies and of their environments is such that there can be no one best way to organize. What is proposed, however, is that ways of thinking about public organizations can be developed so that managers faced with problems, choices, and opportunities might be able to act more effectively than they would otherwise be equipped to do.

How shall we think about public bureaucracies if not actually organize them? The model of the firm used by economists is clearly inappropriate. Whereas firms may be thought of as maximizers—whether or not they *actually* maximize efficiency is immaterial—this model or metaphor is clearly inappropriate for public agencies where efficiency measures are elusive if not nonexistent. A very different model for thinking about bureaucracies is required. Such a model, I believe, has its roots in Weber's work on bureaucracy; but it is fraught with contradictory elements, paradox if you will, that Weber either ignored or did not describe because they were not present at the time of his work. Rather than starting with a typological discussion of division of labor and hierarchy, and moving swiftly to the conclusion that organizations possessing these elements are maximally efficient, one should pause to ask what the implications of hierarchy, that is to say pervasive hierarchy, are for other elements in organizations. The appropriate metaphor for public bureaucracies, then, is not that of the maximizer that can alter structural arrangements in order to eliminate unnecessary costs, but that of the Jacob's ladder on which change at one rung is transmitted swiftly and determinately to the next. Pervasive hierarchy, and the primacy of conformity as a value, yield the following paradoxes in public bureaucracies.

*Openness yet rule boundedness.* Normally, one thinks of rule-bound organizations as closed from the environment. The more rules, the greater the propensity of officials to do that for which the rules allow and to ignore everything else. But if rules originate externally, and if they are imposed upon successive layers of hierarchy through conformity mechanisms, then rule boundedness becomes a manifestation of openness rather than a source of closedness. To be sure, responding to environmental inputs by devising rules can be cumbersome and awkward (i.e., rules specifying exceptions to rules may be needed), but it is instrumentally effective insofar as new rules elaborated by public authorities create the presumption, if not the fact, of their enforcement. Openness and rule boundedness, then, are usually not inconsistent, although they can be at odds when new environmental inputs are in conflict with existing regulations.

*Inseparability of technical-core from boundary-spanning functions.* Pervasive hierarchy also limits the ability of organizations to separate core-technical from boundary-spanning activities because elements of both are present at every level, save for the lowest. All public bureaucracies are nested in larger structures of government, and these larger structures are crucial elements in their immediate environments. For this reason, demarcations between organization and environment are vague, and some buffering of the environment must take place at every level. "Sunshine" laws and acts requiring complete disclosure of government actions allow the public direct access to individual agencies, again demanding boundary spanning at every level. To be sure, public agencies like private ones, and perhaps more so than in the private sector, may designate specialized boundary-spanning positions, especially positions involving coordination of activities of different agencies. But this only means that nonhierarchical boundary-spanning activities are explicitly authorized for certain positions, not that they are confined to these positions. The inseparability of technical-core from boundary-spanning functions renders cause-and-effect knowledge, hence calculable measures of efficiency, very difficult to develop in public bureaucracies. Only where operating-level work routines can be standardized, hence insulated, from the vicissitudes of hierarchy and public scrutiny are even imperfect measures of efficiency possible.

*Change threatens, yet little changes.* The character of change in public bureaucracies is also shaped by pervasive hierarchy. Hierarchical dominance renders change both uncontrollable and inevitable for organizations, the former because planning cannot anticipate what decision makers at higher levels will do, the latter because new conformity criteria must be met or at least appear to be met. Uncontrollable and inevitable change is normally perceived unfavorably and may be the source of considerable anxiety among the public work force. At the same time, fundamental change is infrequent and sometimes nonexistent. The same conformity mechanisms that render change uncontrollable and inevitable once decided upon by hierarchical superiors also constrain severely the freedom of action of the latter, requiring that changes they propose be consistent with the preferences and policies of those who are, in turn, their superiors. Precisely because change is at once threatening but unlikely, proposals for change and reorganization in public bureaucracies assume a special function as signals indicating what superiors might do if not otherwise constrained.

### The role of public management

What, then, is the role of public management amidst these paradoxical elements of bureaucracy? It should be remembered that if bureaucracy operated as Weber said it does—like a well-oiled machine—proactive management would not be an important element. Management activities assume salience, however, when the structure of organizations create either ambiguities or conditions operating against organizational goals. Openness despite rule boundedness, the inseparability of technical core from boundary-spanning activities, and the continual uncertainty generated by the possibility of change despite its remoteness requires managers to develop preferences. These would include, for example, preferences for rule enforcement as opposed to accommodation to other exigencies, for protection of critical activities as opposed to uniform application of rules and rule changes to all activities, for change despite entrenched resistance, or for organizational stability despite environmental shifts. These choices are, importantly, unregulated by the discipline of the market in the absence of tangible outputs from administrative activities. They are also complex in that subunit interests, personal preferences and career prospects, and policies eminating from the larger structure of government must be balanced.

Precisely because of the ambiguities surrounding choices in bureaucracies, no model of technical rationality can anticipate, much less guide, the behavior of managers of public agencies whose activities are rule bound and outputs nondescript. A political as opposed to a rational model of behavior is most appropriate for such circumstances. The literature is rife with descriptive studies of this approach to management (e.g., Selznick, 1949; Lindblom, 1959), and they need not be reviewed here. The important point, for present purposes, is that research covering many organizations over a lengthy interval cannot attempt to capture the nuances of behavior that are the essence of the managerial process in public organizations as well as in private ones to the extent that calculable bases for decisions are absent from the latter. This is a deficiency of our research design, but one hopes that the limitation is more than offset by a focus on patterns of structural change in organizations over time.

For finance agencies, there are some suggestions offered by our results. First of all, it appears that despite the importance of finance administration, the public either does not understand or does not have a preference for any of the diverse organizational arrangements available for this activity. Infrequent reorganization, more frequent loss of key functions such as budgeting and data processing, and the instability of organizational structures below the departmental level suggest that individual department heads on their professional association (the Municipal Finance Officers Association of the United States and Canada) could do much more to make the activities of finance agencies known and understood, hence organizational arrangements stabilized, than has been done in the past. We have no evidence proving that frequent organizational changes undermine effectiveness or that stability does not; but it is difficult to imagine that continuity and comparability, essential to bureaus whose mission is to maintain accurate records, are aided by recurring organizational change. Second, even though finance directors were usually the innovators who introduced electronic data-processing to local governments but have since lost control of computer facilities, this does not preclude their taking advantage of innovative uses of computing at this time. For example, modeling or forecasting of local or regional economies are needed for revenue projections along with more routine accounting activities. The failure to make use of existing data bases and technologies with which to analyze them will mean, ultimately, that these activities will flow elsewhere in local governments, further eroding the domains of finance agencies. Again, although there is no evidence to prove this, it seems most efficient to have agencies that have been the sources of fiscal data for local governments also conduct analytic studies with these data. The basic premise here, as before, is that a strong finance directorate minimizes confusion and duplication in fiscal affairs. This premise also conditions a third suggestion, mainly that information concerning fiscal conditions and data supplied for independent audits of local-government units emanate from a single, centralized finance directorate. Because the accuracy of disclosure statements and audits is always a matter of judgment, year-to-year consistency may be as important an element in building confidence as are financial results themselves. To be sure, periodic reorganization may be necessary for finance agencies, but the attrition of functions observed here and the resulting instability of internal structure would not seems to contribute to the quality of administration.

In terms of the categories elaborated above, finance officials seem to have opted for rule boundedness, and they have failed to protect the core functions of budgeting and data processing despite their importance for fiscal affairs. Rather than altering their agencies as the environment shifted, they have resisted change, which, in turn, has had to be imposed externally. A preference for maintaining existing organizational arrangements, then, has led to inconsistencies with the environment, with the resulting pattern of attrition and periodic reorganization. If finance officials were more comfortable with openness, with nurturing and protecting new activities rather than subjecting them to existing standards, and with changing organizational forms as new technologies displaced old ones, then pervasive organizational decline punctuated by occasional but total reorganization might not have been found. Whether most public agencies respond to environmental changes as managers of finance agencies do, of course, is a matter for other research studies to determine.

### Concluding comments: implications for sociological research

The empirical research reported in this volume is a study of public bureaucracies, not of a representative sample of organizations of all types, and not of social aggregates generally. Nonetheless, the research has been informed primarily by theories with high sociological content if not of sociological origin. If sociology consists of the study of groups or of social aggregates—the language used to describe the sociological unit of analysis is unimportant so long as its meaning is clear—then research on organizational structures ought to have some implications for the study of social structures generally. There are three ways in which I wish to trace these implications. First of all, the question of whether research conducted over time captures greater variations than are permitted by cross-sectional comparisons should be explored. Second, whether or not time itself, aside from variations in phenomena captured over time, is an important variable for the study of social structures also needs discussion. Third, there are, I think, some important parallels between the results presented here concerning change in public bureaucracies and processes of change in social structures generally. I do not want to argue that finance agencies are microcosms of the social universe, but at the same time it is difficult not to draw inferences about change processes in units other than organizations. Whether or not the inferences are correct, of course, is a task for further research to determine.

*Capturing variation over time*

There has been a long tradition of panel or longitudinal research in sociology. Panel or longitudinal designs have conventionally been employed for several purposes including trend analysis, analysis of social processes, and detection of causal relations. Trend analysis, of course, is directed toward identifying gross changes in critical variables over time. Public-opinion studies, market-research panels, and the like are often oriented toward this end. In organizational studies, however, identification of trends is rarely an objective, as trends tend to operate much more slowly with organizations than with individual people. Panel designs have also been used to illuminate social processes, particularly processes culminating in some discrete end such as voting choices or the decision to adopt or not to adopt a particular innovation. The work of Lazarsfeld and his colleagues (e.g. see Lazarsfeld et al. 1948; Berelson et al. 1954; and Katz and Lazarsfeld, 1955) exemplifies this application of panel techniques. Finally, as indicated in Chapter 2, the panel approach can also be used to help specify causal relations among variables more precisely than is possible in cross-sectional studies, albeit with some limitations. In trend and process analysis, it should be noted, events occurring at particular times (or panel "waves") are themselves important. Indeed, trends and processes are not understandable without reference to a time sequence of events. The use of panel or longitudinal data for causal analysis, by contrast, treats time as a means of generating additional information about the units studied but does not pay special attention to exogenous events occurring at each time point. In other words, the behavior of the unit studied is treated as independent of time when panel studies are aimed primarily at elucidating causal relations among variables.

Whereas the original intention of the research study reported here was to utilize panel analysis for the third purpose, the testing of causal models with information collected over time, the initial results suggested that data collection over an extended interval also extended greatly the range of variation in environments and organizations. Variation in the environment increases over time to the extent that organizations share a common environment or common elements in the environment. If, in the extreme instance, all organizations of a given type had the same environment, then environmental elements would be invariant at any one point and change only over time. Even for organizations working in wholly different environments, there remains the possibility that environmental shifts over time are greater than across organizations at any point, hence increased variation is introduced by the panel or longitudinal approach. Organizational variations are also augmented over time, although this effect is not so pronounced as for environments. But if all organizations of a type are patterned after a common model, or if substantial organizational innovation occurs in the midst of a panel study, then the longitudinal approach may capture much more variation than is available cross-sectionally.

A fundamental issue to be faced in sociology is whether forms of social organization of all sorts, not only large-scale organizations, have sufficient autonomy from other structures so that cross-sectional comparisons can capture meaningful variation. The study of finance agencies reported here suggests that elements of organizations are less separable from larger social structures than has been previously assumed. The literature on communities and states, mainly in the tradition of political science, questions the independence of supposedly autonomous units (see Rose, 1973). And sociological theories of world systems (Wallerstein, 1974) also raise the issue of whether nation-states can be treated as separable entities. If shared environments together with the effects of imitation and modeling, the latter usually described in terms of diffusion processes, create strong similarities among structures of a given type at any one point, then requisite variation may be observable only over substantial intervals, sometimes many years.

It should be noted that in extending observations over time in order to capture additional variation in social structures, the distinction between sociological and historical analysis loses significance. Patterned variations in structure over time are almost always the result of fundamental political, economic, and technological shifts at the societal level. Such transformations are usually the subject of history. Their effects, needless to say, lie well within the purview of sociology as well as of the other social sciences, but their identification and description require historical analysis. I do not mean to argue that all variation is historical rather than contemporary, hence that sociology ought to direct itself solely to cliometric studies. I do mean to suggest, however, that comparative research on social structures of any sort, not only organizations, must consider the possibility that variations over time are as great as those across units at any single point. This possibility requires that some effort must be made to capture these historical variations.

### Time as a variable

There is another way that time enters into social research, namely as a variable itself. Any theory of age, of course, has a time component. Age, for example, increases mortality rates, may increase political conservatism, and is hypothesized to contribute to organizational and urban ossification (see Liebert, 1976). More generally, any dynamic model specifying rates of change has an implicit time component, and the testing of such models requires panel or longitudinal data.

A question not yet addressed by sociology but requiring consideration is whether generic structural processes are influenced by time independent of exogenous forces. For example, we need to know whether the deteriorating fit between most finance agencies and their environments observed in this study holds generally for most organizations and social organizational forms. If this is the case, then it may be that organization and accommodation to the environment are inherently opposed. Fit with the environment may be greatest at the time social structures are formed, and then deteriorate slowly until old structures must be either reorganized or wholly replaced by new ones. To be sure, the effect of time in this instance could be reduced to other things, in particular the principle of organization, which requires a modicum of constancy even in a shifting environment. But concepts such as organizational constancy and environment change themselves contain the element of time – the *rate* at which change occurs is crucial.

Let me carry this idea somewhat further in order to indicate some of the theoretical possibilities that are opened when time is considered as a variable in sociological analysis. First of all, there is the possibility that different rates of change in social structures correspond to fundamentally different social processes. Relatively slow, incremental change, for example, may be indicative of normalcy, of the resistance of organizing forces to environmental encroachments. Rapid change, by contrast, may indicate that reorganization, the replacement of organizational forms, is occurring. Secondly, differences in rates of change by level or location may also help in identifying the structural underpinnings of complex social systems. Finance agencies, it has been noted, reorganize infrequently, but there is but slight organizational stability at the level of divisions and sections even though technological imperatives (i.e., the procedures used in conducting the work of accounting, auditing, and the like) would seem to operate with as much force at the subunit as at the departmental level. It may be that political and institutional elements sustain organizational structures much more effectively than technological imperatives. More generally, an examination of rates of structural change by level or location in society might be able to address the question of whether beliefs and institutions or more tangible forces of production constitute the core elements of social structure. If different rates of change in fact correspond to fundamentally different social processes, and if differences in rates of change by level or location help identify the structural bases of complex systems, then the effort and expense needed to adduce these data will have been fully justified.

In sum, the element of time has barely entered into social research, even though the language of sociology is fraught with terms like stability, change, equilibrium, and the like. Time can be built into social research only by collecting or reconstructing data over time. There is no alternative. The failure of social research to incorporate the element of time more explicitly has precluded the testing of some very fundamental ideas in the social sciences.

### Parallels between organizations and other social structures

The study of organizational structures by sociologists is but one approach to the study of social structures of all sorts. Organizational structures are studied, in part, because of their convenience. Whereas the structure of small groups can be quite amorphous, and consistent accounts of the structures of communities or of nation-states may be elusive or obtainable only at extreme cost, organizational structures tend to be somewhat stable and accessible. It is true that, unlike other social-structure forms, organizations tend to be hierarchical whereas groups, communities, and societies may be more interconnected; but this does not preclude generalization from observations on organizations, and it may even be an advantage.

A basic parallel between organizations and social systems generally is in the way they are bounded. Conventionally, we speak of "environment" and "organization" in dealing in the realm of large-scale organizations. For social systems generally, the parallel distinction is between exogenous and endogenous elements. Exogenous elements are those over which systems have relatively little control—causality runs primarily from them to endogenous elements. The latter, endogenous elements, may be ordered in a way such that change in any one of them has implications for some or all of the others. The distinction between environment and organization, between exogenous and endogenous elements, then, is not a matter for empirical research. It is a matter of definition, a point from which research begins. Given these definitions, however, and assuming certain parallels between organizations and social systems generally, one might hypothesize that most social change is caused exogenously rather than by change in endogenous elements. Furthermore, it might be argued that fundamental change is rapid rather than incremental, and that it is mediated somewhat by pressure points or buffering mechanisms such as the character of political leadership and of barriers erected by diverse institutional complexes. Within social systems, one might hypothesize greater differences over time than across subunits of a given type at any one point, but residual effects of origins due to exceptionally rapid rates of change at the time of formation or reorganization. One might also expect less stability in the relations among elements of social structures than in the rules used to construct these relations.

Aside from the mechanisms triggering and mediating change, parallels between the extensiveness of rules in organizations and their extensiveness in social systems of all types are to be expected. Just as egalitarian tendencies have resulted in personnel rules designed to assure "merit" standards in bureaucracies, rules have been increasingly relied upon by societies to assure fairness of treatment and equality among citizens. Indeed, bureaucratization of the nation-state has wrought a fundamental transformation whereby rules themselves have become the primary means through which social change is accomplished. The logic of bureaucracy when applied to entire societies yields the same dilemmas as within organizations themselves: pervasive conformity criteria despite the imperatives of efficiency, and vulnerability to higher authority despite rule boundedness. This may not be a desirable state of affairs, but it may be inevitable until we begin consciously to design alternatives to bureaucratic forms of administration.

It is conventional to end a research monograph with an appeal for more research to cope with unanswered questions. Clearly, more extensive studies of bureaucracy would be useful, perhaps studies making explicit comparisons of public and private-sector organizations in order to determine whether hierarchy and rule boundedness actually generate openness and vulnerability to the environment, as well as historical and comparative studies that capture differences in larger environments. But research results do not constitute the intellectual core of sociology or of any of the other social sciences. Instead, ideas or theories that describe empirical reality only imperfectly and that cannot be tested fully are central to the enterprise. A fundamental idea of sociology is the primacy of social structure in ordering human behavior. The study of public bureaucracies described here presents results on only one type of social structure and over only a limited span of time. Yet it is not without implications for ideas asserting the primacy of social structure. One implication pointing to the need for greater theoretical development is that formal representations of structures such as administrative hierarchies and the core elements of social structure may not be the same things. Structure may consist of the underlying principles and understandings used to construct formal representations such as hierarchies, but not of the representations themselves. The content of such principles and understandings needs to be specified theoretically if it is to be addressed directly in research studies. Another implication is that social systems are much less well bounded than categorizations such as small group, large-scale organization, community, society, and nation-state would suggest. If organizations are dominated by their environments, and if variation occurs more over time than across units of a similar type, then it may hold generally that less inclusive units are the creatures of more inclusive ones or even the most inclusive one, society as a whole. If true, then the implication for theory is that attention must be shifted toward systemic properties and away from properties of units whose organization is largely determined at higher levels. The implication for research is fundamental, for we have no convenient technologies that can identify causal laws operating in a complex social system of which there is but one instance.

All of this is not to rule out future studies of organizations, but it is to indicate that we should not lose sight of the fundamental sociological question—what are the core elements of social structure and their interrelations?—in the minutiae of research. Indeed, my own research on local-government finance agencies continues, extending through the use of historical and archival sources the time span over which organizations and their environments are described, hence the range of variation of both to be explained. The ongoing research, then, renders this book an interim report. I look forward to knowing whether the results outlined above can be both confirmed and extended as the process of change in public bureaucracies is examined in greater depth.

# Questionnaire items used in constructing variables

1 *Department size*
How many full-time employees, *including* full-time temporaries, are there in (NAME OF DEPARTMENT)? (Not full-time equivalents.)

2 *Divisions*
A. According to our information you have the following divisions (or bureaus) in your department: (READ FROM LIST BELOW)
B. Is this correct?    Yes . . . . . . . . . . . . . . . . . . . . . . . . . . .1
NO (RECORD CORRECTIONS
BELOW) . . . . . . . . . . . . . . . . . . . . .2

3 *Levels of supervision*
For each level of supervision, please tell me the number of employees at that level.
First, let's take the highest level . . .

| Level of supervision | A. How many employees are at that level? (RECORD NO.) |
|---|---|
| Highest | |
| 2nd | |
| 3rd | ———— |
| 4th | ———— |
| 5th | ———— |
| 6th | ———— |
| 7th | ———— |
| 8th | ———— |

*Note:* The questions above were administered to division heads, and interviewers were guided by these instructions:

> Starting with the highest level of supervision in the division, ask A for each level. The highest level will, of course, include the head of the division. If he has a "deputy," that person should be included on the same level. If you enter more than "one" for number of employees at the *highest* level, record all job titles that are on the level (i.e., "head of division and his deputy").
>
> This table should cover *all* employees in the division, the lowest level being those with no subordinates, who have no supervisory duties.

The number of levels in a *department* was computed by taking the mean number of levels across divisions and adding one for the department head's office.

4 *Sections*
Is this division divided
into subdivisions or
sections?                           Yes (ASK A & B) ...............1
                                    No ..........................2
(IF YES):
A. How many subdivisions (sections) are there?
B. How many of these subdivisions (sections) have their own supervisors?

*Note:* Only sections with their own supervisors were counted as sections. Divisions with no such sections were coded as having one section so that the number of sections could not be less than the number of divisions in a department.

5 *Span of control*
Refer to the items used to compute levels of supervision. For each division, the number of employees at the lowest level was divided by the number at the level immediately above. The mean of this ratio across divisions is the average departmental span of control at the lowest level.

6 *Formalization*
a. Placement of entry-level employees
Are most employees placed in entry-level nonsupervisory jobs

through civil service (or a similar system such as a uniform employee code) or through political appointment?

Civil service . . . . . . . . . . . . . . . . . .1
Political appointment . . . . . . . . . . .2
Other (SPECIFY)163

b. Written promotion criteria
Are there written regulations that govern the criteria for promotion?

Yes . . . . . . . . . . . . . . . . . . . . . . . . .1
No . . . . . . . . . . . . . . . . . . . . . . . . .2

c. Length of probationary period
How long is the probationary period for a new employee?

_____ months

d. Elected department head
How does the head of this department obtain his job – through political appointment, civil service appointment, or election?

Political appointment . . . . . . . . . . .1
Civil service . . . . . . . . . . . . . . . . . .2
Election . . . . . . . . . . . . . . . . . . . . . .3
Other (SPECIFY) . . . . . . . . . . . . . .4

e. Employees covered by civil service
How many different job titles are represented in your department?
i. How many job titles are covered by civil service (or a similar system such as a uniform employee code)?
ii. How many employees are there in these job titles?

*Note:* Items a, b, c, and d above were combined into an index of formalization of the personnel process. The index runs from zero to one; it is the proportion of responses to these items consistent with civil service or "merit" personnel standards, that is, entry-level placement through civil service, written regulations governing promotions, probationary period of six months or longer, and nonelection of department head.

7 *Responsibilities*
(HAND RESPONDENT CARD A.) Here is a list of activities for which (department of finance/comptroller's office) may be responsible. For each activity listed, please tell me whether your department has full responsibility, shares responsibility, or does not have responsibility. (READ ITEM 1 AND CIRCLE APPROPRIATE CODE IN COLUMN A. THEN ASK B AND/OR C, AS DESIGNATED. REPEAT FOR ITEMS 2–13.)

| Activity | A. Extent of responsibility in this department | B. What division of this department has responsibility? | C. What other department has (partial/full) responsibility? |
|---|---|---|---|
| 1) Maintains records of balance in government funds. | Full (ASK B)....1<br>Shares (ASK B & C)..........2<br>Doesn't have (ASK C) .....3 | | |
| 2) Preaudits disbursements | Full (ASK B)....1<br>Shares (ASK B & C)..........2<br>Doesn't have (ASK C) .....3 | | |
| 3) Postaudits other departments | Full (ASK B)....1<br>Shares (ASK B & C)..........2<br>Doesn't have (ASK C) .....3 | | |
| 4) Is responsible for revenue administration (tax collection) | Full (ASK B)....1<br>Shares (ASK B & C)..........2<br>Doesn't have (ASK C) .....3 | | |
| 5) Assesses real-estate taxes | Full (ASK B)....1<br>Shares (ASK B & C)..........2<br>Doesn't have (ASK C) .....3 | | |
| 6) Is responsible for purchasing | Full (ASK B)....1<br>Shares (ASK B & C)..........2<br>Doesn't have (ASK C) .....3 | | |
| 7) Manages government real estate and property | Full (ASK B)....1<br>Shares (ASK B & C)..........2<br>Doesn't have (ASK C) .....3 | | |

| Activity | A.<br>Extent of responsibility in this department | B.<br>What division of this department has responsibility? | C.<br>What other department has (partial/full) responsibility? |
|---|---|---|---|
| 8) Prepare operating budget. (THIS SHOULD BE THE DIVISION/DE-PARTMENT NAMED IN Q. 2 OF THE SCREENER) | Full (ASK B) . . . .1<br>Shares (ASK B & C) . . . . . . . . . .2<br>Doesn't have (Ask C) . . . . . .3 | | |
| 9) Prepares capital budget | Full (ASK B) . . . .1<br>Shares (ASK B & C) . . . . . . . . . .2<br>Doesn't have (ASK C) . . . . .3 | | |
| 10) Is responsible for investment management | Full (ASK B) . . . .1<br>Shares (ASK B & C) . . . . . . . . . .2<br>Doesn't have (ASK C) . . . . .3 | | |
| 11) Is responsible for utility accounting and collections | Full (ASK B) . . . .1<br>Shares (ASK B & C) . . . . . . . . . .2<br>Doesn't have (ASK C) . . . . .3 | | |
| 12) Is responsible for insurance management | Full (ASK B)( . . .1<br>Shares (ASK B & C) . . . . . . . . . .2<br>Doesn't have (ASK C) . . . . .3 | | |
| 13) Is responsible for fixed asset accounting | Full (ASK B) . . . .1<br>Shares (ASK B & C) . . . . . . . . . .2<br>Doesn't have (ASK C) . . . . .3 | | |

*Note:* The index of responsibilities is the number of activities listed above for which a department has *full* responsibility.

8 *Competitors*
The index of competitors is the *number of other departments* listed in column C above which either share major fiscal responsibilities with the focal finance agency or have full responsibility for these activities.

9 *Demand variables*
a. General fund budget
What is the annual budget of the (NAME OF CITY, COUNTY, OR STATE) general—or corporate—fund that you administer?
b. Total funds administered
What is the total budget of *all* funds that you administer?
c. Government employees
What is the full time equivalent number of employees who work in the government of (NAME OF CITY, COUNTY, OR STATE)? (THIS REFERS TO EMPLOYEES WHO WORK IN DEPARTMENTS FOR WHICH THE FINANCE DEPARTMENT ADMINISTERS FUNDS.)
d. Population
Population figures are taken from the 1960 and 1970 Census of Population. In Chapters 3 and 4, save for Table 23 of Chapter 5, 1965 population, the mean of 1960 and 1970 populations, is used.

10 *Variables describing leadership conditions*
a. Tenure in office
How long have you/has the head of this department) held (your/his) present position?

_____years

b. Dependence on higher authority
See item 6d above.
c. Time spent with head of government
(HAND RESPONDENT CARD B.) We are interested in the percentage of time spent by (you/the head of the department) with the persons listed on this card, over an average month or year.

Please tell me what percentages of time (you/head of department) spend with

1) The head of government of (CITY, COUNTY, STATE) . . . . . . . . . . . . . . . . . . . . . . . . . . . . . . . . . . . . . ._____%
2) Heads of other departments . . . . . . . . . . . . . . . . . . . . . . . ._____%
3) Officials of other local and state governments and federal agencies . . . . . . . . . . . . . . . . . . . . . . . . . . . . . . . . . . . . . . ._____%
4) Community and business leaders who are not government officials . . . . . . . . . . . . . . . . . . . . . . . . . . . . . . . . . . . . . ._____%
5) Division heads in this department . . . . . . . . . . . . . . . . . ._____%
6) Other personnel in this department . . . . . . . . . . . . . . . ._____%
7) Working alone with reports, budget, correspondence, etc. . . . . . . . . . . . . . . . . . . . . . . . . . . . . . . . . . . . . . . . . . ._____%
8) Others (SPECIFY HERE) . . . . . . . . . . . . . . . . . . . . . . . . . . ._____%
100%

11 *Additional variables describing budgeting and data-processing units*
a. Budgeting units
i. How many employees did (NAME OF BUDGET UNIT) have in 1966?
ii. In what year was (NAME OF BUDGET UNIT) organized?
b. Data-processing units
i. How many employees did (NAME OF DATA-PROCESSING UNIT) have in 1966?
ii. In what year was (NAME OF DATA-PROCESSING UNIT) organized?

12. *Index of automation*
Please tell me which of the following equipment, if any, you use for these activities. First, payroll—do you use bookkeeping machines, punch-card equipment, or a computer for the payroll activities? (CIRCLE CODE IN COLUMN A BELOW FOR EACH TYPE OF EQUIPMENT THAT APPLIES, OR FOR "NONE OF THESE." IF "NONE" ASK STARRED (*) QUESTION. REPEAT LIST OF EQUIPMENT FOR EACH ACTIVITY—B, C, AND D.)

|  | A.<br>Payroll | B.<br>Budget ac-<br>counting | C.<br>Cost ac-<br>counting | D.<br>Billing (for<br>taxes, fees) |
|---|---|---|---|---|
| Bookkeeping machines | 1 | 1 | 1 | 1 |
| Punch-card equipment | 2 | 2 | 2 | 2 |
| Computer | 3 | 3 | 3 | 3 |
| None of these | * | * | * | * |
| *Is the department<br>responsible for this<br>activity | Yes No | Yes No | Yes No | Yes No |
|  | 4   5 | 4   5 | 4   5 | 4   5 |

*Note:* The index of automation runs from zero to one; it is the proportion of the four activities (A−D) for which a department is responsible that are done using computers.

13. *Delegation of decision-making authority*
   a. Delegation of substantive decisions
   What kinds of decisions can division heads make without approval of the head of the department? (PROBE FULLY, AND THEN ASK SPECIFICALLY ABOUT ANY OF THE FOLLOWING ITEMS RESPONDENT HAS NOT MENTIONED.) Can they make decisions about work assignments? Can they make decisions about budget allocations? Can they make decisions about accounting procedures?
   b. Delegation of personnel decisions
   (Do you/Does the head of this department) officially recommend promotion and dismissal of employees, or do you delegate this authority to someone else?

   > Department head .............1
   > Someone else (ASK A) .........2

   A. (IF SOMEONE ELSE): What is the title of the person who makes such recommendations?
   In what proportion do the opinions of division heads count in making decisions about promotions and dismissals?

   > _____percent

   *Note:* For item 13a, delegation of decision-making authority in the three substantive areas was coded along with statements about the department head's general policy in delegating authority.

14 *Year department was organized*
   In what year was this department organized?

# Cities, counties, and states covered in 1966 and 1972 surveys of finance agencies

Birmingham, Ala.
State of Alaska
State of Arizona
Phoenix, Ariz.
Tucson, Ariz.
Maricopa Co., Ariz.
State of Arkansas
State of California
Anaheim, Calif.
Burbank, Calif.
Downey, Calif.
Fresno *City*, Calif.
Fullerton, Calif.
Garden Grove, Calif.
Glendale, Calif.
Long Beach, Calif.
Los Angeles *City*, Calif.
Oakland, Calif.
Pasadena, Calif.
Riverside *City*, Calif.
Sacramento *City*, Calif.
San Diego *City*, Calif.
San Francisco *City*, Calif.
San Jose, Calif.
Santa Ana, Calif.
Santa Barbara *City*, Calif.
Santa Clara *City*, Calif.
Santa Monica, Calif.
Stockton, Calif.
Sunnyvale, Calif.

Torrance, Calif.
Alameda Co., Calif.
Contra Costa Co., Calif.
Fresno Co., Calif.
Humboldt Co., Calif.
Kern Co., Calif.
Los Angeles Co., Calif.
Marin Co., Calif.
Orange Co., Calif.
Riverside Co., Calif.
Sacramento Co., Calif.
San Bernardino Co., Calif.
San Mateo *City*, Calif.
Santa Clara Co., Calif.
Sonoma Co., Calif.
Ventura Co., Calif.
State of Colorado
Denver *City* and Co., Colo.
State of Connecticut
Bridgeport, Conn.
Greenwich (*town*), Conn.
Hartford *City*, Conn.
New Haven *City*, Conn.
Stamford, Conn.
West Hartford (*town*), Conn.
State of Delaware
District of Columbia
State of Florida
Fort Lauderdale, Fla.
Jacksonville, Fla.

Miami, Fla.
Orlando, Fla.
Pensacola, Fla.
St. Petersburg, Fla.
Tampa, Fla.
West Palm Beach, Fla.
Dade Co., Fla.
Pinellas Co., Fla.
Polk Co., Fla.
Atlanta, Ga.
Savannah, Ga.
State of Hawaii
Honolulu *City* and Co.,
  Hawaii
State of Idaho
State of Illinois
Chicago, Ill.
Joliet, Ill.
Oak Park, Ill.
Springfield, Ill.
Cook Co., Ill.
State of Indiana
Indianapolis, Ind.
Lake Co., Ind.
Marion Co., Ind.
St. Joseph Co., Ind.
State of Iowa
Des Moines, Iowa
Sioux City, Iowa
State of Kansas
Topeka, Kan.
Wichita, Kan.
State of Kentucky
Covington, Ky.
Lexington, Ky.
Louisville, Ky.
Baton Rouge, La.
Monroe, La.
New Orleans, La.
Shreveport, La.
Jefferson Co., La.
State of Maine
Portland, Me.
State of Maryland
Baltimore *City*, Md.

Anne Arundel Co., Md.
Baltimore Co., Md.
Montgomery Co., Md.
State of Massachusetts
Boston, Mass.
Cambridge, Mass.
Springfield, Mass.
State of Michigan
Dearborn, Mich.
Detroit, Mich.
Flint, Mich.
Lansing, Mich.
Pontiac, Mich.
Saginaw *City*, Mich.
Genesee Co., Mich.
Macomb Co., Mich.
Oakland Co., Mich.
Wayne Co., Mich.
State of Minnesota
Duluth, Minn.
Minneapolis, Minn.
Hennepin Co., Minn.
Ramsey Co., Minn.
Harrison Co., Miss.
State of Missouri
Independence, Mo.
Kansas City, Mo.
St. Louis *City*, Mo.
St. Joseph, Mo.
Springfield, Mo.
University City, Mo.
St. Louis Co., Mo.
State of Montana
State of Nebraska
Lincoln, Neb.
Omaha, Neb.
Douglas Co., Neb.
Las Vegas, Nev.
State of New Hampshire
Bayonne, N.J.
Elizabeth, N.J.
Irvington, N.J.
Jersey City, N.J.
Newark, N.J.
Passaic *City*, N.J.

Trenton, N.J.
Union City *City*, N.J.
Essex Co., N.J.
State of New Mexico
Albuquerque, N.M.
State of New York
Albany *City*, N.Y.
Buffalo, N.Y.
Niagara Falls, N.Y.
Rochester, N.Y.
Schenectady *City*, N.Y.
Syracuse, N.Y.
Troy, N.Y.
Yonkers, N.Y.
Erie Co., N.Y.
Monroe Co., N.Y.
Nassau Co., N.Y.
Onondaga Co., N.Y.
Suffolk Co., N.Y.
Westchester Co., N.Y.
Charlotte, N.C.
Durham *City*, N.C.
Greensboro, N.C.
High Point, N.C.
Raleigh, N.C.
Winston-Salem, N.C.
State of North Dakota
State of Ohio
Akron,O.
Cincinnati, O.
Cleveland, O.
Dayton, O.
Hamilton *City*, O.
Springfield, O.
Youngstown, O.
Butler Co., O.
Franklin Co., O.
Hamilton Co., O.
Lake Co., O.
Lorain Co., O.
Mahoning Co., O.
Montgomery Co., O.
Stark Co., O.
Summit Co., O.
Trumbull Co., O.
State of Oklahoma

Oklahoma City *City*, Okla.
State of Oregon
Portland, Ore.
Multnomah Co., Ore.
Allentown, Pa.
Altoona, Pa.
Chester *City*, Pa.
Harrisburg, Pa.
Lancaster, Pa.
Philadelphia *City*, Pa.
Luzerne Co., Pa.
State of Rhode Island
Cranston, R.I.
Pawtucket, R.I.
Providence *City*, R.I.
Warwick, R.I.
Columbia, S.C.
Greenville *City*, S.C.
State of Tennessee
Chattanooga, Tenn.
Knoxville, Tenn.
Nashville, Tenn.
State of Texas
Amarillo, Tex.
Austin, Tex.
Beaumont, Tex.
Corpus Christi, Tex.
Dallas *City*, Tex.
Fort Worth, Tex.
Galveston *City*, Tex.
Lubbock *City*, Tex.
Midland, Tex.
Odessa, Tex.
Port Arthur, Tex.
San Antonio, Tex.
Wichita Falls, Tex.
Bexar Co., Tex.
Harris Co., Tex.
Jefferson Co., Tex.
State of Utah
Ogden, Utah
State of Vermont
State of Virginia
Alexandria, Va.
Arlington *City*, Va.
Norfolk, Va.

Richmond, Va.
Fairfax Co., Va.
Henrico Co., Va.
State of Washington
Seattle, Wash.
Spokane *City*, Wash.
Tacoma, Wash.

Snohomish Co., Wash.
Spokane Co., Wash.
State of West Virginia
State of Wisconsin
Milwaukee, Wis.
Milwaukee Co., Wis.

# NOTES

### Introduction

1 I am referring, of course, to Max Weber's (1946) classic essay, "Bureaucracy."
2 Needless to say, I have made some changes in the transcripts of the interview in order to preserve the anonymity of respondents and their agencies.
3 The functions of local governments are usually handled by departments. Departments are, in turn, divided into divisions (or, sometimes, bureaus), and large divisions are split into sections. This terminology is different from industrial firms and even universities where work is typically divided into divisions, and then departments.
4 Local-government obligations are, of course, exempt from federal taxation and yield somewhat lower interest (currently around 6 percent) than other bonds. There is always the temptation to borrow excessively and invest the surplus at a high interest rate; this is called arbitrage. Treasury regulations prohibit it, and the successful finance director approaches but never crosses the fine line between shrewd money management and arbitrage.
5 Several states also have departments of administration. They are similar to the Office of Management and the Budget at the federal level.

### 1. Issues in organizational theory

1 Vernon Dibble's (1965) essay, "The Organization of Traditional Authority," is one of the best accounts of nonbureaucratic administration by notables. Although traditional authority had many defects, one benefit, according to Dibble, was that dissenting views would be funneled upward to superiors precisely because freeholders were not tied to bureaucratic

careers. Disagreements could be tolerated, Dibble points out, because traditional administration served to perpetuate rule by the gentry. Bureaucracies that recruit members without regard to social origin are less tolerant of dissent because of the absence of an overriding class interest among officials.

2  See S.M. Lipset's (1950) *Agrarian Socialism* for an account of the limits of elected officials' power when pitted against a conservative bureaucracy. Lipset's study of Canadian politics is corroborated by Ezra Suleiman's (1974) account of behavior in the top echelons of the French Civil Service.

3  Outstanding examples of comparative studies of authority systems include Reinhard Bendix's (1956) *Work and Authority in Industry* and his (1964) *Nation Building and Citizenship*.

4  See Chinoy's *Automobile Workers and the American Dream* (1955) and Blauner's (1964) *Alienation and Freedom* for illustrations of some of the deleterious effects of intensive division of labor in industry.

5  Several mathamatical models of the effects of size on organizational structure have been developed, and they suggest that almost any reasonable set of assumptions consistent with Weber's yield increasing vertical and horizontal differentiation with size. See Meyer (1971), Hummon (1971), Mayhew et al. (1972), Specht (1973), and others.

### 2. Organizational research

1  For convenience, all variables are assumed to be in standard form, that is,
$$x = \frac{x_1 - \bar{x}}{\sigma_x}$$

This permits omission of constants from regression models, and it eliminates the need to distinguish metric regression coefficients from standardized regression of path coefficients.

2  The diagram illustrates how past causal processes are reflected in present associations. In the first interval, between $t_0$ and $t_1$, $x$

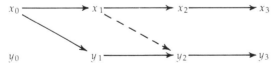

clearly caused $y$, and $y$ otherwise had little stability. Between $t_1$ and $t_2$, $y$ acquired more stability, and the impact of $x$ on $y$ decreased. Finally, in the third interval, both $x$ and $y$ were essentially stable, and no causal paths operate. The association of $x_3$ with $y_3$, then, is the product of past but not current causal processes.

I suspect that this pattern is much more common than is appreciated and is a major source of difficulty in drawing causal inferences from static comparisons of complex social structures.

### 3. The concept of organizational structure

1  In subsequent chapters, the 1965 population of cities, counties, and states is used as an independent variable. It is computed as the mean of 1960 and 1970 population figures.
2  Autocorrelations of the logarithms of the four demand variables are as follows:

| | |
|---|---|
| General fund | .7605 |
| Total funds | .7402 |
| Government employees | .7733 |
| Population | .9692 |

### 4. Some effects of leadership

1  By leadership I mean characteristics of top positions in finance departments, not the numerous acts of leading that leaders are called upon to perform. Perhaps "headship" would be more appropriate, but I am following Lieberson and O'Connor's (1972) use of the term "leadership."
2  My perspective is slightly different from that of Thompson (1967), who argues that different parts of organizations face different degrees of uncertainty, least in the technical core and most at the boundaries. The argument here is that uncertainty in organizations varies over time and from organization to organization owing to characteristics of leaders.
3  Not all of these differences in autocorrelations are statistically significant. The test for significance of differences between correlations is described by Blalock (1972: 405–7). Should the reader doubt the importance of these differences, he is asked to suspend his disbelief for a while.
4  Department heads, some of their deputies, and all division heads were interviewed; information on levels of supervision and the number of sections was provided by the latter.
5  Here are the exact figures: of 93 departments with stable leadership between 1960 and 1966, only 39 kept the same leadership through 1972. But of 122 that had changed leaders in the five years before 1966, 63 had stable leadership between 1966 and 1972. In other words, turnover in leadership positions is not consistently high for some finance departments and consistently low for others. Quite the opposite: Stability in one period is followed by succession in the next and vice versa.

6 Here are the tabulations.

*Tabulations concerning 1965–66 structural change*

|  | 1966 Tenure of department head | |
|---|---|---|
|  | 0−5 Years | 6+ Years |
| 1965–66 Structural change: | | |
| Yes | 45% | 19% |
| No | 55% | 81% |
|  | 100% | 100% |
|  | (120) | (93) |
|  | 1965–66 Structural change | |
|  | Yes | No |
| 1972 Tenure of department head: | | |
| 0–5 years | 49% | 55% |
| 6+ years | 51% | 45% |
|  | 100% | 100% |
|  | (72) | (141) |

7 Here are the autocorrelations with governmental reorganization controlled.

*Autocorrelations of structural variables by governmental reorganization and 1966 tenure of department head*

|  | Government reorganization | | | |
|---|---|---|---|---|
|  | Yes | | No | |
|  | Tenure 0–5 years [a] | Tenure 6+ years [a] | Tenure 0–5 years [a] | Tenure 6+ years[a] |
| Size | .7179 | .9838 | .9492 | .9785 |
| Divisions | .0715 | .4200 | .5263 | .7016 |
| Levels | .3190 | .6310 | .5659 | .6375 |
| Sections | .5134 | .7534 | .5886 | .7356 |

[a] 1966 Tenure of department head.

8 Data-processing units are almost always called data processing, systems, or some like term. Units in charge of budgeting are more heterogeneous. Some are planning and development offices,

some are executive agencies not unlike the Office of Management and Budget in the federal bureaucracy, and others are divisions of finance or administration departments called simply "budget."

### 5. Organizational domains

1 Stinchcombe (1965) discusses liabilities of newness, but my research suggests that new bureaus, unlike business enterprises, grow more rapidly than others. Perhaps this is because the liabilities facing most new organizations – Stinchcombe lists the need to learn new roles, development of new organizational routines, reliance on social relations among strangers and the acquisition of a clientele – do not plague bureaus formed out of old ones or do not affect them as much as others. Clearly, some research is required in this area.

2 This is a variant of the cross-lagged path model in which a dependent variable at a later time is regressed on lagged dependent and independent variables. See Heise (1970) for a full description of the model.

3 The effects of leadership reported in Chapter 4 hold for finance departments but not comptrollers' offices.

4 Needless to say, the small number of departments of administration makes it impossible to group cases to control for additional variables.

### 6. The process of bureaucratization

1 This is not to deny that the federal government had imposed specific merit-system requirements on state and local governments prior to the 1970 Intergovernmental Personnel Act. Quite the opposite: Some 150 district personnel requirements, some of them contradictory, had already been attached to various grant-in-aid programs. These requirements were greatly simplified in the 1971 "Standards for a Merit System of Administration" promulgated by the Departments of Health, Education, and Welfare; Defense; and Labor; and further simplification was proposed by the Advisory Council on Intergovernmental Governmental Personnel Policy in its 1973 report (U.S. Senate Committee on Government Operations 1974:4-5). The advisory council recommended that a set of uniform personnel standards be applied in the administration of all federal grants-in-aid to states and localities, with the sole exception of revenue-sharing funds.

2 Charles Bidwell has suggested that organizations in shared

environments may diverge over time. He cites in private correspondence the example of midwestern colleges founded in the late nineteenth and twentieth centuries. These institutions were initially similar but became differentiated due to demands of controlling bodies, local constituencies, and the like. Divergence unrelated to time of formation, of course, cannot be captured in the model in Figure 6. It may well be that local conditions have caused some divergences in finance agencies over time, but our lack of information about these conditions renders it difficult to gauge their effects.

3  Only Starbuck (1965) has argued that age affects the degree of formalization in organizations, but there has been no empiricial confirmation of this claim. Although it is possible that orga- nizational age influences bureaucratization apart from time of origin (i.e., cohort) or effects of the environment (i.e., period), neither the data nor justification for the strong assumptions needed to separate the effects of cohort, period, and age exists. For a discussion of the problem of cohort, year, and age, see Mason et al. (1973). The literature also suggests that time of origin is more important than age. Aiken and Hage (1968:921–2) found no correlates of age in their study of sixteen health and welfare agencies; Pugh et al. (1969a:94) found a negative but nonsig- nificant relationship of age with impersonality of origins of fity-four diverse organizations in the Birmingham, England, area. Only Kimberly's recent (1975) study of sheltered workshops has corroborated Stinchcombe's results. Kimberly found post–World War II workshops to be more oriented toward rehabilitation than pre–World War II agencies. This in all likelihood reflects changing beliefs about the appropriate functions for sheltered workshops rather than effects of age per se.

4  Procedures for selecting department heads have been least affected by civil service laws. Environmental forces have not had much impact, and a strong effect of era of origin occurs in Section D of Table 17. It could be argued, though not proved, that the differences between the correlations of era of origin with whether the department head is elected and the correlation of era with the other items in Table 17 are indicative of the magnitude of environmental effects on the other items from the time of origin to the present.

5  The first measure of delegation is coded zero if the department head officially recommends promotions and dismissals and one if someone below him does; the second measure is coded zero if the division heads' influence in promotion decisions is less than 80 percent and one if their influence, as reported by the department head, is greater than 80 percent.

### 7. Implications

1  Indeed, we are pursuing this subject in historical studies of city administration. The same results — relative stability at the departmental level but instability below — obtains. See Meyer (1978) for a discussion of these results.

2  This brief discussion does not cover the complexities of assessing effectiveness or the larger literature on the topic. The reader is referred to Price's (1968) propositional inventory on organizational effectiveness as well as to studies by Hirsch (1975), Pennings (1975), and Yuchtman and Seashore (1967).

# BIBLIOGRAPHY

Aiken, M., and Hage, J. "Organizational Interdependence and Intraorganizational Structure." *American Sociological Review* 33 (1968) 912–30.

Aldrich, H. E. "Technology and Organizational Structure: A Reexamination of the Findings of the Aston Group." *Administrative Science Quarterly* 17 (1972).

– and Pfeffer, J. "Environments of Organizations." *Annual Review of Sociology* 2 (1976) 79–106.

Anderson, T. E., and Warkov, S. "Organizational Size and Functional Complexity: A Study of Administration in Hospitals." *American Sociological Review* 26 (1961) 23–28.

Bendix, R. *Work Authority in Industry.* New York: Wiley, 1956.

– *Nation Building and Citizenship.* New York: Wiley, 1964.

Berelson, B. R.; Lazarsfeld, P. F.; and McPhee, W. N. *Voting.* Chicago: University of Chicago Press, 1954.

Blalock, H. M., Jr. *Social Statistics.* New York: McGraw-Hill, 1972.

Blau, P. M. *The Dynamics of Bureaucracy.* Chicago: University of Chicago Press, 1955.

– "Critical Remarks on Weber's Theory of Authority." *American Political Science Review* 57 (1963) 305–16.

– "The Hierarchy of Authority in Organizations." *American Journal of Sociology* 73 (1968) 453–67.

– "A Formal Theory of Differentiation in Organizations." *American Sociological Review* 35 (1970) 201–18.

– "Interdependence and Hierarchy in Organizations." *Social Science Research* 1 (1972) 1–24.

– and Schoenherr, R. A. *The Structure of Organizations.* New York: Basic Books, 1971.

Blauner, R. *Alienation and Freedom.* Chicago: University of Chicago Press, 1964.

Burns, T., and Stalker, G.M. *The Management of Innovation*. London:
Tavistock, 1961.

Campbell, J. P.; Dunnette, M. D.; Lawler, E. E.; and Weick, K. E. Jr.
*Managerial Behavior, Performance, and Effectiveness*. New York:
McGraw-Hill, 1970.

Chinoy, E. *Automobile Workers and the American Dream*. Boston: Beacon
Press, 1955.

Crozier, M. *The Bureaucratic Phenomenon*. Chicago: University of Chicago
Press, 1964.

Dahl, R. *Who Governs?* New Haven, Conn.: Yale University Press, 1961.

Dibble, V. K. "The Organization of Traditional Authority: English County
Government, 1558 to 1640." In J. G. March, ed. *Handbook of Organizations*, Chicago: Rand McNally, 1965.

Downs, A. *Inside Bureaucracy*. Boston: Little, Brown, 1967.

Emery, F. W., and Trist, E. L. "The Causal Texture of Organizational
Environments." *Human Relations* 18 (1965) 12−31.

Gordon, G., and Becker, S. "Organizational Size and Managerial
Succession: A Re-examination." *American Journal of Sociology* 70 (1964)
215−22.

Gouldner, A.W. *Patterns of Industrial Bureaucracy*. Glencoe, Illinois: Free
Press, 1954.

− "Organizational Analysis." In R.K. Merton, L. Broom, and L.S. Cottrell,
Jr., eds. *Sociology Today*. New York: Basic Books, 1959.

Graen, G.; Dansereau, F., Jr.; and Minami, T. "Dysfunctional Leadership
Styles." *Organizational Behavior and Human Performance* 7 (1972) 216−236.

Griffith, E.S. *A History of American City Governments: The Progressive Years
and Their Aftermath, 1900−1920*. New York: Praeger, 1974.

Grusky, O. "Corporate Size, Bureaucratization, and Managerial
Succession." *American Journal of Sociology* 67 (1961) 261−269.

− "Managerial Succession and Organizational Effectiveness." *American
Journal of Sociology* 69 (1963) 21−31.

Gulick, L., and Urwick, L., eds., *Papers on the Science of Administration*.
New York: Institute of Public Administration, 1937.

Hage, J., "Relationship of Centralization to Other Organizational Properties." *Administrative Science Quarterly* 12 (1967) 503−19.

− and Aiken M. *Social Change in Complex Organizations*. New York:
Random House, 1970.

− "Program Change and Organizational Properties: A Comparative
Analysis." *American Journal of Sociology* 72 (1967) 503−19.

Halberstam, D. *The Best and the Brightest*. New York: Random House, 1972.

Hall, R.H. "The Concept of Bureaucracy: An Empirical Assessment."
*American Journal of Sociology* 69 (1963) 32−40.

− *Organizations: Structure and Process*: Englewood Cliffs, N.J.: Prentice-
Hall, 1972.

− Haas, J. E.; and Johnson, J. N. "Organizational Size, Complexity, and
Formalization." *American Sociological Review* 32 (1967) 903−12.

Hannan, M. T., and Freeman, J. "The Population Ecology of Organizations." *American Journal of Sociology* 82 (1977) 929–64.

Heise, D. R. "Causal Inference From Panel Data." In E.F. Borgatta. ed. *Sociological Methodology 1970.* San Francisco: Jossey-Bass, 3–26.

Hickson, D.J.; Pugh, D.S.; and Pheysey, D.C. "Operations Technology and Organization Structure: An Empirical Reappraisal." *Administrative Science Quarterly* 14 (1969) 378–95.

– Hinings, C.R.; Lee, C.A.; Schneck, R.E.; and Pennings, J.M. "A Strategic Contingencies' Theory of Intraorganizational Power." *Administrative Science Quarterly* 16 (1971) 216–29.

Hirsch, P.M. "Organizational Effectiveness and the Institutional Environment." *Administrative Science Quarterly* 20 (1975) 327–44.

Hummon, N.A. "Notes on Blau's 'A Formal Theory of Differentiation in Organizations.' " *American Sociological Review* 36 (1971) 297–303.

Katz, D., and Kahn, R. L. *The Social Psychology of Organizations.* New York: Wiley, 1966.

Katz, E., and Lazarsfeld, P. F. *Personal Influence.* New York: Free Press, 1955.

Kaufman, H. *Are Government Organizations Immortal?* Washington: Brookings, 1976.

Kimberly, J. E. "Environmental Constraints and Organizational Structure: A Comparative Analysis of Rehabilitation Organizations." *Administrative Science Quarterly* 20 (1975) 1–9.

Kimberly, J. R. "Organizational Size and the Structuralist Perspective: A Review, Critique, and Proposal." *Administrative Science Quarterly* 21 (1976) 571–97.

Kriesberg, L. "Careers, Organizational Size and Succession." *American Journal of Sociology* 68 (1962) 355–59.

Lawrence, P. R., and Lorsch, J. W. *Organizational and Environment.* Boston: Harvard Business School, 1967a.

– "Differentiation and Integration in Complex Organizations." *Administrative Science Quarterly* 12 (1967b) 1–47.

Lazarsfeld, P. F.; Berelson, B. R.: and Gaudet, H. *The People's Choice.* 2nd ed. New York: Columbia University Press, 1948.

Levine, S., and White, P. E. "Exchange as a Framework for the Study of Interorganizational Relationships." *Administrative Science Quarterly* 5 (1961) 583–601.

Lieberson, S., and O'Connor, J. F. "Leadership and Organizational Performance: A Study of Large Corporations." *American Sociological Review* 37 (1972), 117–30.

Liebert, R.J. *Disintegration and Political Action.* New York: Academic Press, 1976.

Lindblom, C.E. "The Science of Muddling Through." *Public Administration Review* 19 (1959) 79–88.

Lipset, S.M. *Agrarian Socialism*. Berkeley: University of California Press, 1950.

March, J. G., and Olsen, J. P. *Ambiguity and Choice in Organizations*. Bergen: Universitetsforlaget, 1976.

Mason, K.O.; Mason, W.M.; Winsborough, H.H.; and Poole, W.K. "Some Methodological Issues in Cohort Analysis or Archival Data." *American Sociological Review* 38 (1973) 242−58.

Mayhew, B.H,: McPherson, J.M.; Levinger, R.L.; and James, J.F. "System Size and Structural Differentiation in Organizations: A Baseline Generator For Two Major Theoretical Propositions." *American Sociological Review* 37 (1972) 629−33.

Merton, R.K. "Bureaucratic Structure and Personality." *Social Forces* 17 (1940) 560−68.

Meyer, J.W., and Rowan, B. "Institutionalized Organizations: Formal Structure as Myth and Ceremony." *American Journal of Sociology* 83 (1977) 340−63.

Meyer, M.W. "The Two Authority Structures of Bureaucratic Organizations." *Administrative Science Quarterly* 13 (1968) 211−18.

− "Some Constraints in Analyzing Data on Organizational Structures." *American Sociological Review* 36 (1971) 294−329.

− *Bureaucratic Structure and Authority*. New York: Harper & Row, 1972a.

− "Size and Structure of Organizations: A Causal Analysis." *American Sociological Review* 37 (1972b) 434−40.

− *Theory of Organizational Structure*. Indianapolis: Bobbs-Merrill, 1977.

− "Social Change and Organizational Structure." Paper delivered to the IX World Congress of Sociology, Uppsala, Sweden, August, 1978.

Mintzberg, H. *The Nature of Managerial Work*. New York: Harper & Row, 1973.

Mitau, G.T. *State and Local Government: Politics and Process*. New York: Scribner, 1966.

National Civil Service League. *A Model Public Personnel Administration Law*. 1970.

Niskanen, W.A., Jr. *Bureaucracy and Representative Government*. Chicago: Aldine, 1971.

Pennings, J. "The Relevance of the Structural Contingency Model for Organizational Effectiveness." *Administrative Science Quarterly*, 20 (1975) 393−410.

Perrow, C. "A Framewcrk for the Comparative Analysis of Organizations." *American Sociological Review* 32 (1967) 194−208.

Phillips, J.C. *Municipal Government and Administration in America*. New York: Macmillan, 1960.

Pondy, L.R. "Effects of Size, Complexity, and Ownership on Administrative Intensity." *Administrative Science Quarterly* 14(1969) 47−60.

Price, J.L. *Organizational Effectiveness*. Homewood, Illinois: Irwin, 1968.

Pugh, D.S.; Hickson, D.J.; Hinings, C.R.; MacDonald, K.M.; Turner, C.; and Lupton, T. "A Conceptual Scheme for Organizational Analysis." *Administrative Science Quarterly* 8 (1963) 301–07.

– Hickson, D.J.; Hinings, C.R.; and Turner, C. "Dimensions of Organization Structure." *Administrative Science Quarterly* 13 (1968) 65–06.

– Hickson, D.J.; Hinings, C. R.; and Turner, C. "The Context of Organization Structures." *Administrative Science Quarterly* 14 (1969a) 91–114.

– Hickson, D.J.; and Hinings, C.R. "An Empirical Taxonomy of Structures of Work Organizations." *Administrative Science Quarterly,* 14 (1969b) 115–26.

Rose, A. "National and Local Forces in State Politics." *American Political Science Review* 67 (1973) 1162–73.

Rushing, W.R. "Effects of Industry Size and Division of Labor on Administration." *Administrative Science Quarterly* 12 (1967) 273–95.

Selznick. P. *TVA and the Grass Roots.* Berkeley: University of California Press, 1949.

– *Leadership in Administration.* New York: Harper & Row, 1957.

Specht, D.A. "System Size and Structural Differentiation in Organizations: An Alternative Baseline Generator." *American Sociological Review* 38 (1973) 479–80.

Starbuck, W. "Organizational Growth and Development." In J.G. March, ed. *Handbook of Organizations.* Chicago: Rand McNally, 1965.

Stinchcombe, A.L. "Bureaucratic and Craft Administration of Production." *Administrative Science Quarterly* 4 (1959) 168–87.

– "Social Structure and Organizations." In J.G. March, ed. *Handbook of Organizations.* Chicago: Rand McNally, 1965.

Stogdill, R.N. *Handbook of Leadership.* Chicago: Rand McNally, 1974.

– and Coons. A.E. *Leader Behavior: Its Description and Measurement.* Columbus: Bureau of Business Research, Ohio State University, 1957.

Suleiman, E.N. *Politics, Power, and Bureaucracy in France.* Princeton: Princeton University Press, 1974.

Taylor, F.W. *The Principles of Scientific Management.* New York: Harper, 1911.

Terreberry, S. "The Evolution of Organizational Environments." *Administrative Science Quarterly* 12 (1968) 590–613.

Terrien, F.W., and Mills, D.L. "The Effect of Changing Size Upon the Internal Structure of Organizations." *American Sociological Review* 20 (1955) 11–13.

Thompson, J.D. *Organizations in Action.* New York: McGraw-Hill, 1967.

Tosi, H.; Aldag, R.; and Storey, R. "On the Measurement of the Environment: An Assessment of the Lawrence and Lorsch Environmental Uncertainty Scale." *Administrative Science Quarterly* 18 (1973) 27–36.

Tullock, G. *The Politics of Bureaucracy.* Washington D.C.: Public Affairs, 1965.

Udy, S.H., Jr. " 'Bureaucracy' and 'Rationality' in Weber's Organization Theory." *American Sociological Review* 24 (1959) 791–95.

U.S. Congress. "An Act to Regulate and Improve the Civil Service of the United States." In *United States Statutes at Large,* 1881–1883, *22,* 403–07. Washington D.C.: Government Printing Office.

– "An Act to Amend the Social Security Act, and for Other Purposes." In *United States Statutes at Large,* 1939, *84,* 1360–1402. Washington D.C.: Government Printing Office.

– "An Act to Reinforce the Federal System by Strengthening the Personnel Resources of State and Local Governments." In *United States Statutes at Large,* 1970–71, *84,* 1909–29. Washington D.C.: Government Printing Office.

U.S. Senate Committee on Governmental operations. *More Effective Public Service: The First Report to the President and the Congress by the Advisory Council on Intergovernmental Personnel Policy*–January, 1973. Washington D. C.: Government Printing office, 1974.

Von Mises, L. *Bureaucracy.* New Haven, Conn.: Yale University Press, 1944.

Wallerstein, I. *The Modern World System.* New York: Academic Press, 1974.

Weber, M. "Bureaucracy." In H. Gerth and C.W. Mills, eds. *From Max Weber: Essays in Sociology.* New York: Oxford University Press, 1946.

– *The Methodology of the Social Sciences.* Translated by E. Shils and H. Finch. New York: Free Press, 1949.

Weick, K. E. *The Social Psychology of Organizing.* Reading, Mass.: Addison-Wesley, 1969.

– "Educational Organizations as Loosely Coupled Systems." *Administrative Science Quarterly* 21 (1976) 1–19.

Wilensky, H. L. *The Welfare State and Equality.* Berkeley: University of California Press, 1975.

Williamson, O. *Markets and Hierarchies: Analysis and Antitrust Implications.* New York: Free Press, 1975.

Woodward, J. *Industrial Organization: Theory and Practice.* London: Oxford University Press, 1965.

Yuchtman, E., and Seashore, S. "A System Resource Approach to Organizational Effectiveness." *American Sociological Review* 32 (1967) 891–903.

# INDEX